Notes on Heartbreak

Notes on Heartbreak

Annie Lord

First published in Great Britain in 2022 by Trapeze,
an imprint of The Orion Publishing Group Ltd
Carmelite House, 50 Victoria Embankment
London EC4Y 0DZ

An Hachette UK Company

13 5 7 9 10 8 6 4 2

A CIP catalogue record for this book is
available from the British Library.

ISBN (Hardback) 978 1 3987 0548 7
ISBN (Export Trade Paperback) 978 1 3987 0550 0
ISBN (eBook) 978 1 3987 0551 7
ISBN (Audio) 978 1 3987 0552 4

Typeset by Born Group
Printed and bound in Great Britain by Clays Ltd, Elcograf S.p.A.

www.orionbooks.co.uk

For Schmoo*

*Mum

After he ended it, I got my phone out and started to dial Joe's number. Then I remembered that Joe is now my ex-boyfriend and I don't get to call him anymore.

I wonder what would happen if he were able to comfort me, if he were still my boyfriend and not the guy who has just dumped me. Walking to the Tube station, I'd hear his voice on the other end of the phone line shout, 'Fuck that guy!' and then the long rasp as he tugs from a tightly rolled cigarette. He'd be standing in Adidas trackies, leaning out of the kitchen window, lips blowing smoke outside, even though the wind just blew it back indoors.

'Everything seemed so normal. We were having burgers in a restaurant with my dad and brother and I said, "Shall we get some onion rings as well?" and Joe said, "Sure," and I said, "Are you going to get bacon with yours?" and he said, "If you are," and then we talked about how now is a strange time to do a *Die Hard* sequel, given that masculinity doesn't seem to save the day anymore, and then we discussed how fancy ketchup is never as good as Heinz and what the best way is to stop people sitting next to you on public transport. He didn't kiss me, but I just thought that was because my dad was there.'

'I'd kiss you,' he would say.

'That's because you're my boyfriend.'

'True. Anyway, carry on.'

'Then my dad left to get the train home, and my brother said, "Want to get another drink?" and – *how weird is this?* – Joe was like, "Yeah."'

'*What?*'

'Yeah, we had two pints at the Old Royal Oak.'

'Honestly, fuck this guy.'

'And then we said bye to my brother, and as soon as he was out of hearing distance, Joe pulled me to the side of the road and just said, "I want to be on my own."'

'And he was completely normal at dinner?'

'Yeah.'

'I don't get it. It sounded like you guys were really getting on.'

'Yeah, I mean, we'd had sex every night for, like, two weeks.'

When I get home an hour later and open the door, his eyebrows would slant down with sympathy, and he'd hug me so tightly I'd feel pressure gathering around the bones of my face. Then he'd pull me by the wrist to the living room, where he would've been lying on the sofa in front of one of those experimental black-and-white films; the ones he watches when I'm not there to ask what's going on. '*I don't understand, like, is it a dream sequence or did that guy really just remove his own eyeball and then send it in a box to his mum?*'

And he'd say, 'Sit down,' and ask, 'Tea?' and I'd say yes, hoping it would be better than the ones he usually makes me, knowing it wouldn't be. When the mug arrives the teabag would still be in there, floating in the milky brownness.

'Finish off what you started,' I'd joke, and he'd say, 'It's brewing,' again and again until it's cold, or I've given up and drunk it. I hate it when the wet paper of the bag brushes against the top of my lip, but the fact he is trying to help would make my chest as hot and gooey as a chocolate fondant. Or I'd get annoyed at his lack of effort. *'My boyfriend just dumped me, and you've not even put enough milk in. You know I like sugar in it, right? Why do I have to do everything?'*

I pretend I would play nice because it hurts knowing that so often I haven't. He would roll me a cigarette, even though he only has dust left and I can roll one myself better than he can, I actually reckon. And then he would hold my feet between his big bony hands because it's my favourite thing in the world. Mum said when I was a baby I cried until she did that for me, and since I moved away from home to live with him, he took up this duty of care. Now he's my 999 number, my 'In Case of Emergency' on the form, the person I would ring when my boyfriend dumped me.

Eventually, he would say, 'Right, I'm off to bed,' which really means, 'We're off to bed,' since he has to get up at 7 a.m. for work, and I always wake him up if I get into

IX

bed after him because he's a bad sleeper. There are always so many monsters walking through his dreams, leaving him tooth-grinding and back-scratching all night.

In the bathroom, I'd watch him use my expensive Clarins Restorative Night Cream, and this time I wouldn't tell him that he needs to buy his own, and I'd use his toothbrush because I like the hard bristles of his one better, and he wouldn't tell me that's disgusting – he'd know you shouldn't pick a fight with someone who's just been dumped.

In the darkness of the bedroom, I'd feel his finger sliding up and down my thigh, and I'd know that he wants to fuck. I'd sit thinking about it for a while because my body is so closed off from me sometimes, as though I'm living in the same house as someone I no longer talk to. But in the end I would think about what he'd done for me that day and concentrate on throwing myself into a yes. Animating each limb with what wanting looks like, moving over to sit on him, taking off my T-shirt. Then his hand would loop around my neck and pull me down, and I'd collapse like something that was already breaking. We'd press our mouths together so hard I'd feel the ridges of his teeth from behind the softness of his lips and his hot breath running down my ear and into me until everything on the inside tickled and wheezed.

'I need you,' I'd say, not quite sure what I'm talking about anymore – for forever, or inside me? Then I'd be climbing down his chest, pulling off his underwear, and since I am sad he'd know I'm not in the mood to choke

x

on him, so instead he'd turn me over again and I'd pull a pillow over my face, and under there everything would start to drift away, as though I was floating to the bottom of a pond with rocks in my pockets. *Thump-thump-thump* and my whole body would be squeezing tighter, coiling towards him like sunflowers turning to the sun, and I'd get cramp in my foot because it felt so good it's like my body needed something to sting to put the pleasure into perspective.

Afterwards, he'd roll off me, and I'd think, *Annie, you really should make more of an effort, he'll get bored soon*, and all his limbs would be as slack and heavy as rubber car tyres. He'd arrange himself on the bed with his face down, arms pinned to his side, legs out straight in a way that no one else could possibly find comfortable.

'You look like a little rocket,' I'd say, and a laugh muffled by the mattress would break out from the sides of his lips. 'Or a sardine in a can.'

Silence then. But I'd add: 'Can we make sure we always stay in the same can?'

Hearing no response, I would move to get comfy, but when I stretch my leg out he'd say, 'This is my side,' and I'd say, 'It isn't,' pointing to the centre of the bedhead, which we're meant to exist on separate halves of. We can both see it now because our eyes have adjusted to the light. Everything looks frosted blue, even though really it's black, and there's a scary outline of a body where his shirt is hung up outside the wardrobe, ready for work tomorrow.

'What are you thinking about?' I'd ask, and he'd shut me up by wrapping his arms all the way around me and jokingly covering my mouth, as though ready for murder. When his hand slackens off me, I'd fall asleep, feeling better than I did when he found me.

Except he wasn't there that night, because he really did end our five-year relationship on the side of the road at King's Cross station. And he really did break my heart. It feels like the worst act of betrayal in the world, to have the one who's meant to help get rid of my pain be the one making it.

What really happened is, he went back home to his mum's flat in West London. And I was in bed on my own, stuck, waiting for my leg to hit the scratch of his long thigh hair against the stubble of my own, to hear the tinny sound of the philosophy podcast he listens to as he sleeps leaking out of the sides of his headphones, for someone to croak, half-asleep, 'Can you pass the water?' And even though I knew he wasn't there, I slept on my side of the bed, knowing this logic no longer mattered, wishing it still did.

SALT

I

I don't feel anything at first. I'm actually laughing by the time I get home from dinner.

'You'll never fucking believe what's just happened,' I tell our flatmate Molly, and she pauses *Mario Kart* and bites her lip, bracing for the punchline. 'He dumped me,' I say, and she jerks back so suddenly the cat jumps off her knees and runs into another room.

'I'm sorry' just feel like two words so she hands me a joint, when normally she'd say 'if you transfer me a fiver' first, and I thank her as my mind fizzles out into something like flat cola. Romance feels like a bad idea, so we watch a film where men with serrated butcher knives are chasing women. The baddy pulls a body up and her neck creaks against the rope he closes around it.

'What did you say to him?' Molly shouts back from the kitchen, where she's pouring herself a giant bowl of Crunchy Nut.

'At first I thought he was just saying he wanted to move out and I was like, "If you think you'd be more comfortable that way then sure," and then I realised what he meant and so I said, "You know this means you won't get to see me ever again?" and he sort of nodded. He couldn't even look at me, and then I said, "Have a nice life," and walked off.'

'Nice,' says Moll. 'Bet he was gutted.'

'I did feel a bit like I was in *Real Housewives of Beverly Hills* or something. You know when they drop a fiery comeback before the commercial break.'

'If only you'd had a drink you could've thrown at him.'

They say it takes half the length of a relationship to get over its ending. Has anyone managed to get over it in a night? I want to wake up out of a coma two and a half years from now having missed the entire thing. A doctor shining one of those tiny torches in my eyes.

'Morning, it's 2022 and you've forgotten all about him and you have a new boyfriend and great hair.'

I text Josh, a guy from back home that I worked in a pub with. Joe didn't want me to be friends with him because he knew there was something between us. It makes me feel giddy, as though what I'm doing is against the rules. I'm allowed to do whatever I want now. Josh responds with a voice note:

'Now then, Annie Lord, tell me you're out tonight?'

There's something so hot about someone referring to you by your full name. It reminds me of being told off by a teacher. I listen to it again. I like how his thick Yorkshire accent curls over the Ts until they disappear, smooth as a beach pebble. Josh sends a photo from where he sits in the pub, gums shining pink through his smile, beer froth bubbles popping on his top lip. I message other nearly-sort-of-but-not-quite men and try to build some kind of scaffolding of attention that will prevent me from ever hitting the ground.

'What's he said?' asks Moll, but Josh has stopped replying.

I wonder if I should ring my parents, but then I remember the way Dad held onto Joe's shoulders after dinner.

'You're a good lad, aren't you?' he said, and then slapped him hard on the back in that way men do when they don't want shows of affection to seem affectionate. I want Dad to preserve Joe in his head that way because what if Joe changes his mind and I've already told my parents? It would be tense next time he comes over for dinner.

There's all this adrenaline in me; it sparks in my stomach like electricity, it heaves through my lungs. I suppose I'm anxious, but it feels more like anticipation, as though I'm off to a house party later or going on holiday in the morning. I remind myself of what has happened, but I can't yet feel the solidity of understanding close down around me. All my wires are tangled up.

What was it that made Joe end it? Stopping and turning around under the shadow of a big glass office building, so nervous he was scraping the sole of one Reebok against the other.

'I think I just need to be on my own.'

Was it my bloated too-much-plastic-cheese stomach? Or when I made him list the Kardashians in order of hotness and then screamed that he was wrong when he placed Kourtney so far down? Or perhaps I was so perfect that it made him think it was time to cut me out before he hurt me more than was necessary.

Not that any of this seems necessary.

He must have been planning it for a while; no one breaks up with someone after five years on a whim. Knowing that he was keeping all this private knowledge from me is hurtful. I thought I knew everything he was thinking, which friends he was annoyed with, the consistency he liked his porridge. I should have known he was about to break up with me. We always made decisions as a team. Maybe that's why he did it, because he wanted to start making decisions all on his own.

I wonder if I am focusing on the idea that he kept this secret because the reality of him actually leaving is too big to comprehend. I can't picture what that would look like. I can see a house without his belongings, I can see me cooking for one, but he's always there, getting jealous, bumping into me at parties; he always comes back.

I'm so stoned my head dissipates into this murky puddle. I breathe and then I look over at Moll and wonder if the last breath I took was weird. I nearly say something about one of the characters' outfits, but then I decide it's too much effort to complete the thought, so just say 'as if' instead. The film ends and Moll gathers up her laptop and the blankets she brought down from the room she shares with Danny.

Just before going up to bed, she turns around and says: 'You can't take him back, you know.' I nod at her but I'm not even sure I know what 'back' would look like.

The next morning I wake up and book a train home to my parents' house in Leeds because it feels like something that a person who has just been dumped would do. It's there on the 11.15 North Eastern service that I feel my heart break. Walkers sharing-packets, pre-downloaded episodes of *The Wire*, the guard's voice saying, 'We will shortly be arriving at Stevenage' – and something in my chest snaps; the separate halves of it drift apart like rubbish in the ocean caught by two different tides.

I met you on the way to our first lecture. I walked into the big red university building rubbing my arms because September didn't feel as summery as I thought it would when I set off in a crop top. I got lost in the long corridors, every turn met with the same yellow flecked paint and worn-out carpets, room 11a where 12b should be.

'Did you say you're looking for the Philosophy Department?' you ask, a few paces behind me.

'I didn't,' I reply. 'But that is where I'm going actually.'

Together we found a map, worked out which floor we had to get to and squeezed into the packed lift, my face pressed too close to your chest, my backpack nudging the girl behind me.

We will dissect this moment years later when we know each other better. Maintaining an air of smugness over our former selves who knew so little about what would pass between us. I'll tell you that I couldn't stop giggling at everything you said. You'll say, I know. You'll say you thought I was hot, though. And I'll wonder how that was possible given my tangerine-orange box-dyed hair, eyebrows shaved into little half-moons.

When we walked inside the room, I pulled out a chair and you picked the one next to me. I could see the bones of your shoulders poking up through your white shirt. 'Lion' said a swirling tattoo on the soft underside of your forearm. I don't know who calls you that, but you could be one: skin the colour of a well-brewed cup of tea; floppy posh-boy curls; a huge mouth, big enough to fit a fist into, bigger when laughter is falling out of it.

You sat with one leg over the other, like how girls are supposed to sit. Damp feet from walking over wet grass with those holes in your Vans. You made your jeans look expensive even though there was a safety pin over the busted zip.

One day you will ask me who the best-looking person I ever met was and I will make up some lifeguard from a family holiday in Wales because it's embarrassing that the answer is you.

After Custard Creams and a slideshow about how, if we are lucky, philosophy might help us get a job in advertising, I followed you out of the lecture theatre. You and a girl called Esme smoked and talked about friends of friends in West London. 'Such a small world!' *Maybe your world is just small?* I thought, but didn't say. Back then I still believed that everything that came out of my mouth was stupid. You talked about the house parties you both went to last night and I placed a palm over my Freshers' Wristband. I couldn't believe how cool you were. I couldn't believe I went to a foam party. You and Esme exchanged numbers, then you asked for mine too.

It's hard to describe quite how bad I feel right now. I learn later on that this is normal. Pain is so difficult to convey to others that in 1971 two scientists developed the McGill Pain Questionnaire to help medical patients explain to doctors the precise nature and dimension of their affliction. Overall there are twenty sections, and throughout each the patient must choose which adjective best aligns with what they are feeling.

Is it . . .?
1. Flickering
2. Pulsing
3. Quivering
4. Throbbing
5. Beating
6. Pounding

Is it . . .?
1. Jumping
2. Flashing
3. Shooting

Is it . . .?
1. Pricking
2. Boring
3. Drilling
4. Stabbing

There are another sixty-four adjectives to choose from. I keep looking for the right words, but each time they escape me, like when you turn around to try to see your own shadow. I find that too often words fall short, reducing the overwhelming swell of feeling to an isolated sensation as though it was just one thing and not all of you at that moment.

'It hurts,' I say when I ring my best friend Vicky from somewhere outside Grantham. The same phrase that comes out of me when I have a cold or period pains.

I get off the train and leave the station, and Mum's there in the car park, walking towards me, leaving the door of her Polo wide open. 'Oh, love,' she says, and wraps her arms around my neck so tightly I feel some of the hairs on my head popping out. On the drive home I cry with my head pressed against the warm glass of the window. When I look up, I see that there's a shininess in her eyes too.

'What's wrong with you?' I ask.

'I don't know.'

She brings the corner of her sleeves up to her eyes and dabs away the wet.

'Why are you crying?'

'Because I don't feel happy unless you're happy,' she snaps back at me, the car veering slightly too close to the pavement. Everything is quiet for a bit except the soft whooshing of lorries overtaking us. 'You're only as happy as your least happy child – have you heard that saying?'

Perhaps it doesn't matter that I can't find the words, because those that care can see the right ones written all over the lines in my face.

''Ey up, kiddo,' says Dad when I get inside the house, half embarrassed at the melodramatics of it all. 'Would a tea help? Probably not?' He looks at the ground and then back up again. Then he starts picking at the garden soil that's worked its way under his nails. 'I bought lots of soya milk – is that right? Or is it oat milk that you like? I've forgotten which one you said is burning down the rainforests.'

'I'm just gonna go to bed, I think,' I tell him.

My room hasn't changed much since we moved here when I was eight. Bones, my Beanie Baby, lies mangled from over-squeezing on the bed. Sickly pink pom-pom curtains at the window were Mum's compromise for re-fusing to paint the whole room in fuchsia like I wanted. The shelves are covered with things I didn't like enough to bother to take with me to London, books I'm slightly embarrassed to have read, foundation it took me a long time to admit is too dark for my skin. I've cried a lot in this room: when I hid Dad's cigarettes in my Duplo box because Mrs Fletcher told me that smoking gives you cancer; when I wasn't allowed to see my friend's metal band Decayed Messiah at the Three Horseshoes because it was a school night; when hormones gave me spots, and then again because hormones made me more upset than I should be about spots.

I get under the duvet and scream into my pillow until it's wet with spit. I thrash until the sheet comes off the corner of the bed. And there's that pain again, wriggling out from under the strength of my descriptions.

'I could feel my skull. You know when you feel something you're not meant to feel?' I remember my friend saying when he hit his head coming off a bike, and I remember feeling it in my own head as he said it. While talking, he ran one thumb over the length of his scar. 'Then there was that metallic taste of blood running into the back of my mouth. And my brain seemed to swell up one thousand times the size and there was this heavy bowling ball gliding over its hard floor, scraping off the paintwork.'

If words are dead ends, then metaphors are doors that I can try to open up. When you compare pain to another thing, those that are listening can fill in the abstraction with their own interpretations. My friend's pain was a bowling ball and mine is something like a tarantula who's using my body as her nest. I can feel her pulling up my oesophagus, the lump of her body balancing at the edge of my throat. I swallow her down, but eight legs means she works her way back up again quickly. Fighting the pain is tiring, so eventually I fall asleep and when

I wake up there are a few delicious seconds of quiet when I've forgotten what's happened. But then I feel the bristle of her legs scraping against the pink smoothness of my gut and I remember. It seems like a fault of nature that my unconscious mind could be so cruel.

Maybe now that I can explain the pain a bit more, those who hear me will share in that feeling? Take some of it away with them?

'Oh my God, please, stop,' I said when my friend told me about his head injury. 'You're making me nauseous.'

But just because you know the name of a flower doesn't mean you understand what it is to be one.

It was the Tuesday after Freshers' Week and it felt good to take a break from sambuca shots and Adele 'Set Fire to the Rain' remixes. I was watching *Gossip Girl* on the laptop with my flatmates. My phone buzzed. 'Hey, it's me from philosophy. You out?' It was 12.30 a.m., which meant I probably wouldn't make it into town until 2.30 a.m., and the clubs shut at 3 a.m. I was supposed to think it's not worth it, but I got up.

'Guys, whose room did I leave my make-up bag in?'

Eyelids tacky with fake-eyelash glue, L'Oréal Elnett hairspray dry against the back of my throat, Nina Ricci toffee apple smell, my flatmates' laughter, my new best friend Jess screaming, 'She's literally the worst!' at the laptop as Serena starts kissing Blair's boyfriend again, a Budget Taxis to Perdu in Newcastle's city centre, a plastic bottle of vodka and cranberry mix for the way and a pre-rehearsed excuse about losing my friends, and I found you. The bartenders were loading the dishwasher for the final time, but paying £5 entry didn't seem like a loss.

Walking through Newcastle's cobbled streets, you laughed, and against the dark sky your teeth were tinged grey.

'I only want to be with you,' you told me, so we ran away from your friends to eat bolognaise chips under the metallic of Best Kebab's strip lighting. Our calves pressed together under the table and it felt as though someone was whisking my insides until they thickened. For a moment I thought I heard you say, 'I-love-you,' but you were just saying, 'How could you?' because I nicked a chip from your pile. I imagined the words I wanted to hear being swallowed up with the grease sinking down your gut. At least then they would get to live on in your stomach.

Broken-heart syndrome is a dangerous disorder that causes chest pain, breathlessness and low blood pressure. Most patients recover, but research shows that the condition can scar and weaken the heart muscles. It is known formally as takotsubo cardiomyopathy. The medical world recognises it as a temporary condition where sudden emotional upset or other physical stress can cause the apical ballooning of the heart's left ventricle. It distorts and enlarges so that it's narrowed at the top and swells outwards at the bottom. The Japanese word '*takotsubo*' is the name of an octopus trap with a similar form. The octopus can get into the circular trap, but there's not enough room for it to manoeuvre itself to turn around and get out.

I feel like I've swallowed a gobstopper.

If I had takotsubo cardiomyopathy – a name, a fancy scientific name, to legitimise this feeling – would I feel better?

Mum sits with me while I cry. 'That's it, get it all out,' she says. The palm of her hand rubs my back in circles to dislodge what's choking me, trying to free the octopus from the trap.

2

The day after I get home Mum takes me to see Granny in hospital. She's in ward J45 recovering from a cancer operation that removed most of her bowel. Under the strip lighting you can see through her skin as though she were wrapped in the casing of a crystal dumpling. Blood chugs around purple puffy veins. Tendons ripple as she moves. She says it feels like there's a band around her stomach, pulling tighter and tighter until it's hard to breathe. I want to tell her I feel it too.

I'm scared to tell Granny about Joe, scared that she will forget so that I will have to keep repeating the fact again and again, a fresh wound every time, sticky liquid as another scab is picked away.

'Annie's feeling a bit low, aren't you?' says Mum, patting my leg. 'Joe ended things with her.'

'Oh dear,' Granny says, her eyes so still I wonder if she thinks Mum said something different. But then she sighs. 'You need to have a fling.'

Mum and I laugh, both of us shocked that a woman neither of us has ever heard swear would encourage something so casual. But I'm confused. I thought she liked Joe.

'He's a lovely young man,' she would say every time he came over to eat the ginger biscuits she laid out in a perfect semicircle on a plate. 'So handsome,' she told all the ladies at bridge. 'You can tell he's going to be very successful.'

A nurse comes over and lifts Granny's legs up to try to drain some of the fluid that has built up in her calves.

'Tell Annie about Henry,' Mum says, and then Granny talks about the man before Grandpa. He wanted to join the Air Force, but she wouldn't go with him because that would mean giving up her friends to live in garrisons where you weren't allowed to put pictures on the walls because at any moment you might have to pack up and move to another place where humans were pointing guns at each other.

'He said he would wait for me at the top of my road at 7 p.m. for an hour. If I didn't come, he would know it was over.' She stops for a while. Eyes looking beyond the walls of the ward to something I cannot see. 'I didn't go,' she says.

I wonder if her mum comforted her. If her tears soaked the bed damp. 'Did you cry, Granny?'

'I suppose I did.'

That's the thing about pain: we forget it. Our bodies can withstand more than we give them credit for. Granny knows this more than anyone. Evacuated during the war to the country so that the walls of her home didn't crumble on her seven-year-old knees, stomach rumbling under the covers at night because all there was to eat was boiled eggs, a ruler to the wrists if she dared complain. She's so pale now, the brown of her age spots fading into the white of the bedsheets she lies on.

When it's time to go I feel guilty because I've wanted to leave for a while. It never seems as though you've stayed for long enough. Stupidly, when you don't visit at all you never feel guilty because you can pretend none of it's happening. As we stand up to leave, Granny's painting on mauve lipstick and patting her hair into place so she looks presentable for the doctor.

Before Mum and I walk away she looks over at the old lady in the bed opposite. 'I don't look as bad as that, do I?'

'No,' I laugh. 'You look much better.' When I hug her she feels like a wilting flower, one that keeps going even though there's no sun. I want to be strong like Granny, but I'm not sure I'm made of the same matter as her. She's iron and I'm something like dust.

In Victorian times, women would mourn the death of a loved one by filling small vials called lachrymatory bottles with their tears. By the time the liquid had evaporated the grieving period would be over. You can find these antiques for sale on Etsy.

'Beautiful moon and star design,' writes one seller.

'Essential for any lover of eighteenth-century gothic,' writes another.

There's a reference to the practice of tear-catching in one of the psalms when a pilgrim worn out by the hate of others says to God: 'You have kept an account of my misery; put my tears in your bottle' (Psalm 56:8). The man finds solace in the fact that God keeps a record of his pain, so nothing is wasted.

I like to measure my tears too. To see my suffering quantified, categorised.

I cry until I have a dehydration headache. I cry until my face crumples up like tissue paper and then I take a picture and send it to my friends, and they say, 'I've never seen you look so sad.' I cry until I can't remember when it was that I wasn't crying. I cry until I've worked through more tissues than a person with the flu. I cry until I feel as though I might have given myself the flu. I cry until I'm craving salty foods, anchovies, capers, chips, to replace all the electrolytes I've lost. I cry until it feels as though I could fill my bedroom with tears, the carpet sodden, squelching under my toes, liquid rising up until I'm paddling in it, wetness creeping up the walls until the paint turns damp and flakes away. I'll cry until the skin of my calves becomes pruney, until I can swim around the room, until my belongings start to float out of their drawers and my legs strain from doggy-paddling above the wet.

Eventually, when the liquid hits the ceiling and there's no more room for my head to breathe above the tide, I feel that I might drown in my tears like Alice in her Wonderland.

Granny seemed to come alive when she was talking about Henry. The colour flushed back into her cheeks and she could form full sentences, where usually everything just looped back around to, 'Where are my glasses?'

'Everything is so sharp when you are young,' she smiled. 'When you're old like me you might even miss feeling this bad.'

* * *

A more discerning internet search into lachrymatory bottles reveals that they weren't really used for tear-catching. Art dealers found that people were more likely to buy them if they heard this invented melancholic backstory. These bottles were only used for perfume or vinegar.

If the average one is 4.5 inches high, it would take 200 years to fill a lachrymatory bottle all the way to the top with tears.

Up to 60 per cent of the body is made up of water; does that mean once I have cried all of it out I will be a different person? One filled with a liquid less tainted by sadness?

Tears flush out adrenocorticotropic hormones, which cause high stress levels, so that you feel calmer, while also triggering the release of natural opiate leucine enkephalin, which reduces pain and improves mood.

That's why you feel such an abounding looseness when the tears have all come out, like a blow-up bed drained of air.

I'm sitting on the floor of my room on my fourth day at home when I ring Andy, a mutual friend who I use as a spy.

'What did he look like?' I ask, pulling at loose carpet strands until they unravel.

'Not great. To be expected, I guess,' he says, ordering a coffee on the other end of the line.

'So, he didn't cry or anything then?'

'Not in front of me, no.'

I can see what Joe looked like when Andy spoke to him, a light shrug and then he'd be looking down to rearrange his feet under the smoking-area picnic table so that he could hide the tension in his jaw. *'I'll miss her, but we couldn't carry on how it was going. She was always on my case about stuff, dishes, nights out with the boys, we were arguing a lot.'* And then he wouldn't say anything more because I don't think he'd want to even talk about it because that might make the lip wobble and then the pain might *splish-splosh* onto the floor where someone could see it. Instead, it would be, *'Southampton have been playing well,'* and a discussion of the last film he saw.

When he's on his own, even more distraction. The *New York Times* music podcast on while he crushes garlic under the flat side of a knife, listening to punk or some other genre I don't get so it won't remind him of me. If he never cries, does that mean his grieving process never ends or does it mean he never grieves at all?

I'm back in your university room on Holly Avenue, a Sports Direct mug filled with fag ends, a postcard of two clasped hands from the Picasso Museum blu-tacked to the wall. We're watching this film about abortion called *Lake of Fire* after a 'best documentaries of all time' Google search.

You're pulling your skin around to try to show me the bite marks on your back where a boy in your class bit you in Year 7; your finger touches those small craters where the skin never grew back.

'Ralph did that, you know?'

I pretend it's the first time you told me. A protestor comes into frame and shouts 'sexist bigotry' in a particularly nasal voice. It's not funny, but we have smoked so much it seems like it is. You spit cookie crumbs over the bed. I'm laughing so hard I press my eyelids down until they sting, my breath is asthmatic, we look at each other, desperately, *please stop doing this to me*, a stitch in my side. One lone tear rolls down the steep incline of your cheekbone. You put your tongue out and taste the salt.

By the end he wasn't crying with laughter, but with frustration. I was crying because I knew it would get me what I want. Tears are women's weapons. And like men and their guns, they can be used unfairly; 'crocodile tears'. The phrase comes from the myth that crocodiles cry while eating humans, feigning grief while doing bad things.

I say myth, but in 2007 a scientist fed crocodiles and noticed that the reptiles teared up while eating their food, with some of their eyes frothing and bubbling.

'You can do so much better,' says Moll as I cry down the phone to her. 'He's not worth your tears. Do you remember that time you were making him a stir-fry and you accidentally touched him with the hot pan? He was so angry and it was only an accident.'

'It was a boiling-hot pan,' I say. 'If anything, his response was mild.' As I speak one of my tears hits my phone and slips down the groove at the side of the screen so that for the rest of the call I worry that the circuit board will break and I'll have to buy a new phone because it's not insured. 'He got a big blister from it! I would have bitten his head off if it was the other way round!' I've reached the point in my crying where my breath rattles out in short, sharp bursts. 'It's all my fault!' I say, but the tears make it look like I'm the innocent one.

Why did I get so angry at him for leaving his stuff everywhere? Why did it make me so angry that I took a picture of each untidied-away item and sent it to him as evidence? His suitcase spilling out from under the bed. His clothes leaking out of the drawer. Beer on the mantelpiece. Why did I do it a week later when there was an even smaller collection of things left out? Vape juice. Deodorant. Why did I let cleanliness and order become the language of our love? Believing he couldn't possibly care for me if he left me with his mess, when really he could have just not minded it, like the younger version of me who would throw her coat and shoes in all the wrong places and it would feel light and easy because I never cared where things landed. Why didn't I say, 'I don't care, I love you,' when he replied to the pictures with, 'Sorry, I wasn't thinking because I was excited to get out, sorry'?

Why did I get so annoyed that he didn't want to join our friends Davey and Maya and Jonny and Eve on that couples' holiday to Paris? Why did I keep sending him job applications for stuff he didn't want to do like the ALDI grad scheme or that assistant marketing consultant role? Why didn't I just let him leave his trainers on the floor rather than on the shoe rack? Why didn't I just say, 'You look,' when he asked where the towels were rather than finding them for him on the radiator and then being passive-aggressive for hours after? Why did my shoulders tense up like that when he came over and kissed the bit where they curved down into the collar bone? Why did I say, 'Sorry, I just need a bit of time to myself,' in a voice that made it sound like I wasn't sorry at all?

It's the morning of the fifth day and I've been awake for a couple of hours when Mum walks into my room without knocking. 'I could have been wanking,' I tell her.

She ignores me and says, 'Shall we go get you a bra fitted? You need to get measured. You need some proper support.'

I turn away from her and look outside the window where there's the rumble of cars creeping over the speed limit on the busy road. The sky looks pale and drained, as though the clouds have been feeding on it. 'People my age don't wear bras anymore,' I say, then protest for a while about how I wear boob tubes, halter necks, strappy tops, bikini tops, off-the-shoulder tops, all of which look weird with bras, and when I'm working I sit at home wearing nothing under a T-shirt. But because I'm sad she'll probably pay, so eventually I say, 'Let me get my shoes on.'

It's a small shop on a cobbled back street. Everything is baby pink and black, and in the window white mannequins sit with their heads and legs sliced off, wearing bridal sets. Inside the changing rooms, the store assistant, Mary, runs her hand underneath the thick black band of the push-up she's dressed me in. 'Fits perfectly,' she smiles.

'It's not really my thing,' I say. 'There's too much padding.'

'Try this,' she says. 'It's the Emma, very popular, we have it in turquoise as well.' Then I'm in another medical restraint, thick foam rising up my chest, lace inserts, scaffolding.

'Sorry, it's just really not my thing,' I say.

I can tell Mary doesn't like me from the way her mouth moves into a smile while her eyes sit still, the way she smacks the hangers against each other when searching for what she wants.

'I like stuff like this more,' I tell her, pulling out a sheer black bra from a nearby rack with lots of straps crisscrossing over it. I feel a welt of sadness thinking about how I stopped wearing underwear like this for him. Everything became elasticated, period-stained.

'I'm not sure that would fit you,' says Mary. 'This is for women with a more modest bust.'

A warm, oily tear glosses over my eye and spills, rolling a shiny line down my cheek. I laugh and wipe it away. 'God, why am I crying?'

'She's going through a break-up,' whispers Mum.

'It's getting ridiculous at this point,' I say. 'Just ignore me.'

Mary's shoulders sink down from where stress had pinned them up.

'Now I do *not* miss that feeling,' she says, wrapping her arms around me with so much kindness my tears flood freely as blood from an arterial wound. She lets go and, with her hands on my arms, says: 'You feel like you're going to die, don't you?'

Knowing Mary has gone through the same thing makes me feel less alone with my pain. I should find comfort in that, but instead it just makes me annoyed. A lot of the time the only way to withstand pain is to poeticise it, imagine it as something beautiful, unparalleled. Why suffer for something ordinary?

I want to think of a way to beat Mary's words to describe something more acute. But all I can do is agree because she's right, that is what it feels like: dying.

When I get home I google 'can you die from . . .' and it turns out 'heartbreak' is second only to 'a hangover'.

I resolve to write a love letter because it sounds like something dedicated lovers would do, the diehards. I begin with: 'From the moment I saw you I knew I wanted to belong to you,' and though I feel the words deep in the marrow of my bones, when I read them back, and the ones that follow them, without dreaminess, concentrating on the grammar, the syntax, I see that too many have said this before. So much so that the words have become dead and dumb from overuse.

I try beginning it with: 'I don't like the world without you in it,' and find that again I have been captured in a cliché. I might as well say, 'Love is a drug.' 'You've got the key to my heart.' I might as well run through the rain to the airport and stop him before he gets on a flight. I'm caged up by a wall of Hallmark cards. A Care Bear carried on a love-heart-shaped cloud under the words: 'I'm so glad we found each other.' I try to think of a new way of expressing my love, but it seems all the ways have already been taken.

'I love you' is an exception to this rule. You can say those three words again and again and they only increase with meaning each time. When you've got grey hair and crow's feet, telling someone 'I love you' will mean more than it did when it first tumbled out on a night when you came hard and then rolled off what's now soft and drifted into a deliciously milky half-sleep.

'I love you.'

'What did you say?'

'I love you.'

'I love you too.'

Crying is the only other exception. Roland Barthes says tears are the truest language of love because they are sent from the body. 'Words, what are they?' he asks. 'One tear will say more than all of them.'

In *Bluets*, her memoir about (among other things) love and heartbreak, Maggie Nelson quotes a clinical psychologist who says that although it seems strange to imagine that crying could be anything other than innate and innocuous, in fact, sometimes crying is 'maladaptive, dysfunctional or immature'. This hits me the same way it hits Nelson.

'Well then, as you please,' she responds. 'This is the dysfunction talking. This is the disease talking. This is how much I miss you talking. This is the deepest blue, talking, talking, always talking to you.'

Do you hear me crying from where you sleep at night?

Maybe instead of a letter I should just send a video of myself crying. Or maybe I should cry onto the paper and let him see the stains. I wouldn't ring him up and cry into the answering machine because that's a cliché too.

A couple of days ago I rang my older brother and he started telling me about his break-up with his first girlfriend. The relationship fizzled out after two years. A shared future of Le Creuset pans in volcanic orange and split rent on a studio apartment turned into avoiding each other on the narrow streets of their university town. 'It hurts so much, doesn't it? But you will get through this. It took me a while but now I realise our break-up was the best decision for both of us.'

'Mmm,' I said down the receiver. 'Mmmm,' all the while itching to scream, *'You don't get it! Me and Joe were different!'*

My brother laughed. 'This is quite embarrassing actually. At one point I was so upset I nearly went to her house with a fucking love letter. David was like, "Don't be a moron," and managed to stop me just before I put it into the postbox.'

Knowing that my brother planned to send a love letter makes me feel queasy. Not because he now considers it a moronic decision, but because I hate that he was as dedicated to heartbreak as to write one in the first place.

I wonder what his letter said. Did it begin with 'From the moment I saw you I knew I wanted to belong to you'? Did it list out all their inside jokes? Describe what she was wearing when they first met? Laugh about a stupid argument? Explain why this break-up is all just some big mistake?

I miss Joe so much I want to build a shrine for him. I'd pile each block of rock one on top of the other until my back was breaking. I would chip at the stone with a pick and hammer, ignoring the blood pooling from the places where I knocked against my skin, and then I'd rub the surface into smoothness even if that meant my own skin would be rough with callouses in the end.

I'd render his likeness in solid gold and then sit him atop a huge throne with curling edges and a regally high back. I would place it in Regent's Park in the rose garden that we used to walk around, holding hands and pulling funny faces at babies waddling past in duffle coats and bright wellies. It would be huge – bigger than the one Victoria made for Prince Albert, bigger than the Sphinx, bigger than Nelson's Column. It would poke upwards into the landscape of London so that no one looking across the city could ever miss it.

In the summer, people would sit around the shrine drinking cans and dipping Doritos into hummus, saying, 'Don't worry, the burn will turn into tan.' Tourists would take photos grinning in front of it with selfie sticks. It would be on *Time Out*'s list of Best Free Things to Do in London. Everyone would see the length and breadth of my love, the biggest ever to have existed.

3

It was a few weeks into our second university semester. You were even thinner now. You had spent all your loan and that grant you got for the best mark in the humanities on beer and a coat from Acne. For weeks all you'd eaten was porridge microwaved with water. I didn't know that yet, though, because there were still secrets between us. Soon I would know you well enough to read your facial expression even when your back was turned.

I was late again to the library that morning because I'd spent too much time contouring my nose, but that was OK because you'd saved me a seat with your note-pad. You passed me books with green highlighter on the good quotes, you read my draft and corrected it when I fell into the wrong tense, explained Kant's categorical imperative until I could paraphrase it well enough to get a 2:1.

'Your syntax is off here,' you said and I nodded, only half aware of what syntax was. My brain was always slower than yours, but you always waited for it to catch up. Eyes spidered red from the beam of a laptop screen, I followed you to the canteen where you bought a black coffee. I sipped it and told you it tasted like bin juice.

'What do you like then?' You laughed. 'Strawberry Frappuccinos? Babyccinos? Breast milk?'

Then we laughed until I felt my ab muscles tweak.

Your girlfriend had come down to visit from Edinburgh.

'Is it wrong that I would rather sit in here with you than see her?'

I wasn't supposed to answer your question out loud, so I answered it in my head. *We can be wrong.*

When I walked away from Joe after he told me we were over, I felt incomplete, like I had left something behind – my card maybe, or my phone. An object of importance that it would be difficult to function without. I patted my pockets, dug my fingers into them, but I could feel my phone, my travelcard, the things I needed. I still felt wrong. When I got to the station, I thought about going back and checking the pavement, but I thought that if I had dropped anything it probably would have been taken by someone else by now.

In Plato's *Symposium*, Aristophanes, a famous Greek theatre and comedy writer, explains the myth of soulmates. According to Aristophanes, humans were originally created with four arms, four legs and a head with two faces. Fearing their power, Zeus split them into two separate halves, condemning us to spend the rest of our lives looking for that other part. According to Aristophanes, love is the pursuit of that lost wholeness.

'Each of us is a mere tally of a person, one of two sides of a filleted fish, one half of an original whole. We are all continually searching for our other half.'

That's what I had left behind when I walked away

from Joe – the other half of myself. I feel its departure now in my body. It's not localised as 'the other half' metaphor would suggest, like losing an arm or a leg, but more an all-over lack, something floating out of me, up into the atmosphere like the soul of a dead person rising up, translucent and sparkling, into the sky. What's left of me feels very small – so small I'm not sure if it would even constitute a half.

At first there was pain, but there's not even much of that anymore. Just this dull aching. As though the life is being sucked out of me. I'm so detached from everything it's like I'm watching the world through FaceTime. I spend most of my time watching endless episodes of things I hate: a Netflix documentary about glassblowing, a history series about Hitler's failed art career, another documentary called *Hannibal: The Man Who Hated Rome*.

The tears stop after a while and Mum is happy because she thinks it means I'm getting better. 'You look great, love,' she says.

I look down at myself, snot dried silver on the sleeve of my Sleeping Beauty pyjamas as though a snail has crawled up my arm. I smell like the chilli con carne we ate last night.

'I can't feel anything.'

You'd think departure would be a quiet sound, but it's not, it's noisy. His absence talks to me. I hear him like people with phantom limb syndrome can feel pain where their body part used to be. He's walking out of the shower with the towel tied around his stomach rubbing a hand through his hair, asking, 'Do you know where my phone charger is?' I feel his elbow digging into my chest while I sleep. '*Move,*' I tell him, but then I realise I was just leaning on the corner of my phone. I eat spicy food and can't stop thinking about how bad he was with spice, spitting half-chewed chillies out onto the plate, or, if he was doing all right, he'd say, 'This is hot,' so I'd notice how well he was managing.

Our two halves were so different. You'd think their shapes would prove incompatible. But somehow they slotted together perfectly; it was like someone had engineered them only for each other.

He was suspicious, I trust people.

He did things because he really believed in them, I do things because they will make me look better.

He was academic, I am creative.

He's a big-light person, I'm a lamp person.

He had all these ideas that went nowhere, I am much better at seeing something through.

He was good at grammar, I always put commas in the wrong place.

He knew where he wanted to go, I like following.

He was incredibly arrogant and incredibly insecure at the same time, I think everything I do is kind of all right.

He was always early, I am always late.

I am warm, he was cold.

He was all or nothing, I am consistent.

I am thick, he was thin.

He was tanned, I am pale.

He wanted to be loved, I just want to love.

My nose slotted into his eye socket and it fitted perfectly.

I wonder if it was the opposition of our two halves that made me feel so complete when I was with him? Because together we encompassed everything, a whole universe of planets and moons and black holes and stars and comets burning through the atmosphere.

I liked gossip, ease, never getting out of my pyjamas. I remember telling him about the Kardashians and why I loved their show.

'What actually happens on it?' he asked.

'Fuck all. They just argue over what the best crisp flavour is and walk around in £3,000 tracksuits taking turns to say how being a mum is the most important job in the world. It's so completely empty of meaning I experience it like meditation. If you fill your mind with that much nothing, then there's no room in there for all the other stuff that was stressing you out.' He didn't watch it, but he asked me about what was going on in it and he talked the minutiae with me: *Is Kylie Kris's new favourite? Are Scott and Kourtney soulmates?* He saw that it was important to me in some way, cheered for the nothing like it was a football match.

He liked complex things – subplots and dual meanings, walking fast, starting books and finishing them and immediately opening them up again on page one. I remember when we were at university and I went with him to watch *2001: A Space Odyssey* and I found it so difficult to sit through I couldn't stop tapping my foot on the floor, but after we came out of the cinema and walked through China Town, and the flashing lunch-deal offers and red dragons felt all blurry and surreal, I felt like I was walking through a kaleidoscope or one of those optical illusions where geometric shapes look like they are twirling even though they're still, or that picture of a duck that flips into a rabbit if you look at it from a different perspective. I couldn't believe that a film could have that effect on me.

I feel so disorientated right now, dizzy. I see on the front of a newspaper that it's Thursday and it feels impossible that six days have gone by since he left. When I'm moving it's like I have to remind each foot to go in front of the other. I scroll through Twitter until I realise it's 2 p.m. and I haven't managed to load up that thing I decided to watch three hours ago.

Someone tells me about their grandad getting dementia and I regard their circumstances with the level of empathy reserved for when you hear terrible stories on the news. I know it's bad, but I can't quite comprehend enough to care.

'I'm sorry,' I tell her, feeling sorry for no one but myself.

I am vertical for less than five minutes a day. Moving, half knocked-out, from one cushioned surface to another. Standing up only to eat cold pasta or slices of ham straight from the fridge.

'Want me to get you a plate?' my parents ask, hoping the act of holding a knife and fork might remind me of how I used to move through the world before he told me it was over.

Scientists carried out a study to test the physiological effects of being in a relationship. Thirty-two couples were asked to sit a few feet away from each other in a quiet, calm room but not to speak or touch. They were connected by heart rate and respiration monitors and told to mirror the movements of one another. The findings revealed that both partners showed almost identical patterns of heart rate and respiration.

The couples were then asked to perform the same exercises with a stranger. This time their hearts did not show synchrony, nor did their breathing match.

I learned to breathe in time with the rhythm of his lungs. He turned over in bed and I turned over too.

When we were together it was hard to tell where he ended and I began. It wasn't always like that, but as each year went by our perspectives became closer and closer until he would say ideas at dinner parties, not even knowing it was me that said them first, and I would say 'I' but mean 'we'. '*I don't think abstract art is my kind of thing*'; '*I'm not sure I can be bothered to hear other political views*'; '*I'm not going to go to that birthday, I think I'll have more fun at that other party.*'

Now he's gone I am condemned to spend the rest of my life missing this other arm and leg, feeling like a half-formed thing.

* * *

I've been back home in Leeds for a little over a week now. Haven't done any work since I got here, which I can get away with because I'm freelance but also can't get away with because I still need to pay rent. Moll tells me he's moved out of the flat we share with her and her boyfriend to go back to his mum's house.

Dad knocks on my bedroom door and announces: 'We're going for dinner tonight. Salvo's. We'll set off around seven – that all right?'

And then they spend all day talking about how nice it's going to be so that I know how upset they will be if I don't try.

We walk inside the restaurant. There are exposed brick walls and low-level lighting and sixth-formers in white shirts who rip receipts off card machines with fluid wrists, pirouetting between packed-out tables, arms piled with huge white plates. I order the pasta with spicy sausage meat and Mascarpone because that's what I always get. But, rather than eating it all and mopping up the sauce with garlic bread and ignoring Dad's mocking pig noises as I lean in and steal the spoonfuls of whipped cream piled on top of his tiramisu, the food just gathers in my mouth like vomit.

Being here should be a distraction, but I don't know if you can distract from something like this. Turning away from the hurt, I only feel its influence more. Like the pain is saying, *Look at me while I am talking to you.*

I remember reading a line in Roland Barthes's *Mourning Diary*, which he started writing the day after his mother's death: 'I live in my suffering and that makes me happy. Anything that keeps me from living in my suffering is unbearable to me . . . I ask for nothing but to live in my suffering.' I too don't want to escape the suffering; it's more painful when I try.

Dad asks me about some book I brought home with me and, as I struggle to respond, all I feel is *Joe doesn't want me, he wants to be on his own. I am never going to see him again.* If I give in to the hurt, let it envelop me, everything's less of a struggle.

'Haven't really read it,' I say, and then carry on pushing my pasta tubes into a triangle shape.

In the car on the way home, 5 Live Sport hums out of the radio.

'Do you feel better now you've got out of bed?' Dad asks me.

'Not really.'

Dad makes a 'huh' noise and then turns up the volume so that it's loud, shouting.

Back home, I get into my bed. An hour or so later I wake up from a half-sleep. Downstairs there's the low mumble of my parents talking so as not to be heard.

'How long do you think she'll be like this for?' Dad asks. 'She's going to have to snap out of it at some point.'

I get up and open the door to my room and yell, 'What are you saying about me?' but I haven't used my voice for anything but moaning, so the words barely crawl out of my throat. I walk out onto the landing and scream again: 'I can hear you!'

Dad looks up at me from the bottom of the stairs, the gap between his grey bushy eyebrows pinched with rage. 'Oh, so now we can't fucking talk anymore?'

He slams a door, and it feels like the whole house shakes from the impact.

The next morning, when I'm making a tea, he walks into the kitchen, his face softening outwards. He hugs me so hard my shoulder blades move in their sockets like angel wings.

'I'm sorry,' I tell him. 'I'm just not really myself right now.'

'I know,' he says, and for a moment I think about how lucky I am to have people who love me so much they will let me hate them just in case it helps.

4

Dealing with a break-up is unlike any skill you will ever learn. The world teaches you that in order to fix things you have to *do*. If you want to get better at football, *play more*. If you want to get better at painting, *paint more*. But google 'how to make him want me back' and WikiHow says 'let him contact you', 'give your ex space', 'allow them time to heal'.

Not doing requires more concentration than doing. You have to focus on it because, if you relax for even a second, your thumb might text him without your brain ever granting permission.

It's been nearly two weeks now and each moment is defined by what I do not do. I do not send him the 3,000-word love letter I spent days perfecting. I do not stand outside the shining glass doors of his workplace holding a hot chocolate and a black coffee, saying, 'We should talk.' I do not march across London to where he now sleeps in his old bed in his mum's house, the one with the lumpy mattress and the two planks missing that's so narrow that, when we slept in it, I had to be in his arms because there wasn't enough room for me not to be. I do not go see, touch, shout.

Now 252 hours of not have passed. Millions more minutes of not await me.

Sometimes I worry that the more I want him to text the less of a chance there is that he will, as though I have hexed my phone by hoping. So I put it on airplane mode and throw it across the carpet. Seconds later I crawl towards it on all fours and unlock it again.

I wake up slightly earlier than usual on the eleventh day because I've got a hair appointment. When me and Mum arrive there's still twenty minutes before I'm due, so we sit in the car park across from some ugly student accommodation. While she talks about some article she's read on women living in communes, I pull down my phone's front screen hoping that when I refresh it the 'What have I done?' text will flash on the screen. All I find is a discount from Boohoo.com.

Mum notices and changes the subject.

'When my first boyfriend Michael broke up with me, I would have chopped my arm off and given it to him if it meant he would stay with me.' She takes a leaflet from the dashboard and uses it to pick bits of croissant pastry out of her teeth. 'Thing is, I didn't even like him that much when we were together. I just didn't like that he was the one who made the final decision to end things.'

'How did you cope?' I ask.

'I went to visit my friend in London and spent the whole time drinking rosé on a deckchair in Hyde Park.'

'Did it work?'

'I got up when I found out you had to pay however much an hour to sit on them. Bloody London.'

We both laugh and it feels strange to feel my face pull in a direction that isn't downwards.

'You're doing a lot better than I ever did,' she tells me. 'I absolutely humiliated myself.'

I shrug. 'I don't feel like I'm doing good.'

'You are,' she says, patting my leg with the palm of her hand.

'I keep waiting for him to say that he's changed his mind. I just don't believe this is it.'

I look out of the window. Sometimes I try to think of a future without him, but it's like trying to imagine a new colour. With him I saw it all: we would have a bull-dog and call it Pig; our kids with his gorgeous lips and my gorgeous eyebrows; arguing about interiors because he'd want everything white and granite where I'd want patterned wallpaper and leopard-print sofas and pink chandeliers. We used to joke that he'd be the first one to lose his mind in his old age; I imagined pushing soup between his lips, all their softness now bitten through with cracks.

'The closest I can get to accepting this is to think that one day in the future, when he's got whatever he needs out of his system, he'll ask for me back. Maybe in two years' time or something.'

'Why, do you think he's sleeping with someone else?'

'Mum, as if you would even say that?' I ask, turning away from her again. 'I obviously don't want to hear that.'

She's quiet. Looks so far over me, trying to catch my eyes from an unreachable distance.

'I actually don't think that's so bad, if you let yourself imagine that in the future you'll get back together. As long as you're thinking in a few years' time and not next week or anything, because chances are, by the time you're there, you won't feel anything for him anymore so you won't get disappointed when he doesn't – sorry, *if* he doesn't.'

I walk into the hairdresser's and all around me are women who probably never forget to take their make-up off before they go to sleep after nights out. One of them, who's wearing lots of floaty linen, says to me, 'You're here to see Verity, right?' and then sits me down in front of a mirror so well lit I can see exactly how bad I look. My eyelids are so puffy they could envelop the rest of my body like a sleeping bag. I look diseased. *A case of orbital cellulitis, Graves' disease, conjunctivitis, a fist to the face.* I can't bear to acknowledge that I'm so clichéd as to seek solace from a break-up in a hair salon, so I just let Verity think I'm ugly and bury my face in a magazine.

Parting my hair, Verity presses a comb into the base of my skull and it feels so good, I shiver. She asks, 'What are we looking for today?' and I wonder about changing my hair to an icy astral blonde. Perhaps he would see the colour switch and interpret it as a signal that I'm transitioning into a new woman, one who buys lots of expensive slouchy lounge wear to walk around the house in, uses ashtrays instead of mugs and says things like, '*Well, considering the image through a Hegelian lens . . .*' But then I think of his friends smirking to him at the pub,

'So Annie's got new hair,' and him knocking one of their shoulders as if to say, *Leave her alone*, because it seems almost too easy to make fun of my pathetic attempt at rousing his attention. I end up asking for my hair the way he always liked it: ashy pink, sharp bob, slightly longer on one side than the other. 'Lovely,' says Verity. 'I'll be two seconds – I'm just going to go and mix the colour.'

I look back down at the magazine, where there's an article about Jennifer Aniston's twelfth phantom pregnancy. 'Jen already three months gone?' She's probably just eaten lunch.

If you're dumped, you can do *some* things to get your ex's attention. You just have to make sure that your movements are subtle enough that they won't seem as though you did them on purpose. I will make an Instagram account and post a picture of me taken months earlier on a girls' trip to Liverpool. In it I'm wearing a pink latex dress that makes my ass so shiny and spherical it looks like you could puncture it with a pin. I hope that the new profile will come up on his 'suggested friends' and he will see it and remember how I wore that very same dress at a party with him on New Year's Eve. *Five! Four! Three! Two! One!* And suddenly it was 2018 and our kiss was the first thing I did that year.

I deleted him on Facebook. I told people who can't keep secrets things like, 'I've been thinking about moving to Paris.' I will comment on all of our mutual friends' posts with love hearts, especially if they used to fancy me. I will rent a Jean-Luc Godard film on his dad's

Curzon Home Cinema account that I'm still logged into on my laptop and hope that he will see my choice and think about how clever I am. Maybe he'll even be tortured by nightmares of my body flopped against the torso of another man as I watch it. My ears prickled by his chest hair. My lips damp from the oily pasta sauce he made me and from the saliva on his tongue.

'You look great,' says Mum when she sees my hair. The pain of her being so unthinkingly kind is like a stomach ache. I want to keel over and hold my knees because her love is so limitless it comes back over and over again, even after I've spat in its face.

I get home and he's messaged.

'Hey, I'm not sure whether you want to talk to me at the moment, but I would like to speak about what's going on with the room in Tottenham. We can do it over the phone, or in person, or over text, or whatever is easiest for you. If you still don't feel able to speak then that's fine too, but just let me know.'

Able finally to *do*, I draft and redraft various responses as though I were writing a fucking haiku: 'I don't want to talk'; 'It hurts too much right now'; 'I'm not ready to talk.' I wonder if the space between a 'to' and a 'too' might be big enough to make him want me back. Perhaps one reply will be so perfect it'll make him remember how at one time he liked the sound of my breathing so much he tried to record it on his phone so he could listen to the soft tugging of my breath even when we were apart.

Really, I want to reply with a bullet-pointed list of all the reasons why he's wrong. But, like a well-behaved loveless object, I wait until 10 p.m. to reply, just a few words, hoping that anxiety over my response will keep him awake.

He replies again minutes later. *A sign of thoughtlessness*, I think. But why would he play hard to get with something he doesn't want to 'get' anymore?

'I know this is all very fresh and raw and painful and confusing, but it would be great if we could see each other before we come across each other at a social event. I want us to be as respectful and kind to each other as we can be to each other.' He's repeated 'each other' three times, which shows he could only have read the message over once, maybe twice. Another sign that he doesn't care. 'And I think that would begin if we could have a proper conversation. If you don't want to talk or see me again then that's your call to make, but I don't want that to be the case.'

It isn't a 'What have I done?' text. So I ignore it and cry with my wrists pressing against my eyes until I see neon shapes speckling in and out of my field of vision. I cry because it's pathetic that he still gives me butterflies even when he's talking the logistics of leaving me forever. Because I stuck to all the rules. I became a ghost and he didn't miss me when I disappeared.

5

It was one of those days when it was warm under the sun, freezing cold when it went behind a cloud. Someone had taken out all the books on phenomenology from the library so the essay that we had due soon would be impossible to write. Instead of dealing with it, we went to an art gallery that was so quiet all you could hear was the sound of rubber shoes squeaking against laminate floors. The rooms were filled with big sheets of glass sliced through with yellows, blues and reds like the windows of churches. Jesus in a crown of thorns. Saint Sebastian tied to a tree and shot through with arrows. Joe stood under one and became green, then, as he walked, he was purple; his hand drifted out and touched the yellow light. This room was made to render him in colour. In front of me dust motes flecked through the air. If I had known which ones were his skin, I would have poked my tongue out and let them dissolve there like a communion wafer.

There was no one else in the room so he just turned around and shouted, 'Do you like it?'

'It's beautiful,' I said.

He nodded and turned around, and, looking at his back, I decided to try to impress him. 'I'm not reading the descriptions, though. So much of the time when you see modern art it's all "what happens when you take found objects like wood and plastic bags and recontextualise them to fit the space of the gallery" and then it's just a dumpster heap in the corner.'

He smiled. 'You're funny. Do you know that you're funny?'

Then I smiled.

'I like that you don't just pretend to get things you don't get. You're probably smarter for not getting them, you know? Like, this looks cool, but I'm not sure it means much, but I'd try to make out that it did. You're very honest.'

It's as if some of me was hidden right down in him to begin with and the more I knew him the more I knew myself. I started to speak more in lectures. I said, 'I'm talking,' when people interrupted me. I started wearing short dresses again and stopped trying to look like the cool girls. I made fun of him because his world was small, and he laughed because not everything that came out of me was stupid. When we walked out of the gallery the sky was so blue that when you shut your eyes it shined through them bright pink. We skipped a lecture to lie on the grass with our rucksacks under our heads, comparing the amount of hair on our arms, making excuses to touch.

I sit at the kitchen table and the warm sun tickles my back through the window. The chicken stock simmering on the stove reminds me I need to eat lunch at some point.

I hear Mum come into the house; she's been at Granny's most days this week, sorting through all the belongings ready for when she will eventually leave hospital and go into a home.

Mum sits down with a heavy sigh, and I tell her I like the orange she's repainted the walls in. She says she thinks she should have picked blue, *although blue can make a room feel very cold*. Duck egg, warm okra, broken flint, dick's gristle, syphilis wisp, dog fart, balls' deep – she's undergoing a midlife crisis via colouring the house in varying degrees of muted blue. The granite surface tops become wooden. The roof needs redoing. New taps by the sink. Sometimes I wonder what will happen when the house is finished. After it's shed its skin like a snake, will Mum and Dad find peace? Or will they see a badly installed skirting board and start all over again?

Mum reaches down into her bag to get something. She taps me so I stop staring into space.

'Look at what I found at Granny's today.' She pulls out a reel of photo-booth pictures of herself as a teenager with some guy. 'Did I ever tell you about Nathan?'

I look at the photograph and feel slightly disconcerted by how much I fancy him. He's got vacant, sleepy eyes hiding behind a fringe so long that it tickles the end of his nose. Everything else is all pale denim and puckered lips.

She has spoken about Nathan before. He's the reason she stole her sister's favourite pink cardigan (it stretched because her boobs were two sizes bigger), why she lay on the carpets of dark rooms listening to *Tubular Bells* because she felt its calamitous sound was the only thing capable of understanding the depth of her feeling.

One time Mum and her sisters made a special box filled with things that they hoped would make their dreams come true. Mum put in a cutting from one of Nathan's T-shirts and asked the universe to make him fall in love with her. The three sisters buried it in the garden like witches.

'What was he like?'

'Cheeky. Wasn't into me at all. He used to meet me out the back of the disco car park and he'd lick my hand so my paid-for stamp would go onto him so he could get in for free.'

'What else?'

'Well, he had a scooter that he drove way too fast that I pretended to like riding on the back of.' She reaches over to a stack of newspapers and looks down at the crossword.

'He went to Allerton Grange High School.'

'And?'

'That's it, really.'

Sensing she's done with remembering, I message my best friend Ruchira about the holiday we just booked to Lisbon. I scroll through the Pinterest board Ruchira has made for all the make-up looks we can do when we get there. It's hard to distract from my disappointment. For years Mum loved Nathan and now she's rendered him a cartoon, one that's smudgy and incomplete. How can she no longer see the man she went mad for?

In 'The Glass Essay', Anne Carson goes back to her mother's house on a moor in the North to try to repair her broken heart. In the poem, Carson remembers a conversation she has with her mum in the kitchen:

> *You remember too much,*
> *my mother said to me recently.*

> *Why hold onto all that? And I said,*
> *Where can I put it down?*

I don't want to put it down either. I want to hold onto it until my hand burns. Until the skin peels away in flakes.

'I'll walk you home,' he said when we came out of the nightclub and onto the street. When we got to the door of my halls, he didn't walk off but stood there trying to bite down the smile that was spreading a flash of white across his face.

'If you're quiet,' I said, letting us both in. I didn't allow myself to believe it meant anything that he was here. He was probably just staying over so he was more likely to make our 10 a.m. lecture. His halls were a forty-five-minute drive away from town because he applied so late for accommodation. There was no one there but mature students and people who still thought Ring of Fire was a fun game.

'God, this is a shithole,' he said when he saw the plastic chairs in the living room of my accommodation and the fire-escape doors.

'No worries, mate, if you wanna jump in a taxi back to the suburbs, feel free.'

In the bathroom, I changed into leggings and a crop top as though I normally slept in stuff like that and not the oversized 'Don't Mess with Yorkshire' T-shirts my dad got me when I got into uni, and then I carefully moved a make-up wipe around my eyebrows and mascara because I'd heard too many guys talk about women who 'looked shit without make-up'.

In the bedroom, he was stomping his way out of his trousers. I got under the duvet and tried to shut my eyes, but I was so awake I had to think about pressing the lids closed otherwise they jumped open again. Outside the window some students were chanting, 'One plus one, two plus two, these are sums Northumbria cannot do,' about the nearby former polytechnic. My breathing was loud in my own head. I counted the number of fly corpses in the air gap between the double glazing. Looked for faces in the pebble-dash walls. We'd been lying there for an hour or two when he started it. The tips of his fingers drawing shapes on my back, eventually sliding up the back of my top, working their way down over my ribcage. Normally the moments before being intimate with men felt like psyching myself up for an exam. But right now my body felt like it knew how to move even if I didn't. I pushed my ass back against him lightly enough that it could just be me rearranging myself to get comfy on the bed. And when he never flinched away from that heaviness I moved up and down until I could feel him hardening. He put his hand over the leggings and squeezed the base of me and something in my stomach fell away like rocks tumbling down a cliff face. I got on top of him and his finger was in my mouth and I bit down onto it. I wanted to do more but I couldn't because this wasn't cheating. It was just us being inappropriate.

What would happen if Mum dug up the box in the back of Granny's garden? Would all the memories seep out like the evils from Pandora's box, wrapping themselves around bodies and forcing them to move in ways that hurt them? Would she remember Nathan and what he did to her?

Another afternoon something else about Nathan does come back to Mum. She tells me about it when I walk past where she's sitting in the kitchen, flicking through a Graham & Green homeware catalogue. 'I queued up from five in the morning outside Jumbo Records to buy Bowie's *Aladdin Sane* LP. Nathan was jealous that I got it. I wanted him to like me so much that I offered to swap it for his battered *Space Oddity* album.' Mum looks up from the cowhide rug she's circled on the page with a biro and exhales slowly. 'I'll never forgive myself for doing that for a man.'

Some people recommend writing a long list of everything you hate about an ex as a way of seeing how much better your life could be without them. When she needed to forget Nathan, Mum thought of her lost *Space Oddity* album and it made her angry enough to not want him anymore.

- Never made an effort with my friends, was even rude at points.
- Never remembered to buy milk.
- We always used to argue about that fight we had at my cousin's wedding in France when I flirted with the hot guy in front of him.

I start to write a list, but it makes me sad thinking that the bad could replace the good. That the only way we get over things is to imagine they were less than they were.

'Do you remember when he left your birthday party to go and meet Ali?'

'Do you remember how he used to always talk over you?'

'Didn't you say he stopped cooking?'

When I speak to her on the phone Moll tries to bend Joe into a shape that's so bad I'll decide I don't want him anymore. It should make me feel good, but I don't like it. It hurts when people criticise your ex because you're still in love with them and, now that you have lost them, you love them more than ever. Now the only relationship you share is one in the past tense: *had, held, tasted, touched, breathed, believed.* You can't face the memories being ruined, because that's all you have left.

I will cling onto each one until the scabs on my hands weep.

'I mean, I didn't know him *that* well,' says Aaron, a school friend who has rung me on the way to the pub where she works. 'I liked him, though.' She's talking about Joe. I was sure they had never met.

'Eh, when did you meet him?'

'You both came over to mine when Frankie had just turned two and he read to her for ages while we watched *Real Housewives of Atlanta*.'

I make no sound of recognition.

'He made us tea – because you said he was bad at doing it. He made us all one to prove you wrong? I lent you that top?' Aaron gets more frustrated as none of her prompts restarts my memory.

'*Real Housewives*?'

'Yeah, and then Frankie tried to paint his nails but she just smeared purple all over his hand.'

I still don't remember, and it alarms me. What else have I forgotten?

After his wife died, C.S. Lewis found himself frustrated at the process by which his image of his wife became increasingly inaccurate.

> Slowly, quietly, like snow-flakes – like the small flakes that come when it is going to snow all night – little flakes of me, my impressions, my selections, are settling down on my image of her. The real shape will be quite hidden in the end.

I thought I held Joe in his totality. But really I just remember what I want to remember. I see flirting in the library, cookie crumbs on his stomach, hand-holding in taxis, and all the while, this afternoon of reality TV and cold tea with Aaron has faded away. My mind doesn't lie, I don't make up things about him that never existed. But in choosing what I want to see, my impression of Joe becomes more and more my own. I pick out pieces of him and sew him back together like Frankenstein's monster.

One school of scientists believes that memories are not singular occurrences that we return to, but rather endless repetitions of that memory and the memory of that memory and that memory and so on. There is no stable 'memory fragment', or what is often called a 'trace'; instead, we create a new 'trace' each time to house the thought. Meaning each memory is a mere copy of a copy, each one a more distant reconstruction of the first.

Even if I memorised the deep crease of his eyelid, the little scrape through his eyebrow, the way the bone of his nose veers out slightly more to the right, the mole on the bottom right of his skull, they are only memories of my memories of his skin, his eyelids, his moles – far more a reflection of myself than of him. As time wears on, these images will drift further away from the original. Much like how the first statement in a game of Chinese Whispers is progressively bent out of shape.

'In Scotland the snow sleets.'

'What? No, I said, "Dan's got gross feet."'

There is another way of looking at that first night he slept in my room. In the morning, my flatmate Yla walked

in wearing nothing but a towel, already taking the hairdryer she was asking my permission to borrow. When she
saw him in my bed she screamed and ran out. I laughed and
looked over, expecting to see him doing the same. Instead,
he rubbed his hands deep into his eye sockets as though
trying to smudge away what they'd seen the night before.
His body turned away from me as he put on his jeans.

'God, I was so drunk last night, can't remember
anything.'

When we were queuing up outside the lecture hall, he
went and stood with Esme.

'Where did you get off to last night?' she asked him.

I checked my phone and Yla had messaged. 'Was that
fit philosophy guy in your bed?' 'Details now.' 'His jaw-
line is so chiselled I bet you could slice vegetables on it.'

Telling her that we dry-humped all night didn't sound
as sexy as the way it felt. I left out the part about how he
wished it had never happened.

I asked him about that night years later when we were
in the supermarket. 'I don't remember that,' he said,
squeezing an avocado to check for ripeness.

'Well, it happened,' I told him, but was I telling him
or was I telling myself? Because as soon as he expressed
doubt over my story, I couldn't see it anymore. I wondered if I had felt his hands in places that they weren't,
if I had dreamt hard muscle where there was really bone.
Perhaps he was just rearranging himself in his sleep. I
thought of his hand between my legs, but the image
blurred and distorted, fell out of my head. It was funny

arguing about whether or not it had happened back then in the supermarket, because I had already won. He was mine anyway, so it didn't really matter either way. But now it feels humiliating that something so pivotal to my idea of us could be built out of lies. I don't like this perspective. So when it hits me it's red in my mind. I push it back until it fades to black and then I fill the emptiness with the colours of another love story.

There's a rare condition called highly superior autobiographical memory, or HSAM, which causes people to recall every day of their life with startling accuracy: a white van dangerously overtaking you on the M24 on 8 September 1999 right before you stopped at Little Chef for a full English and a blueberry muffin. A long queue to get popcorn to see *Mean Girls* at the Vue in Kirkstall on 25 June 2004. The sixty or so people who have the condition often say that recovering from loss is impossible when you can't forget.

There's an episode of *This American Life* where a woman with the disorder talks about what happened when her husband died.

'Like, his death has really, like, paralysed me. I will never, ever, ever, ever forget that. I am still in March of 2005.' She tells the presenters that she thinks of her late husband around ten times a day. 'I feel like I'm still standing in the same place. It's like – it's really being stuck. It's being stuck in a moment that you can't – there's no escaping it.'

The presenters ask her how she thinks her life would be different if she could forget.

'I think that I would have been able to move forward. I think I probably would be married today. I don't think I would be so scared.'

We're meant to feel bad for her and her inability to forget, but she feels bad for us: 'I can't imagine what it would be like to not remember my life.' If you never forget you become one of those sad people who stumbles over 'my girlfriend, I mean ex-girlfriend' when talking about the past. Someone who insists their ex wants them back even when you saw on her Instagram that she's already in Marbella – or was it Lisbon? – riding around on the back of a motorbike with her tanned holiday arms around someone new.

I don't care. I want to be stuck in a moment with him forever. I want that condition so that I never have to find out what it's like not to remember him.

6

I've been here in Yorkshire for two weeks. I leave my bed more often now. Still not really showering. Still not really brushing my teeth. I decide to go on a walk to the Beach. The journey there is an adventure. Out of the house and turn left past all the bland cul-de-sacs of houses rendered in beige brick, beige insides, photos taken by a photographer in a shopping centre of kids in pigtails bouncing on trampolines. Then past the fancy houses made out of converted barns, with split-level ceilings, carpets that fill your toes, sheep in the back – not to eat but to call yourself a farmer to your friends down south. Turn down a path through a field thick with tall, stiff corn plants, whose mass of leaves look silky as lapping waves but would slice open your calves if you ran into them. At the end of the field there's a path grown over with nettles. *Private Property,* says a sign that everyone ignores. And then you find it. A bright-blue river, low-hanging tree branches tickling the water. White sand. A traffic cone whose brilliant orange has faded to peach under the sun. *Take home your litter,* wrapped in a plastic pocket nailed against a tree. The Beach isn't paradise, but it felt like it as a teenager. A place to escape parents repeatedly asking, 'So who is it that's going tomorrow?' because they still don't remember any of your friends' names, school lessons when your only joy is getting away with having chewing gum in your mouth. A place where you can feel freedom rolling your shoulders back into their sockets.

It's August so the water is almost warm. I take off my socks and dip my toes in and feel the soft brush of the tide pulling against my ankles. The fish are still here. *Garra rufa*. For a time a number of spas opened that offered *Garra rufa* pedicures; you would pay £8, dip your feet in the tanks and they would nibble the dry skin off your feet until you were smooth again. A few years ago they all closed down. People found out *Garra rufas* were only eating skin because they were being starved in between procedures. In the wild, they eat a mix of detritus, small animals and algae; they never wanted to eat anyone's feet for breakfast. *Garra rufa* come from Asia so I don't know how they have found their way to my tiny town in Yorkshire. Perhaps a spa poured them in the Wharfe after they opened an envelope to find an eviction notice. The little fish still eat feet now. Maybe they learned to like the taste. Or maybe they never learned to want anything different.

I used to come here with Josh, the guy I worked with, the one I texted when I got home after Joe dumped me. When he passed his driving test, he would pick me up in his Nissan Micra and take me here. By the time we got to the farmer's field we would be holding hands. Then we would lie down on the sand and talk until it was so dark I couldn't see where his body ended and the blackness began. I remember one time, when I'd finished telling him something about Sylvia Plath that I definitely misinterpreted, he ran a forefinger from my hairline, down the length of my nose and over my chin and told me: 'You're the cleverest person I've ever met.'

On the drive back I looked over and he was staring at me.

'What?' I asked.

'Nothing,' he said, swallowing something down.

When I got back home, I'd tell Mum, no, he's not my boyfriend and stop interrogating me. At work I would ask him to pick things up from high shelves I probably could have reached if I went on my tiptoes. On quiet shifts he would invent cocktails and name them after me, matching each one to the orange, peach and pink of my ever-changing hair.

Sitting here, I remember the feeling of my head on his chest, a heart jolting under my cheek. Electric pulses again.

After a bit of flirtation in the initial week after Joe dumped me, Josh's messages have grown less frequent and more non-committal.

'I'm not free that weekend 'cause I'm moving house.'

'Work is pretty mad at the minute.'

'Sorry I didn't reply to your last message, got distracted.'

'Just realised I actually have a mate's birthday that day.'

I think of Joe while I sit here at the beach. When I brought him here he ran straight into the water and tripped on a rock, so he was completely submerged before he had time to hold his nose. He made that dick joke all men tend to make when they get into cold water. But today I thought of Josh first. Next time I come here I might not think of Joe at all.

I sit down in the sand and the wind whistles against my ears, turning them pink. Coldness squeezes my teeth against my gums. As the wind breaks against my bones it feels like I'm being cleaned. The thought doesn't comfort me; it makes me think of all that I am losing.

It was the Easter holidays and I had come to London for your birthday night out. Your girlfriend wasn't there – I didn't know why. Your friend Malcolm was dancing with me, spinning me around with his hands until beer sloshed out of the can, sticky onto my wrist. He had big hair, thick and dark and curly, and it bounced through the air in slow motion when he danced. I thought all your friends, your London friends, wouldn't like me, but he bought me a drink and waited for me outside the cloakroom while I put my coat away.

'I like your accent,' he said, and I smiled because everyone back in Leeds said I don't have one. I told him stories about annoying people in my uni halls. The guy who screamed, 'Who nosed the Brie!' when we had a cheese night. The other one who compensated for his lack of personality by wearing a Primark monkey onesie on every night out. I was drunk so none of my stories connected to each other, but Malcolm said, 'You're funny,' and pulled me back onto the dance floor with him.

When Malcolm went to the toilet, Joe came up behind me and whispered in my ear, 'He likes you.' There was blood smeared on his cuff from sore nail beds. 'He's got a girlfriend, you know.'

I laughed. 'So have you.'

He stepped back. 'What's that supposed to mean?'

We never normally acknowledged what we did. I helped hide his actions from him because I wanted him to keep committing them.

I didn't answer, I just walked off, but then his hand was on mine and I felt its shape with so much precision it was like on crime scenes when they spray white around the bodies of the dead. And then I was dancing under those blue lights again. Spin, spin, spinning until the yellow of a girl's fluffy jacket whooshed into the lilac of someone's hair into the navy of someone's trousers and everything was a soft rainbow. The music changed and we stopped for a moment.

'We don't have to do this if it's making you feel uncomfortable.'

'No,' I said, and then I was back to being the one responsible for making these bad things happen.

'It's hard to control myself when I'm around you.'

At the end of the night we piled onto the bus and Malcolm fell asleep on his own shoulder. When it was time

for everyone to get off and change onto the 237, Malcom
was still knocked out in the back.

'Leave him,' said Joe.

'What's wrong with you, mate?' our friend Mark
asked, shaking his head at Joe and tapping Malcolm's
arm until his eyes opened.

'*Joking.*'

'No, you weren't.'

It's dinner and Dad makes my favourite pasta. I eat
enough of it that I have to lean over to make extra space
for it to sit in my stomach. Tomato sauce, 'nduja, white
penne, Gorgonzola, Parmesan. Then I take the salad
bowl and pick the cucumbers out with my fingers like
I used to do when this kitchen was where I ate dinner
every night. Dad turns on the TV and announces that
the brown-haired guy is going to win this round of *Mas-
terChef* even though it's obvious because he just made a
raw Jerusalem artichoke chocolate delice that makes all
the judges moan as though in the early stages of orgasm.

'Wow,' Gregg pauses, 'now *that's* what I call a dessert.'

When the brown-haired guy makes it through to the
final Dad fist-pumps and then walks to the fridge to get a
bottle of sparkling water for another white wine spritzer.
He sits down and starts reading about Man United on
his phone. Rather than tapping with alternate thumbs,
he prods at the screen with one forefinger. It's the litmus
test of a boomer; anyone under forty uses their thumbs.
I tell him that when the revolution comes we will use

texting as a measure of who gets to live and who is shoved under the guillotine for being part of the generation that made us pay university fees and rented out their second homes. He laughs, Taste the Difference wine fizzing on his tongue. He makes a cross shape with his hands as though I were a vampire allergic to Jesus references, then he shouts, 'TEENAGE!'. One of his favourite jokes. Growing up, it annoyed me almost as much as when someone accused me of being tired. More so than when someone accused me of being hormonal.

The episode ends. Someone's telling the camera how much this means to them.

'Can I leave the table?' I ask, already standing up.

'Where?' Another favourite joke. He's said it to me every dinnertime since he first came up with it when me and my brother were still tiny.

For some reason, tonight it makes me laugh. And as I'm walking to my room I realise I didn't think of Joe throughout the whole of dinner. And I only think of him now because I force myself to. Just to make sure it still hurts.

It was the start of second year. We had just got back from the summer holidays and I'd gone round to his new university house. I had covered over the bright orange on my hair with a more sophisticated dark auburn. I'd brought a picture into a tattoo shop of Rihanna's henna-style hand tattoo and asked them to do the same thing but on my foot. One of our mutual friends, Jonny, said it looked like I was wearing a sandal. But Joe seemed to think it was cool. I smiled and asked about his summer.

'It was all right,' he said.

I thought about what his version of an 'all right' summer looked like: going to his friend's holiday home in the Lake District. Canoes on water. Sun-bleached arm hair. Flies buzzing around plastic containers of M&S olives and feta cheese in the park. Apricot skies as they walked back from house parties hosted by women with long, beaded earrings bought from stalls set up on the backstreets of Greek villages.

He asked about my summer.

'Yeah, it was all right,' I said back to him. I told him about working at the Old Royal Oak, handing out endless John Smith's Smooths to men in tweed flat caps who said things to me like, 'If I was your dad I'd still be bathing you.'

Emptying ashtrays, £5 an hour, a security camera over the bar so the boss can see if I'm working even when he's not there, polishing the cutlery while the men say something offensive that ends with 'we're all thinking it'.

I'm not even sure why I did it. I had applied for the job because I was deep in my overdraft and because I didn't know what else to do with myself. Jess was going to Thailand and she didn't invite me. I hadn't got an internship. When nothing decent presented itself I was almost determined to have a bad time. Turning up to work looking like shit and then finding myself too embarrassed by my face to look anyone in the eye. Forgetting to write in my overtime on the sheet on the back of the staffroom door.

Joe smiled at me. 'I bet you learned more there than all of us put together.'

At university we were taught about the lie of the information economy. Blair thought we'd all get smarter, but it just means we all sit inside, working in offices until our heads ache with filling out health-and-safety forms. Or something like that. What I was doing seemed to work against this logic.

Another lecture was about eudaimonia and what makes a good life. Joe was impressed because we were confused, over-intellectualised students who condemned 'selling out' without really knowing what it meant. Whatever it was, working in a pub sounded like its opposite.

He was wrong, though. I didn't learn anything. Just sat portioning up the time I had to be there into more easily divided chunks. *So there are five and a half hours until the end of my shift, which means eleven more halves of an hour and just twenty-two sets of fifteen minutes.* But hearing him say that made it feel more like I'd learned something. As though knowing the miserableness of the world was enough to fight against it. All those empty minutes became filled.

'Jess went to Thailand,' I said, rolling my eyes at the cliché, suddenly feeling rather superior.

He laughed.

'She was doing this charity thing where you go and teach English,' I said. 'So colonial, right?' Even though secretly I wanted to do something like that. Quad bikes and beach parties. I was just too scared to do it on my own. My home, all pink and womb-like, calling me back.

'Christ, yeah,' he said. He looped his finger around mine and held it under the table where no one else could see.

I'm on Instagram and I didn't mean to see him, but he flashes up in the background of someone else's story. His newly bleached, snowy-white hair, a jacket I've never seen before, joy speckled through the blue of his eyes, his teeth absorbing the flash of the camera lens. I click off it quickly, but I still see him. Girls with bony shoulders and long necks sitting on his knee at pubs asking if he remembers that party they went to as teenagers where some guy lost his finger in an overhead fan. Men slapping his shoulders – 'Don't worry mate, you'll absolutely clean up.' Something wrenches around my insides like metal bolts. Why do I sit here holding onto us until my hand bleeds? Why should I alone shoulder the burden of memory when he is so quick to throw it away? Pulling my hairs out of his jumpers. Deleting from his phone all the nudes I sent him. Squinting so that the image of my body becomes blurred in between the gaps in his eyelashes. I can forget too, I can push him away. I want to snog men that I'll regret snogging in the morning, and fall over and bruise my knees, have that fling Granny was talking about. Ruchira sends me a link to a night out she's going to at the weekend. I buy a ticket and also one for the train back to London the next morning.

Mum drives me to the station and when we get there

she buys me a cheese and ham toastie from Pret and I eat it quickly, and then pick the crumbs of burnt cheese off the now-see-through paper wrapping with my fingers. She's staring at the announcement board, unable to relax until the platform has been called, even though I tell her it will be platform eight and we are forty minutes early. I tear the toastie paper into thin shreds. Mum tuts at the pile I make, shakes her head. Love rises thick and warm in my chest, a gooey custard.

'You're the best mum in the world. Sorry I'm horrible.'

She smiles, her hand picking through my baby hairs; she's trying to work out if my natural hair colour is still blonde because it still annoys her that I dyed it. She loved me so much, growing up; it taught me how to love another properly, without ever bending.

The train pulls into the platform.

'Did you forget your railcard?' 'Have you got your laptop charger?' 'Ring me.' I'm about to walk through the barriers when Mum grabs my wrist and pulls me back to her hard enough that I swing towards her. 'You're going to be all right, you know?'

I nod even though I don't believe her, and as I do I'm reminded of a line from a Sharon Olds poem she wrote after her husband divorced her:

> *I guess that's how people go on, without*
> *knowing how.*

Seat 46b. I sit there and watch the green of England blur

past. Before I left the house Dad gave me a freezer bag filled with meals. Met with the warm bodies of the train, they have started to defrost and orange oil drips through the freezer-bag zip and onto the seat next to me. *Sorry, sorry*, lots of apologising until I manage to sort out the situation, hiding the bag in the back of the luggage rack.

I put in headphones and turn the sound up so loud that something seems to squeeze against my eardrum. I'm going to really miss missing him, I think. I wish I didn't have to forget how great he was in order to feel OK about what's happened. I wish he wasn't a 'was' but an 'is'. I wish he didn't have to be caged up in the past tense. But I need to let go, watch things topple out of my hands and crack against the floor. I lean on my tear ducts until they break, liquid running down my cheeks and onto my chest where it feels all sticky. I cry so much it feels as though my insides are breaking out of my body, the tarantula I swallowed back in my bedroom climbing out of my mouth again, its legs running down my chest onto the plastic fold-out table and onto the thick red carpet of the aisle.

Just before the second-year Christmas holidays, you invited me to dinner: I assumed it would just be pizza at Francesca's, but you brought me somewhere I knew you couldn't afford. When the waiter asked if you wanted to try the wine you joked: 'How can the wine be corked if it's a screw top?'

I thought the comment made you look like an arsehole.

The food arrived: pink meat lost in the middle of a big white plate. You ate like you were doing an impression of someone eating food and got embarrassed when you tried to chew the lemongrass. You kept changing the position of your arm but found comfort nowhere. You decided you were going to make me yours, and it made you a different man.

You asked after my family when normally we just gossiped about our lecturers: how Natalie must have been a dancer in a past life because her back is so straight, the nature of Dr Flanagan's sex life (we decided it almost certainly involved asphyxiation). We walked out and bought a bottle of red wine at the Co-op and sat drinking at the edge of Jesmond Dene until purple crusted into the cracks of our lips.

'I guess you can tell how I feel about you at this point.'

Somehow it was you that said this and not me. It was a strange feeling, realising I was inside the moment I had been waiting for forever. Nothing could be as perfect as the way I scripted it in my mind, but it took on a more beautiful form in the harsh grip of reality. We were kissing and it was clumsy, our teeth bumping, our tongues pressing at the wrong times. It was too wet. But we carried on until blood swelled to the surface of our lips, until redness blurred outside lip lines, until your stubble scratched my chin pink, until jaws stiffened, until we were back at mine and there was lilac light seeping through the blinds, and it was morning, and nothing could get me out of my bed because you were in it.

That was it. We found things on each other's bodies and named them. The skin tag on the base of your skull was your nubbin. My belly was a 'she' and you told me never to lose her. I learned to like coffee, I learned to like smoking. When I poured a drink, I poured two. When we were in bed together I dipped my nose and then my chin in your eye socket because it meant 'thank you' in the weird secret language we made up. The word 'baby' stopped being disgusting. I sat on the turned-down toilet seat while you showered because you liked having me there even when I didn't say anything. I could tell you were near just by the sound of your trainers hitting the ground. I knew if you were annoyed just by the way your breath sounded down a phone line. We had inside jokes that no one else found funny. Like how we came home from a party and you tried to type into Google 'who are Drake's best mates' and all that you typed was a blur of nonsensical words, so that when we said something that doesn't make sense we'd ask, 'Who are Drake's best mates?' You were always texting people, 'Where's Annie?' because never losing me was your responsibility.

One evening I was in bed with you. I should have set off to my friend's house for dinner fifteen minutes before. I was trying to get up, but you kept pulling me back down again. I felt your hands on my back tracing the letters 'I--l-o-v-e--y-o-u'. I didn't move.

'Say it back,' you told me. I'd had these words in me for so long, I was afraid of them touching the air. I couldn't let them out right away.

'Say it,' you told me again, and I did.

'I love you.'

I love you.

I love you.

I love you.

I love you.

I still do. I'll try my best to forget, but I think I'll love you for all my life.

SKIN

7

Ruchira and I crouch in the shadow of a big yellow wheelie bin and watch as hot piss sinks past our ankles. We take turns drinking from the rum-and-Coke mix until the fizz stings through our nostrils. Stand in the queue with our fingers tucked into the right passport page, ready for the bouncer to make a joke about what we used to do to our eyebrows. When we walk inside the club I think I see him flash through the crowd on the way to the smoking area, but then he turns around and it's just someone else with a bleached buzzcut. When I'm at the supermarket or in my bed and I feel his presence this clearly I normally end up crying, but here there's enough to distract me. That's why I came out and why I've been out most nights since I got back to London. The music radiates out of my chest bones. I keep drinking until I reach the level of drunk where I'm sober enough to re-alise there's no point worrying about anything. I push him right back into the darkness, the black sky leaking through the windows, the shadows bending out of peo-ple's backs, and eventually he disappears.

I feel as though I've dropped something and don't care where it's gone. My hips are as fluid as running taps, my hands unfurling flowers that blossom above me. I roll my head back, too relaxed to hold it up. A topless guy takes his glittering cowboy hat, puts it on my head and spins me around under his arm. When he leaves I lean over to the girl next to me in a bikini top: 'You look so hot,' I tell her. 'It makes me want to take my top off.'

'What?' she yells, and I press down the tragus in her ear while I talk into it because that helps to block out crowd sounds. It was Joe who taught me that. It's probably why I hear him in my head now, asking why I'm listening to Jungle when I hate this kind of music. But then it's easier to ignore him when this girl's here clapping and yelling, 'Do it!' as I pull my shirt over my head and then shimmy my shoulders back and forth.

'We should all be like this all the time!' she shouts, and then introduces me to every single one of her eight friends. Jamie, Lenny, Tara, Sara, Carrie, Molly, Lucy, Enya. We take a picture together and I laugh at my reflection in her phone screen because my eyes shine in it like a bat's.

'You're lucky,' says my friend Yla when I go to the pub with her a few days later. 'When Matt and I broke up, I cried on pretty much every night out.'

'Why's that, do you think?' I ask her, leaning forward, the uneven table wobbling under my elbows.

'I dunno,' she says. 'My friends kept looking at me with this concerned face, like I could see them thinking, *Is she OK?* And I know it's nice that they care, but knowing they were worrying about me . . .'

'It was harder to distract yourself from how you were feeling?'

Yla nods, rubbing Vaseline on her lips so that they glimmer in the soft orange lamplight of the pub. She drops it back into her bag and then flicks her slick black hair behind her shoulder.

'It's like when babies fall over,' I say.

'What do you mean?'

'Well, you know when babies hurt themselves, there's always those few seconds where they're quiet and they're just looking around, just before they start to cry? I read once it's because they're watching to see how people react. So when they see their parents frowning they cry because now they know that scrape on their knee and the weird burning sensation that came with it is a bad thing.' I pause for a second. 'Basically, you know to be sad because your friends look sad when they look at you.'

She stirs the straw in her gin and tonic so that the ice cubes clink around the glass. 'So the baby becomes the pain reflected on their parent's face?' she says.

'Exactly.'

'Do people not look at you like you're sad?'

'They did in the beginning.'

'And now?'

'I tell them not to, I tell them I want to have fun.'

'What about when you're on your own?'

'I'm literally never on my own.'

'Sounds healthy,' says Yla, making a sarcastic thumbs-up, and in response I give her the finger and we both laugh, then I get up off the stool because it's my turn to buy a round.

* * *

In *A Widow's Story*, the memoir she wrote about her husband Ray's passing, Joyce Carol Oates describes a weekend she spent with a friend. Despite her pain, she was able to make small talk, contribute to conversations on the latest political scandal. To make sense of how she managed such a feat, Oates refers to an idea from the philosopher Leibniz. According to him, the universe is continuously collapsing and continuously reassembling itself, through eternity. In her grief, Oates sees herself in this endless process of renewal and destruction.

> I've come to think of my 'self' – my personality – as
> an entity that collapses when I am alone and unper-
> ceived by others; but then, as if by magic, when I am
> with other people, my 'personality' reassembles itself.

I see myself in this process too, it's why I cling on so hard to other people, because social etiquette demands that I hold myself together in some sort of shape. Alone, I just disintegrate.

It's a Friday and I'm drinking at the birthday of some friend of a friend I've never met. They say that nothing good ever happens after 2 a.m. but I like to stay for the bad bits. Everyone heads to this club in Hackney, but because me and Ruchira haven't bought tickets in advance it's twenty quid on the door.

'Let's go to G-A-Y,' I say, and then I order the Uber before she can say no, but when we get there it's a two-hour wait to get inside. 'I'm tempted to just call it quits,' she says.

'But it's Friday!'

'But me and Ryan are . . .'

'Ooh Ryan, Ryan, Ryan, Ryan,' I say, not because I actually think she talks about him too much, but because I don't want to be on my own. Without anyone else I'll just sit around at home in that room that smells of Joe, feeling like my insides are being scraped out with an ice-cream scoop.

'It's Friday!' I say again and Ruchira nods, follows me into the kebab shop where I make lots of jokes so she doesn't get sleepy when she's eating. My chicken doner is cradled in my arms like a newborn baby.

'You have to support the neck!' I shout, and it works; she's laughing so hard chips spill out of her lips. I get a long streak of garlic sauce in my hair and pretend it was the result of an expensive dye job.

'Oh yes, just a balayage, please, some subtle highlights.'

Our friend Adham texts to say he's at Five Miles so we order another Uber and run to the corner shop and back out again with two cans for the road. Fifteen minutes later the Uber arrives, but as soon as we get in the car Adham says they're leaving because it's dead so we should meet him at his house in Tottenham. We manage to change the route but almost straight away Adham texts again to say that, actually, we can't go there because their flatmate Rudy has a job interview in the morning and needs a good sleep.

'I might just get out here,' says Ruchira, looking at the route back on her phone. 'I can get the Northern line to Clapham and then walk to mine from there.'

'Wait,' I say, covering her phone with my hand. I have a free house and we're only about a twenty-minute drive from there anyway, aren't we? And it's only 3 a.m. So I ask the Uber driver to change the route for the third time and then update Adham, who comes over with a load of his friends. Every time it looks like one of them is ready to leave I ask them a conversation starter like, 'Is cheating ever acceptable?' Someone's alarm goes because it's the time they usually wake up for work. I pour everyone gin and orange squash mixed with tap water because there's no tonic left, and repeatedly say, 'It's surprisingly nice!' hoping they will agree with me. One by one they crawl up to bed looking like old men.

'Wanna chat?' I whisper to Ruchira as I slide under the duvet next to her.

'Sleep,' she says, her hand palming me in the face.

A while ago I went out for dinner with my friend Hannah who had lost her dad about six months earlier. 'How're things, with your dad and all?' I asked her. I was afraid to bring it up, but I did because I figured it would be weirder not to.

'I just don't think about it,' she said. 'I know that if I did it would ruin me and I wouldn't get out of bed and I wouldn't work, so I just put it away in this box and one day in a few years' time, when I'm ready, I'll open it.'

I didn't think it sounded healthy to keep all that pain inside. Wouldn't it start to rot? Crawl out into her dreams? Fuck up her relationship with her kids?

It makes more sense to me now. Not what it's like to lose a dad, but why Hannah wouldn't want to confront her feelings. When I was in Leeds I spent too long alone with my thoughts. I let them break me apart into pieces and it was awful finding myself all scattered over the floor. So I get dressed up and go out and say funny things and lose my friends and sit on the floor of the smoking area talking to some lovely girl with pink eyebrows about how she stops them from smudging and when we're done talking I stand up and brush all the little rocks from the concrete out of my skin and run onto the dance floor with her tiny soft hand in mine.

When I wake up the next morning my mouth is so dry I have to peel my tongue like Sellotape off my palate. I feel two organs ache on either side of me and wonder if it's my kidneys. I remember last night thinking that if I got a pint of water and put it on my bedside table I would appreciate it, but I didn't do it. The house is quiet because Moll and Danny have gone for lunch with his parents. That's when you come for me, and this time it's difficult to push you away because you're bigger than all of the distractions. I message people asking what they're doing but it will be a while before they reply. You crawl out of the drawers where so many of your clothes still sit, stir in the dust that clogs the radiator, your hairs that thread through the carpet. I think of my thigh resting across your lower back, dipping my nose in your eye sockets to wake you up. 'Honestly, I don't think I can go,' you said one morning. We were hungover, arguing about whose turn it was to get food and it was always me so I tried to make a stand.

'Yes, you can, babe,' I said, kicking the duvet off the bed so that you rolled around in mock agony, clutching your legs. I took the water bottle next to me and held it over your head, a bulb of water swaying back and forth, threatening to drop. And then I squeezed and a spurt slapped cold against your stomach so that you jolted up on impact.

'You bitch!' you shouted, joking. And you pushed me down and sat on me and I saw the whole length of you stretching out. You leaned down and dipped your tongue in my mouth and I tried to reach up to you, running my hands through your hair, but you held them down, crushing my wrists into the pillow. Not being able to do anything might be my favourite thing in the world and you understood that. Afterwards, you were droopy, spent, a deflated birthday balloon. 'Baabe,' you crooned, so I went and got fried chicken and we ate it cross-legged on the bed with tea towels from the kitchen so it felt less gross. You picked a film and I loaded it up but it buffered for a while so we just watched the dots spinning in a circle and listened to the sound of each other sucking meat off bones.

'Don't do that,' you said as you caught me wiping my greasy hands on the duvet cover.

'I didn't,' I told you, lying. And we stayed like that all day in the sort of bliss where you start arguments not because anything needs to be resolved, but because the flaws make you realise just how perfect everything else is.

'God, I miss you so much,' I say aloud, because your presence in the room is so strong it feels as though you can hear me. 'Why won't you leave me alone?' Pain stretches out through my body like a yawn. I hold the duvet as though it could fill up the black hole that's opened up inside me and I cry in there until kids are walking past my window on their way home from school.

After a while, Jonny replies to my text. 'I'm at the Red Lion with a couple of work friends if you wanna join?'

'I'll be there in an hour or so,' I say, and I pull my heavy body out of bed, kick off the duvet, put on my face.

8

'When's Joe gonna pick up the rest of his stuff?' Moll asks as I walk past the open door of the living room.

'Not sure,' I say, watching as she bends the PlayStation controller the way she wants her car to go, furiously hitting one of the buttons with her thumb. 'Do you think he left it on purpose?'

'It was probably just too much for the taxi.'

'So you don't think he might have done it so he has to come back here? Like, even if he doesn't want to get back with me, he's probably finding it difficult to admit it's fully over and if he's still got stuff here then it's not quite over?'

Moll pauses the game, chews her lip. 'Yeah, I mean, I'm sure he's struggling too.'

'Do you think?'

She stands up, wrapping her dressing gown tightly around herself. 'How much actually is there?' she asks, following me into the room. 'As if he left that,' she says, pointing up at the big picture sitting over the fireplace. It's an illustration of a scene in the 1928 silent film *The Passion of Joan of Arc* carved out in jagged white and black pencil strokes. She nudges the chest of drawers with her foot. 'Is this all his too?' she asks.

'The bottom two drawers, yeah, and there's stuff in the wardrobe.'

She opens one of the drawers, dragging out the clothes so they sit in a mucky puddle tangled around her feet. 'I mean, what even is this?' she asks. 'You're not a storage facility,' and then she holds up a white T-shirt covered in coffee stains, and then another long-sleeved one with white and navy stripes.

I remember you at university wearing that top. That time I was lying with my legs around you in a room where the radiator was turned up to full and it stank of sex. 'I should go,' I said, because I'd been invited to this girl's night in with some of Jess's friends and I was already late enough to have to apologise. But when I got up you reached out, pulled me back onto the bed and unclasped the bra I had just put on. 'Stay.'

'I can't,' I said, putting the bra back over my shoulders.

'Stay,' you said, pulling down my knickers, taking off my socks.

I let myself have twenty more seconds under the covers before moving again. I used to do that when I was getting up for school in between alarms. Coming away from you felt like pulling off a wax strip. It was something I had to force. It didn't feel natural. I wouldn't be surprised if leaving you made my skin come out in hives.

Now I was late enough to have to apologise and not be forgiven. When I arrived all the girls were sitting around eating crisps and talking over each other. Phoebe thought it would be a good idea to empty all the different flavours into one big bowl to make a lucky dip. Pickled onion,

Worcester sauce, prawn cocktail all swirled together. The clashing tastes left a dull synthetic tang in the back of my mouth. After a few handfuls, I looked at my phone front camera and my tongue was orange. I tried to join in their conversations about Brad Pitt getting better with age, how boring one of them found their compulsory Renaissance art course. I listened, I nodded. But I could feel your presence running underneath every moment, like you were a song no one else was listening to. All the others were staying over on mattresses and sofa pillows, but around 11 p.m. I got up to leave. 'Are you going back to Joe's?' Phoebe asked.

'No,' I said, not quite sure why I had felt the need to lie.

When I was about to walk out of the door I could hear the girls talking about something in hushed tones. I couldn't make out any words, but I convinced myself they were talking about me. I walked home with a twisted stomach. *I'm just not really into the same things as them anymore*, I told myself. *Sometimes you drift from people and that's OK.*

When I got back to yours you were halfway through a film. I put a T-shirt on and slipped into bed. It was boiling under there. The temperature simmering at the point just before you slip into sweating. It was nice because it meant that we were permanently drowsy. There were gunshots coming from the laptop. You moved a piece of hair that was hiding my eyes. I thought when I fell in love it wouldn't be disgusting like it was with other people – we wouldn't speak in baby voices or force people to walk off the pavement and onto the road because we couldn't bear to let go of each other's hands even for a second – but there I was, staring into your eyes because you were more interesting to me than any film we could have chosen to watch. Love feels like cherishing a little yellow duckling in your hands. That's a disgusting way of describing something, but it turns out love is fucking disgusting.

'So when's he going to come and get it?' Moll asks. 'Annie?'

'I don't know,' I say, snapping, grabbing the clothes she's pulled out and putting them back into the drawers. 'I don't know if he's found somewhere to live yet and he had just paid the rent when he moved out so I probably owe him money, technically, and I mean, he barely has any clothes.'

Moll leans against the wall with her arms crossed. I've known her since school. We used to sit together in the library condensing our notes about the Cold War onto prompt cards we could read before the history exam. Telling my parents I was sleeping over at hers when really we were going out. I suppose she can tell when I'm hiding something.

'You don't want him to take the stuff, do you?' she asks.

I shake my head.

I like that I have the long-sleeved T-shirt here. His socks. These things are all that tie him to me. Once they're gone there will be no reason for us to talk. And it seems so unfair to get annoyed at him for doing something that makes me feel so much better.

'That's exactly why it's not OK for you to have it.'

9

I'm going on my first date since Joe ended it with me about a month ago. I can't really remember what this guy looks like so I'm not sure who I'm looking for when I stand outside the station waiting for him. I said yes when he asked me out because it makes me feel less bad about the fact that I know Joe will be dating too. Me and this guy didn't speak for long when we met. I was sitting opposite the Portaloos at Notting Hill Carnival waiting for some friends to come out and he said, 'Your boyfriend's brave leaving you out here on your own,' and me and all the other girls he must have said it to laughed awkwardly, tucked hair behind our ears, passed our phones over to get his number or pretended we were actually in a relationship. He rang my phone to check what I'd given him wasn't fake and then, when it buzzed in my hand, he drifted away on the current of the crowd he came in on. But the man walking towards me must be him because there's the nod of recognition and he's about my age and I think, *No-no-no-no-maybe-no-maybe?* He's wearing a silky floral bomber that I hate. His jeans are too skinny. I imagine Joe saying, 'Maybe go up a size?' like he used to at university when I went off with men when we weren't together and the thought of it annoys me like it annoyed me back then. 'You could do so much better,' he'd say, and I'd think, *Yeah, but* you *are the so much better and you're not getting with me so what do you expect me to do?*

We go to a bar and at first I don't know how I'm supposed to be. I've never really dated before. There were just bathrooms at house parties and then there was Joe. I tell him I've just come out of a five-year relationship and his lips tighten shut and he says, 'Must have been a real captivating guy,' and I realise that's not something you say on a first date. So then I change the subject to a fall-out I had with my friend a few weeks ago over not responding to her WhatsApp messages and he says, 'Does that happen a lot?' and I realise you shouldn't say stuff that's so personal. But I get better at being who he wants me to be. When I say 'path' he makes me repeat it back to him because he says I sound Northern, so I tell him other things about where I'm from that make it sound more exotic. That people from home say 'me sen', meaning myself. When I can't light my cigarette he takes it out of my hand and says, 'Let me do it,' with so much conviction that I let him do other things I can do because he must like doing them. Like Google Map us to a bar I know the way to or explain how mortgages work. When he says he plans to learn choreography for the first dance when he gets married, like you see on all those viral Facebook clips, I lie and say it's cute. Avoid saying 'that's weird' when he mentions that Ronaldo's his favourite football player. Parts of me slip away. I don't mind watching them leave.

I didn't need to bend around Joe; we fitted together like jigsaw pieces, like the people in that Plato story with two sets of arms and legs, cartwheeling across the Earth. Or in 'Lovesong', the poem Ted Hughes wrote after his estranged wife Sylvia Plath killed herself, where he describes how in their sleep they became tangled up in each other. Their heads falling apart like the two sides of a lopped melon, her limbs now his and his now hers, both taking the other's brain hostage. Until the morning when they 'wore each other's face'.

I feel amputated without those other parts of me. I need to fit with someone else so that I feel whole again. That filled to the brim feeling that is love. Water pouring over a cup.

Failing that, I hope these men can give me something to fill up the gaps, an inch, a quarter. A funny impression of how I walk like a dinosaur in heels; holding onto my bag so that it's easier for me to take off my coat.

I open Hinge. There's a guy with floppy brown hair. A moustache. He's wearing combat trousers. Big, baggy, stripy T-shirts. In one he's in a bar singing into a microphone. 'Were you doing karaoke here?' I type into the app.

'I was.'

'Do you have the voice of an angel?'

'Like a bag of cats being swung into a wall,' he tells me.

'Me too, I can't sing for shit.'

'Duet with me and I'll look better.'

'What shall we sing?'

'"Señorita" by Justin Timberlake.'

I can't think of anything funny to say in response so I just stop answering.

Black PU strappy bodysuit. £4. I click and add it to my basket. I'm online shopping now. Scrolling and scrolling until my eyeballs shrink in their sockets.

Shape mocha slinky zip-detail short-sleeved mini-dress. £11. Add to basket.

Grey marl joggers with cuffed hem. £14. Add one and then two because maybe I'm a 10 and not a 12 now.

I spend hours adding and refining. Maybe I don't need those gold twisted hoops. Maybe I'd look like a dick in those. Remove.

Page 114 of 11,732.

Twenty-per-cent-off voucher code taken from an influencer's Instagram post. Next-day delivery because last time I accidentally pressed the button where you can pay £7.99 and get it free for a year. It means I'm now loyal to this site over the other Miss Queen, Slay Sister, LA Girl (based in Sunderland), So Classy, Princess Polly, Baby Star, Oh Catherine, Oh-So-Cheap-Because-We-Pay-Our-Factory-Workers-£3.50-an-hour-no-overtime.

Normally I'd hate myself for doing this, filling fish with microfibres that block their digestive tracts, putting child workers in factories with walls that threaten to crumble down. But I have safely compartmentalised the guilt in a part of my brain I have no quick access to. If anything would make me feel better right now, I'd do it. What's hurting seems far away. But I feel the dopamine rush like a kick in the teeth.

A notification pops up because I've matched with someone else. After two hellos he says, 'Drink?' and I say yes because he's doing a PhD and I know that sort of thing would make Joe jealous. I say something early on in our date about how I don't get economics because isn't it all just a bunch of nonsensical made-up numbers based on nothing and why does 'the deficit' even matter if America is the richest country in the world and it's in billions of pounds of debt, like why don't we just spend more and get richer? He laughs but it sounds like a sigh. Later, when I ask what his dissertation is about, he doesn't answer the question. 'Just post-war stuff,' he says, shaking his head. 'It would take me ages to explain.'

He thinks I'm dumb and I can tell he doesn't want me to be, so I start saying big words. Pushing them into sentences where they don't belong. 'Well, yeah, I guess that's subjective. His films are somewhat of a misnomer.' Say something about the French psychoanalyst Lacan, which is not even tangentially related to our conversation. When I hear myself, I recoil every time I say 'like'. Once, Joe commented on how much I say that word and I replied: 'Saying "like" is just another way of slowing speech down so you have more time to think, and loads of private-school kids speak really slow in order to do that anyway, and isn't it the same thing but one's dismissed because it's been portrayed a certain way? Taking time to think is never a bad thing.'

And he said, 'Yeah, you're probably right.'

'Did you like him?' asks Ruchira when I ring her on the way home from the date.

'I'm not sure,' I say. 'I think he thought I was a bit dumb and I'm not sure I asked him enough questions,' and then I tell her about other things that might have been wrong – the pub we were at was too noisy, Tuesday's an odd day for a date.

'Did you like him, though?' she asks.

'Yeah, yeah. I mean –' I go to say something else but can't find the words. I hadn't really thought about that part.

'You know, if you're not ready for this yet, it's absolutely fine,' she says. 'Don't put pressure on yourself to move on.'

I start crying and the cries come out like big gusts of wind that shake through me. 'I just feel so empty.'

A day or so later, I open Hinge again. The first match I get is six foot four. In one picture he's covered in paint sleeping in a broken camping chair. Another is a webcam picture of him in a white shirt in a sparse office like Joe used to send me when his boss at the estate agent's went to the toilet. He's from Newcastle. His profile asks: 'How would you rate . . . mixing ketchup and mayonnaise?'

'Low,' I reply.

'Ah, shame. But you're talking about gravy?' he says, because on my profile I answered the prompt 'What I'd order for the table . . .' with 'more gravy'.

'You don't like gravy?' I ask. 'Are you OK?'

'It's all right. I'm not asking for more of it, though. Ketchup and mayonnaise on the other hand . . .'

'I'll help myself to your gravy then.'

Eventually, the chat ebbs away and he stops replying. I have hundreds of conversations like this. He is one of 134 matches. I'm not sure what number I am for him. I find that the trick is to do short replies because if they're too long then people feel pressured to also write something long and, faced with that obligation, they will just respond to someone else. Never start with 'How are you?' or something open-ended because they'll just reply, 'Good, you?' and the conversation will continue down this path of dull pleasantries. Instead, go off some stupid specific thing on their profile, like gravy, accents, sombreros, Thai curries, fold-up chairs, pistachio ice cream. Reply constantly for forty-eight hours to measure how weird they are; if you haven't organised a date by the end of that time it will most likely never happen and you'll turn into pen pals who only message when self-esteem is low. Don't expect anyone to be funny because even if they're funny in person, no one ever is over message. That's where apps get confusing, though. What then is there to go off? Just looks? That's difficult, because at this point they all look the same because the algorithm has codified my type: a bony face, a small hoop in one ear, one slightly bizarre arty picture of, say, a bunch of dying dandelions or a deflated balloon on a roadside. Perhaps then you should go off their interests? The book they're holding in one of their pictures that you've read? Which of the men that you discuss gravy with should you actually meet?

'Are you gonna laugh at me if it's tall and pink?' asks one guy as he orders a raspberry cocktail, worrying that my drink will come in a manly tumbler and his a girly flute. We're almost halfway through September and I've been on enough dates by now to know from the way he's grinning that he wants me to make fun of his choice of drink. So I do when it arrives. I bite in other ways too. I call him Oliver Twist when he tells me he went to a cheap private school and when I don't believe him he gets a picture up of the Portakabins they used to teach him in. I say it must have been really hard learning Latin. 'Fuck you!' he says, his whole face throwing itself back towards the sky as if the laugh was enough to bend the alignment of his head, break his spine.

I'm getting so good at this now. I mould around men like cake mixture sinking into a baking tray. Give them my arms and legs and, like a shop assistant, ask them: *'Are these all right for you or would you like to try them in a different size?'*

When my granny married my grandpa she stopped going to church. He didn't ask her to as far as anyone knows.

Maybe he just didn't think that stuff was important and so she stopped thinking it was important too, because men are meant to be the most important thing in our lives, so what they don't value starts to feel insignificant. Maybe that's why she didn't go and sit on that pew near all the cold stone and the big windows in her nice stiff skirt. She didn't sing or run her fingers over the buttery leather binding of the Bible in her hands. Instead, she went to the rugby with him, wearing two pairs of tights to keep warm, and then she brought Welsh rarebit and home-baked cakes to him on a tea trolley and they ate them in front of the telly. She probably didn't even realise she was losing her religion.

In historian Thomas Laqueur's *Making Sex: Body and Gender from the Greeks to Freud*, he says that before the eighteenth century they believed the vagina was an inverted penis. Not a unique organ with its own needs and wants, but a perfectly moulded space whose value comes only from accommodating another object's shape.

If you actually look closely at an X-ray of a vagina it looks like a flower. All these tubes explode out like long stems; swollen pink glands become petals – it's somewhere between a rose and a tulip.

I still can't remember what he looks like, that guy from Notting Hill Carnival that I went on a date with, so when he arrives at Finsbury Park it takes a second before I smile back at him and walk over. We go to buy some alcohol from the shop and when we're at the till he pulls the cans I'm holding out of my hands. Even though it's a nice thing because he's paying, I find it so annoying that he just took them from me. We walk into the park and sit on a bench, and I don't know how we get onto it but we start listing the best carbs, and I say why would you ever eat couscous 'cause it's basically pasta that tastes worse? And he says, no, it's a grain, and I'm like, no, it's made out of wheat and then he googles it and when he sees that I'm right he says, same texture as a grain, though, and for a second he looks so much younger, almost childlike, his shoulders rounded over while he rearranges his feet on the floor.

I get the ick – that sudden, slightly sick feeling where you find someone you previously thought attractive all at once extremely unattractive and everything they do is infuriating. Not because this guy got something wrong, but because he looked so pathetic when he realised.

He's not the only one who gives me the ick. I get it because one guy waits for me to say 'table for two' even though he's standing in front of me, because one guy says he 'felt like superman' when he snorted coke for the first time, because one guy begins a sentence with 'the thing with girls, right . . .', because one guy holds his cutlery between his fist and bites down on the fork when taking things off it, because one guy meets me holding an umbrella, because one guy's legs are dangling off a bar stool, because one guy presses the traffic-light button and actually waits for the green man and I've already crossed over and am standing waiting at the other side of the road, because one guy has all this white stuff between his teeth, because one guy's shoulders hunch upwards when he gets cold, because I accidentally imagined one guy wearing a dressing gown, because I accidentally imagined another standing naked in the bathroom waiting for the shower to heat up.

A week after we last met I send the guy from Notting Hill Carnival a text saying I'm not ready to date. His response is so nice; my heart turns purple for how nice it is. 'No worries, Annie, it's been so lovely getting to know you. Thanks for making me smile!'

I go to the pub with someone I used to work with. He's coming home with me so we go to the Overground together. I used to want him all the time when I couldn't have him. But now he can be mine, I realise what I wanted was a fantasy I built up in my head. He's drunk. He turned up drunk and then he carried on drinking. He walks down the platform and pisses on the train tracks. When we get on the train he smokes out of the little window even though he had that rolly tucked behind his ear for the whole of the long walk to the station. 'You're going to get us kicked off,' I say.

'You're going to get us kicked off,' he says, parroting my words back to me in a higher-pitched voice. I don't want him to come to mine anymore, but saying that seems harder than just letting it happen. He goes to pick up a paper and when he does he drops his beer and a pool of amber sinks towards the feet of the people opposite. 'Don't worry,' he tells me, patting my hand. 'No one's going to die.'

At the door to the house, I think again about how I could just say, 'I'm not feeling this, sorry,' but the more I rehearse the phrase the harder it becomes to squeeze it out. It's like I have hot mashed potato in my mouth. In bed, he swipes past my clit like he's scanning items on the Sainsbury's self-checkout machine. Then, almost without warning, he's inside me, moving in me with this aggressive circle motion. My brain rehearses the words I might use to correct him, how his face might break apart like a smashed plate if I did, how he might leave my room walking smaller. So I swallow those words back down, try to find other ways, moaning when he moves more in the way of something I would like, shuffling to different angles. But every time I just end up on my back again counting all the cracks in the ceiling as he draws those same circles into my cervix. It feels like someone's rooting around in me for something they need to remove. After a while I give up and lie there, thinking of England.

He might not have minded if I spoke up. He might not have been offended but actually grateful for some direction. But each man doesn't exist in isolation. They are connected to a whole spider web of other men: the ones I see on TV who seemingly make women come as soon as they lift them onto a desk; the soon-to-be men at college who prodded my shoulder and said, 'I bet you like it rough . . .' with a face that was all screwed up, as if women wanting anything was disgusting; the men from work who said, 'I know,' before I'd finished explaining my feelings towards the news story we were discussing, and the men from history who started all of this, like the god Jupiter in Ovid's *Metamorphoses*, who turned Io into a cow so that she couldn't talk but only moo.

The next day he's still in my bed and there are holes in the bedsheet from when the ash from a cigarette dropped onto it. He lights another one. 'Can you open the window?' I ask and he does, but he's not really blowing the smoke out of it. Clouds sink back into the room and I feel as though I can see smoke settling in my curtains, on my skin.

'It stinks in here,' I say.

'I don't really have a sense of smell,' he says. 'That's why my flatmates come and smoke in my room.'

'All of your flatmates?'

'Yeah, 'cause they don't want their rooms to smell and I can't smell it in my own so I don't really mind.'

I crinkle my nose. It feels as though he's keeping me from work even though I wasn't planning on doing any today. His cig keeps going out. He pats the duvet, trying to find the lighter. 'I need to go see my friend,' I say.

'Don't worry, I'll get out of your hair,' he says. 'Once I've finished this,' and he raises a mug of instant coffee I brought him earlier. He takes tiny, noisy sips from the mug.

While he sits here with me it feels as though it will be so long before I'm alone again. And knowing that feeling of aloneness is so far away I start to long for it even though I've been avoiding it for months. For a moment I stop wanting to find a man and instead I just want myself, my arms wrapped around my own shoulders, holding myself tight. I want to lock myself in my room watching films until my eyes sting, soak in a bath until my hands prune. I realise all you need for happiness is yourself; no one else needs to help you achieve anything, to help you feel it. The obviousness hits me like a revelation. Aloneness still feels so distant, but then he's saying, 'I should probably get on with my day,' and he's getting dressed, tapping his pockets asking, 'Have I left anything?' And then he's walking out of the door.

The quiet afterwards is precious. Like when you're a teenager and there are a few hours before your parents get home from work and start asking you lots of questions like, *'Tell me you handed that form in? Did you lose that nice water bottle I gave you?'*

The day stretches out in front of me, inviting and warm, like something I can take by both hands and rub my face into.

But a few hours later I'm thinking of that cute face Joe would make, pulling up his hood, ears sticking out either side, a big grin so that he looked like a monkey, and then I'm loading up Hinge and I'm saying, 'Do you come with the dog?' to a picture of a man holding a puppy. That's the thing with revelations: they come and then you ignore what they show you and continue on in the way you behaved before. It's only in retrospect that you look back and recognise that this moment of clarity was the moment where you began to change – the start, the beginning, all you could ever hope for.

10

I've always been obsessed with eating. When people say, 'I'm starving, I forgot to eat dinner,' I can't get my head around how that's possible. At 11.20 I'm looking at the clock and thinking about lunch. At 11.55 I'm spooning the food onto a plate and opening the microwave. When I go to bed I relax by telling myself that when I wake up I'll get to eat again. I often think about how lucky we are to eat three times a day. What if we'd ended up like bears who have to starve through the winter hibernation period? I wonder what they dream about during those months. Teeth dripping with deer blood, a still-breathing fish slippering around in their jaw, the crunch as they break through the spine. When I'm eating something delicious – say, a big, golden, spongey pile of pancakes with bacon and maple syrup and caster sugar – when the salt squeezes against my tongue and the grease coats the roof of my mouth until it's furry, I think about how unfortunate it is that I've nearly emptied the plate and how sad I am that it would be socially unacceptable to order a second one. If I'm hungry, I can't concentrate. I wonder if I have low blood sugar or whether I'm just intolerant of the feeling.

I get a snack and return to my desk, but seconds later I'm back at the cupboard, licking Nutella off a teaspoon.

On the lid of the jar it tells you that's eighty calories. Sometimes I hide this information under my fingers, telling myself if I don't see the number it won't go into me. In restaurants I'm always the one asking, 'Are we getting starters?' The one who's disappointed when everyone answers the question 'Pudding?' with, 'Shall we get one to share?' I'm so excited to eat things I put them in my mouth when they are too hot to enjoy. Spitting the rest of the pork and prawn dumpling out because it burned my tongue. I've finished my popcorn before the film starts, advent calendars before Christmas. When there's food in front of me I can't not eat it. When they bring out those aniseed sweets after a curry, I pick up so many of them they're pouring through the gaps between my fingers. I don't even like them; they go down like medicine.

I like putting enough ketchup on things that you can't taste what it's coating. I use crisps like edible spoons. I find that food is best when it's deep-fried or inside bread or both. Halloumi squeaking like cleanness against the roof of my mouth; pushing peanut butter off the end of a spoon onto thick, gelatinous white bread; chocolate straight out of the fridge snapping in between my two front teeth. I like peach juice running down my chin and sticking my hair into knots that hurt to brush out. I like cutting through the grease of fish and chips with a hot tea. I like doing things the wrong way round: eating cereal for dinner and cold pizza for breakfast.

But now that he's dumped me I don't eat. I actually don't even want to. Feeding myself has become a function, like brushing my teeth or clipping my toenails. Trying not to think of him takes so much effort there's no room in my brain for anything else. He's the best diet I've ever been on.

I've tried other diets before. In fact, the reason that I ordinarily obsess about food so much is precisely because I dieted. Most women I know started restricting themselves when they were about sixteen. I was lucky in that way. I got a few more years of freedom. My first diet started during my first term at university. After weeks of cheap wine, garlic-sauce-smeared kebabs, cheesy chips and beer, I became bigger and when I took off my jeans I could see the outline of the button and zip pressed into my stomach. I decided this was a bad thing, having grown up with *Heat* magazine's 'Kerry Katona's Let Herself Go' headlines and evidence-based research on what type of female body men tend to go for. My flatmate was already dieting so I followed her rules: dark chocolate is fine; milk chocolate is bad. Don't eat after 7 p.m. Carbs are bad. Protein is good. Everything became brown: brown rice, brown pasta, brown bread. Eat little and often. Drink a pint of lemon water when you wake up.

I was always useless at sticking to the rules. I didn't eat less, I just pushed food into these weird dark corners. While waiting for the kettle to boil I'd throw down the cold chips someone had left on the side after a night out, eat three bowls of cereal in a row. If I broke a rule, I couldn't stop. Once I'd seen that this whole moral checklist was completely made up and so easily breakable, I couldn't keep myself from extending entirely beyond its limits. So when I ate a digestive biscuit I had to finish the whole packet.

This lack of appetite should be a relief. It was tiring thinking about food as much as I did. A few times I tried to go back to how it was before the first diet when I would just eat when I was hungry and not eat when I wasn't. It didn't work. If I relaxed the rules I'd end up binge-eating and then after that guilt would make me go back on the diet again. I would dream of ways out of the cycle, be jealous of those I thought already had such an escape. Like this girl called Emily I met when I was working at a pub. She had a fast metabolism due to her hyperthyroidism, a condition that occurs when your thyroid gland produces too much of the hormone thyroxine. 'My heart rate is really fast,' she explained. 'It's difficult for me to put on weight.' She had daily injections to lessen the symptoms of this disorder and I couldn't understand why she'd give up the ability to never put on weight. 'Because I'm tired all the time,' she said, and then held out her hand so I could see the tremor the hyperthyroidism gave her. I knew it was wrong, but to me, staying thin still seemed like something worth keeping.

I thought the same thing when I was at school and our biology teacher told us about tapeworms. Apparently if you swallow one you don't put on weight because the worm steals the food you eat from inside your stomach and then it shits it out without you ever absorbing any of the nutrients. I remember thinking about how much I would eat if I had a tapeworm. Lots of those curries that have so much coconut milk and brown sugar in them they taste like puddings. Bread dipped into the centre of a gooey yellow Camembert. Now I don't want any of it.

There is a scientific reason for my loss of interest in food. When you're heartbroken your body enters 'fight' mode. Your sympathetic nervous system kicks in – that's the system that allows your body to respond quickly in the event of an emergency. Your pupils dilate, the pulmonary alveoli widen, and your heart starts to beat faster. To help you escape danger, the body suppresses hunger so you have one less thing to think about. You also have fewer constrictions and relaxations of the muscles in your stomach and bowels, which consequently slows the digestion of food.

Mum likes eating Lindor chocolates from the fridge, and when she's finished one box Dad puts another in its place. In fact, there are often three boxes stacked up ready, waiting. He brings her croissants on Saturday morning, bacon sandwiches on Sundays, carbonara when she's busy with work.

Food is love in many ways, or at least it's one of its messengers, like flowers or paying someone to fly a plane with a dedicated love note trailing through the sky behind it.

When I do manage to eat I tend to have fish fingers, potato smiles or sausage, mash and beans. The sort of thing you eat when you're a child and you have a separate dinnertime from your parents. The idea of anything remotely challenging – say, pomegranate seeds on a salad, olives, lots of spices – is disgusting to me.

You leaned forward and wiped a bit of curry from my chin.

'Mucky pup,' you smiled. We were in an Ethiopian restaurant tearing away bits of bread and scooping up the red, yellow and green of different curries. Another dish came out and we groaned. I said I couldn't, but then, without telling it to, my hand was launching it into my mouth.

'It tastes a bit like chocolate,' I said, because it had that same richness. Feeling fullness coming on, we ate faster, getting as much in as possible before the body had time to send the brain a signal to stop. I leaned back in my chair, blowing air out of my lips so hard they wobbled. I wanted to be drunk, but the wine was soaked up by the carbs so all I got was a headache.

'I'm so full I think food will start coming out of my nose soon,' you said, and then while you were still talking you grabbed the roll of injera bread between your hands and took huge bites out of it, as though it were a burrito. It was a meal in its own right. I laughed at you. 'Why do you do that?'

'I don't know.'

And we laughed again, both of us bursting at the seams.

* * *

I look in the mirror and my stomach is almost flat. I've got gaps between my legs and I've lost the small pad of fat under my chin. I've never had a flat stomach before, but now my belly's nearly gone except for a small dome at the bottom.

'Nothing tastes as good as skinny feels,' said Kate Moss, supposedly. But being skinny doesn't feel that good at all. It doesn't feel like anything.

'I love your tummy.' You used to say that all the time. When we started going out none of my clothes fitted anymore. I'd been eating loads of tuna-melt paninis from the library café. Coco Pops in bed. When you ate, I ate, but my weight went up while your body shape never changed. When you were signed up to a modelling agency the person writing your stats down into a computer said you had the metabolism of a twelve-year-old. One afternoon we were in a gallery walking around echoey rooms with hands behind our backs because that's how it feels you should walk in art galleries. I stopped in front of a Renaissance nude of a woman. You came up from behind, looped your arms around me and whispered in my ear so close it tickled: 'You have a body a bit like that.' I looked at the painting. Her flesh was overwhelming, like a big sofa with even bigger cushions. The sort you always fall asleep on even when you're enjoying the movie. She had a belly, but it didn't look like a flaw; it looked luxurious. As though curves meant also having curves on your stomach, not just on your boobs and your bum.

Later, when we were in bed together, you took a handful of my tummy. 'I love it,' you said, and the soft rolls moved in your fingers like warm bread dough. Sometimes I hated that you paid so much attention to my stomach, giving it a name and a personality. But other times I thought perhaps it was better to acknowledge it. If you never said anything, it would be the same as saying it was better if it wasn't there. 'I love it,' you said, and I tried to see what you saw. Appreciating that at the very least it made a good pillow for you to rest your head on when we watched TV.

Before you, I thought you only got love if you were skinny, but you can have your cake and eat it and have a man too.

In second year, when we went home for the Easter holidays, we spoke almost every night. I would sit at my kitchen table watching my bunched-up legs reflected in the black of the window, fearing that there was a monster behind it that I couldn't see. All day I'd soak up as many interesting things as possible from my quiet streets to tell you about. The bit in my book about the uselessness of art in igniting real-world change that I knew your cynical self would like to hear about. The red kites, massive birds with copper wings who flew over this part of Yorkshire thanks to a successful local breeding programme. You were there in the screens I looked at, the pictures I saw, the conversations I repeated in my head, but you weren't there enough to stop the old world order creeping in. I did YouTube workout videos. I went for long walks. I started following food rules. I suppose I wanted to do something for you, shake your love like a maraca, smack it in the face. I was better at losing weight with you as my end goal. I fasted so that in the end I could feast. It was never something you asked for.

'You look great,' you said when you picked me up from the train station.

'I thought you liked my tummy?' I asked.

'I dunno,' you said, your hands flying up in frustration and then smacking back down against your sides. 'You just look good.'

I'm not sure if you loved me so much that I always looked good to you. Or if you loved me so much you'd tell me I looked good even when I didn't. I suppose it should have made me happy, but I hated that it felt like an inexact science, something malleable that could send me in the wrong direction.

It didn't matter anyway. The weight came back on and you grabbed onto it like it was something perfect and not something to lose.

Over time I learned to love my body through your love. Through borrowing your eyes.

But now you're gone and my eyes no longer like what they see.

When I walk inside the gym it's cold and smells like chemical disinfectant and cucumber deodorant. Protein bars shine from behind curled metal rods. It's quiet because no one speaks to each other; occasionally the smack of a hand against a back when men hug, the squeak of trainers against the linoleum floor. A woman opens the door to the next room for me, her eyebrows shaved off and replaced with the faded grey-blue of tattooed ink, her shoulders high like clipped wings.

I'm using the kettlebell, swinging it between my legs. I think the pain into the slice of muscle I want to work; this time it's my glutes. All the thoughts in my brain close around this one isolated motion and my body's delivery of it. I'm no longer a body but a machine made of tiny levers that I can twiddle away at. I'm an assembly line making nothing.

I have a to-do list and I enjoy crossing out tasks from it so much that sometimes I write things I've already done just so that I can enjoy the satisfaction of striking through them.

- Give Ruchira that book back when I see her
- Go to the gym
- Food shopping
- Invoices
- Tax return

It starts to feel as though things haven't happened unless I've put them on the list. So more goes on, stuff that's supposed to happen without being on a to-do list.

- Reply to that guy on Hinge
- Read
- Masturbate
- Watch a film

I remember seeing the comedian Katherine Ryan live. She made a joke about Kim Kardashian and how people say she's famous for no reason. But she is famous for a reason, Katherine said: she's a world champion in the sport of hotness. Think of all those 5 a.m. workouts, blood facials, filler injections – she's a fucking athlete.

After a couple of weeks I start calling working out 'training', although what I'm training for isn't a sport.

I squat until it hurts to bend onto a toilet seat. I hold planks until sweat drip-drops off the end of my nose onto the mat and each second feels like a minute. I crunch my existence down to a series of numbers: 10,334 steps, 2,054 calories, an average of 53 minutes in the gym each visit, 25 trips so far this month, 4 sets of 12 with a 20kg weight. Waist 29cm. Chest 36cm. Thigh 24cm. It's as though I am an equation and if all these numbers add up correctly, I can be solved.

You bought me a samosa from the shop, one for you and one for me. I said I'd eat it later when I was hungry but then I was eating it anyway. Bits of pastry crumbling through my hair.

Love is losing control. It's like trying to hold onto water.

* * *

Sometimes I add weights to the end of a bar that I don't think I can lift. I'm down in a squat and I'm squeezing as hard as I can. There's no way I'll be able to get back up again. I anticipate the embarrassment I will feel as the weight clanks behind me, rolls dangerously into the middle of the floor, a member of staff in a blue polo shirt giving me a safety warning. But then I keep squeezing, squeezing and slowly I'm making my way up. And when I walk into the lift on the way out everything in my head feels softer, as though coloured in pale yellow, or flavoured vanilla, and all my problems feel like something I can solve, like the weight I thought I couldn't lift but did.

You build muscles by breaking them. By tearing their fibres so that they become damaged. The body then repairs these damaged fibres by fusing them, increasing the mass and size of the muscle. It's a process called muscle hypertrophy.

Is this what the past month has been? Breaking me down so I can be built back up again stronger?

'For you,' Moll says one morning and throws a package's airy mass into my chest. I tear open the plastic and then the plastic inside that plastic until another one of my clothes orders falls around me. They call it retail therapy, but it feels more like something that's bad for you. Something that oozes out of a syringe.

First, I try on the teal satin strappy midi dress. It gapes off my chest. I throw it in the no pile.

I put on the grey woven cut-out-detail utility co-ord. Too big. They go in the no pile too.

There are some winners. I put on this tight neon-green dress and it squeezes me in so far that it makes me see my body in a different way. There are lines running all through me, cutting me into halves. There's one down the centre of my stomach, along the side of my thigh, underneath my bum. I have cheekbones rather than cheeks. There are soft undulations on my arms from where the muscles break through into waves.

Would he even recognise this body if he felt it under his hands? Would he feel betrayed that it went so far away without him?

They call it a revenge body for a reason, because it stings like a knife in the back.

Later, I'm lying on my pillow, readying for sleep. I let myself imagine what sort of person I will become in this body, in that dress. Walking into the pub, my friend will run over and pick me up and spin me around in a circle and throw me over his shoulder in a fireman's carry and I'll be screaming and begging to be put down, but also laughing, and I have a really great laugh – the sort that's loud and contagious, dragging people right into its centre like a cyclone. I'll bump into a guy I'm having casual sex with and he'll loop his hand around my waist, get annoyed at another man for looking at me, shove him. Everyone will roll their eyes because they worry that he's bad for me because I'm one of those chaotic beautiful people who makes bad decisions. Joe walks in and he'll see the whole thing and feel something deep inside him pull apart like a Christmas cracker. *POP!* and then all the insides will fall out. He'll try to grab my hand, drag me into the corner, but I'll say, 'Stop, too much has happened.'

'But I'm nothing without you. Annie. Wait.'

'What you doing now? We've got people over if you wanna join?' says Jonny one evening, and I put on the green dress and tell him I'll be there in an hour or so. When I get to the party I sit down on the sofa and the cushions of it are so soft I have to lean forwards onto my elbows so I don't feel as though I'm being left behind everyone else. I drink so much my brain turns into this soupy puddle. Someone tells me to stop shouting because of the neighbours. I can't think of anything to say so tell the story about why Bryan Adams was a guest at my aunty and uncle's wedding and most people say they have heard the story before. 'It's a good one, though,' they say. 'Go on.'

On the way home I sit with my face against the cold glass of the bus window feeling slightly deflated because even though I wore the green dress nothing was any different to any other night.

I worked to mould myself into another shape and I thought everything would change, but nothing did. I was the exact same funny but not hilarious, good-looking but not beautiful, clever but not intelligent person I always was.

If people notice a change when you lose weight, it's only because you're more confident and that's attractive. You're still that same you with abs; you're still her with a spare tyre around the waist. All those tiny changes we obsess over are so surface level. It's something behind the eyes that we're drawn to.

So I start eating a lot again. I choose beer instead of gin and slimline tonics, stop buying rice cakes and all those other snacks that taste like cardboard. It feels good for a while, but I know in a few months, when I've put the weight back on, I'll begin thinking that things would be better if I was skinny – imagine some man picking me up and putting me on a kitchen counter, my tiny frame drowning in a trench coat on a crisp autumn day with leaves crunching under my feet. So I start following the rules again and again and again and again and again and again and again and again and again.

11

Our Hinge conversation was boring. But he lives only two streets away so I decided to meet him anyway. Even when he's just a tiny scratch in the distance I can see I've made the right decision. He walks with his hands in his pockets, slow, though he can see me waiting for him. He wears a black Puffa, Adidas trackies similar to Joe's pair, looks a bit like he would have been mean to me at school. Then he's next to me and his eyes are wet from the wind blowing into them.

'You all right?' he asks, leaning down to kiss my cheek, his cold palm slipping slightly under my jacket, resting for a second longer than appropriate on the curve of my waist. Something ripples through me.

'Yeah, I'm good. You good?'

'Yeah, good.'

'Good.'

Nerves have made me so aware of myself I feel like someone's watching us on a surveillance camera. I can't remember how people walk when they're not thinking about walking. I'm slightly ahead of him and when I turn I see that he's looking me up and down from behind, his dark brown eyes prodding into me like a finger.

As we walk he points out the school he went to. Tells me that the corner shop owner, Yesim, used to turn him away when he tried to buy cigs underage because he knew his mum. He's different from me. He knows this area in ways that I don't. I came here on trains, for internships. I looked on Zoopla and found that it was one of the remaining places in London I could afford, and it said it had some big warehouse nightclubs that sounded cool. When me and my friends found a house I paid deposits, agency fees and sent rent to a landlord who bought the place off a family moving further out to Zone 5 because you can get more for your money there and because no one was coming into their shop anymore since Sainsbury's opened over the road. I liked it here so I signed a long lease, leaving the room in my parents' house empty, taking up space somewhere other people wanted to be.

He suggests a pub nearby. I've stood opposite it many times, waiting at the bus stop for the 267 to take me further into the city, but I've never been inside. Neither had Joe. People like us had moved into this area and changed it. Now there were all these expensive cafés that served their tap water with cucumber and mint in it. We didn't want to move into their pub as well. Thought if we did all the conversations would stop so that it became quiet enough to hear chair legs scraping over carpet.

'Bit arrogant,' he says when I try to express this. 'Do you always assume people are going to notice you when you're walking around?'

'No, it's just that –' but I can't finish off the thought because I'm laughing at how right he is.

When we sit down with our drinks we ask each other lots of questions, but I'm only interested in the answers he gives. He has nine siblings. He plays five-a-side. His mum works at the café in the park, the one that has lots of plastic kids' toys outside fading under the sun. His dad lives in Kent. He goes there when he needs air and grass and a high street where you can walk without having to dodge people looking down at their phones. He listens to heavy metal because he googled that you work out better when your heart rate is raised and heavy metal does that. Now he just likes it. Black Sabbath, Slayer, Iron Maiden, or anything else where the guitars sound like they're being crunched up in an incinerator. He just ended it with a girl because she wanted a relationship and he's not ready for that. He was naughty at school. He would organise fights in the playing field. But he did a good job of reffing them. Pulling guys apart when blood started to pour from their noses. Squirting water down their swollen faces. He works as a delivery man, but he also might start selling fitness gear on Amazon because apparently you can put a huge mark-up on it.

'What about you then?' he asks. 'What do you do for a living?'

'I'm a journalist.'

'Are you going to write about me?'

'Not unless you do something interesting.'

He asks me if it's hard to get into. If my parents are proud. Have I ever considered making one of those true-crime podcasts? But I'm sick of myself and all the people I meet who are similar to me. So I ask about him again.

'If you could go on holiday anywhere in the world, where would you go?'

I'm drunk enough that I can feel warmth clouding up my neck from the wine. He goes to the toilet and when he comes back he adjusts where he's sat slightly so that one of his knees rests against my knee. I'm conscious of keeping my leg still because I worry that if I flinch, he'll move it back to where it was before. I realise this is what it is to want someone and I'm reassured that I'm still capable of it. I was trying so hard to force it with the other men, but here it happens without me asking it to. He picks up my hand and runs his thumbs over my nails. Turns them over and traces the lines of the deep creases in my palms.

'Are you reading palms?' I ask.

'No,' he says. 'What's that?'

'Some people think they can predict the future by looking at the lines in your hand.'

He brings my hand close to his face and recoils as though he's seen something terrible.

'What?' I ask.

'Nothing, nothing. Wouldn't want to upset you,' he says, grinning so widely I think I can see every single tooth in his mouth. I go to punch him in the arm for the joke, but he grabs my arm before I reach him, stretches it out and back in so that my bicep tenses.

'Look at these guns,' he says, raising his eyebrows. 'They're almost bigger than mine.'

* * *

Later, when we go out to smoke, it's pouring with rain so we huddle underneath an umbrella, sit on the backs of our jackets so that our trousers don't soak up damp from the rotting wooden bench. A man with a cracked red face and a grey ponytail leans out of the door frame, looks up at the sky, shakes his head, shouts, 'Fucking England!' and then disappears back inside.

'Is this all right?' he asks, putting one hand on my thigh. I nod, swallowing something down.

'Weather's shit, isn't it?' I say.

He laughs out of his nose, stubs the half-smoked cigarette into the ashtray. 'You're cute,' he says.

'No, I'm not,' I say, going to punch him again, but he takes my hand and lowers it and then there's no more play fighting because his hand is sliding around my jaw, into my hair until he's got handfuls of it spilling out between his fingertips. I let my cig drop through my fingers onto the floor.

'Is this all right?' he asks, moving his face closer to mine, lips parted.

I nod.

I think about what that red-faced man would think if he came back outside.

I think about what Joe would think if he saw me with this delivery man, his shoulders so broad they look like they're growing out of his ears.

I think about how my heartbeat seems to have moved down between my legs.

I think about whether or not he can feel it thumping in the seat.

'Is it all right if I kiss you?' he asks.

And I answer by leaning in. His lips are softer, bigger than Joe's. There's not much tongue and it annoys me because I want him to break into my body and crawl around in there, fill it up, spread himself out so that he's pushing himself against the walls of my skin like a crayon colouring right up to the lines. I open up my mouth slightly to let him in, but rather than filling up the emptiness he just settles the kiss around my lips. I can taste the plastic strawberry of my lip gloss. Mint on his breath. His hand is cold and it crawls up the side of my top. I can feel it against my ribcage. I'm not wearing a bra and he stops when he realises this.

But then I feel the end of his index finger moving over my nipple and it's like a wave breaks down the length of my body, frothing and white, sinking out over sand.

'Is this all right?' he says, and this time I manage to speak.

'Yes.'

It comes out as a croak.

When we walk into my room it's like I'm seeing everything in it for the first time. He sits on the bed and looks around him with his hands held in a V on his lap. I worry that the dirty cereal bowls are disgusting. That the pencil illustration of a woman masturbating makes me seem too sexual. Then I think about how pathetic it is that I'm so willing to discard the picture if this man who I've just met doesn't like it.

'You have a lot of books,' he says, seeing what I hadn't noticed.

'Yeah.' I sit next to him on the bed and for a while we pretend we don't know why we're here, having messaged for weeks, having gone out for drinks. As though we might have actually come here to watch that film we used as an excuse to get here in the first place.

'I'm quite drunk. I normally just smoke weed,' he says. And his head is in his hands, rubbing at the temples. I want to look after him. Get him something sugary to eat. Run him a hot bath, which smells like lavender and salt. But he sits up fast, as though hauling himself back into the moment and the role he knows he needs to play in it.

'Come here,' he says, and his lips are back on mine and we are falling into the bed, hurrying.

I sit on him with my hands flat against his chest. His body feels impossibly hard, as though he were a marble sculpture in a gallery. The small mounds of his abs are drawn as tight as knotted rope. I want to look over all of him. Glide my tongue along every inch. Name it all. Run forensics. Learn him like I learned Joe's body. So well it felt like an extension of my own. The bite marks on his back. The small red dot under one eye. His arms, his legs. But I don't get much time to see the delivery man because the kissing is short and then he's pulling my top over my head, and I move off him to pull my jeans down and there's awkward laughing when my socks get all bunched up in the trouser leg and he's so efficient that he's getting naked while I struggle and when he's finished with that he helps me to pull at the socks and as he does he laughs, 'What have you done?' and then they come off so hard he falls back against the bed frame, but apparently he's not got time for any more laughing because he's moved over to me, pushed my knickers to the side and put his hand between my legs.

He doesn't look at me when we have sex, but his dick is going into me. He heaves as though he were doing a workout. Deep breaths as he pushes out the leg press. Arms wrenching the lat pulldown. Air huffs out hard from his nose. Everything in him tightens like screws into bolts. *Squeak-squeak-squeak* goes the bed and I think about how I should have oiled it. His pace quickens. He pulls my legs into the air. My skin slaps against his. I look over and on the top of the book pile is the one Joe brought back from my parents' house about the philosophy of walking. Its shiny paper cover glints in the half-light. I like that it's watching me. Is this what cuckolding is? Getting fucked by another man by the picture he got for his birthday. In the bed we bought on Gumtree together. The sheets from Next I made him transfer half the money for. Would he hate that someone else was in me? Or would it make him feel relieved that I look like I'm doing what moving on is? You have to get under someone to get over them and I'm right under the delivery man, his sweat soaking into my skin.

It seems to go on for ages.

'Wait,' he says. 'I just need a minute.' And I can't tell if that's because he's going to come and he thinks I want it to go on for longer, or because he's lost his boner because he's drunk and he needs a moment to get it back. He seems to be measuring his performance not on how good it feels but on how long he lasts. As though it were a game where the highest number wins.

'You can stop now if you like,' I want to say. *'It's starting to burn.'*

But no sounds come out and the pressing starts again and I'm carried away as though on a ship I am not the captain of.

'I have to go home,' he says at the end of it. 'I left my leftovers cooling in some Tupperware outside the fridge – it will go off if I leave it out overnight.'

'OK.'

'Thanks,' he says, as though he has taken something away from me I shouldn't have given him. He kisses my cheek hard enough that it makes my face move in the opposite direction.

His hoodie is still bunched up around his top as he leaves the room. But he stops when he realises he's forgotten his phone. Lingers for a minute, not wanting to puncture the clean exit. When he does come back in I make it easier for him, pretending to be reading something on my phone, as he looks under the bed, finds it under the pillow.

'Cya' he says.

'Bye.'

* * *

It's mid-afternoon and the delivery man's sitting in my kitchen. After he came back to get his phone he kept coming back and now we've been seeing each other for a few weeks. He's wearing a grey vest and his biceps bulge out of it in such a stereotypically attractive way it's almost embarrassing to look at him. He could be on a pull-out poster in a teenager's magazine. I put my foot on the delivery man's legs and he holds it between his hands. We don't talk much, but silence feels comfortable between us, like a big blanket wrapped around our shoulders.

Moll walks in. She likes the delivery man. 'Want a coffee?' she asks, even though she spends the remains of her student loan on that expensive Moroccan blend that comes in stupidly small packages that she has to reorder online.

'I'd love one.'

'Milk? Sugar?'

'Just black, please.'

I shift my foot around to get his attention, creeping up his thigh. 'I always think black coffee tastes like bin juice,' I say.

His nose crinkles. 'Are you into that?'

'What?'

'I dunno, is it a Leeds thing?'

Me and Moll look at each other with widening eyes. 'No, we don't drink bin juice.'

'I dunno,' he says, shrugging. 'Maybe you guys do it to get high.'

I assume he must be joking. But there's no curling up at the sides of his lips, no flickering in his still, brown irises.

I'm not sure he understands me much either. A few days later, he looks at the books stacked up on one side of the room. 'Have you read all these?' he asks, opening one and flicking through the pages, some of them crisp from wet hands in the bath.

'Most of them.'

'Why would you bother keeping them after you've read them?'

I open my mouth because the answer feels obvious but then I realise I have no answer.

'I suppose it makes you feel clever,' I say after a while. 'It's like you look at them and you can see all the things you've put in your brain.'

He nods, puts the book back carefully in the place he took it from, making sure it's straight. Then he looks up at me again. 'But if it's in your brain, why would you need to see it?'

'I saw my world again through your eyes,' wrote Ted Hughes in his *Birthday Letters*, a collection of poems written in response to the suicide of his estranged wife, Sylvia Plath. When he recalls falling in love with Plath, he also falls in love with her way of regarding the world with fairytale wonder. 'Through your eyes it was foreign.'

To Plath, everything was a mystery, emerging from nowhere 'as if it had appeared to dinner guests in the middle of the table'. Her frenzy woke Hughes up to seeing everything anew.

The delivery man does a similar thing for me. Being with him is like exploring. He scares my old logic away, the one I shared with Joe, like a shaman blessing a house by burning white sage to ward away all the old ghosts.

'Wanna go for a walk?' I text him one morning.

'Sure,' he says, but when he arrives at my door he's confused.

'Like, where do you want to go?' he asks.

'Just around.'

'Fair,' he says, looking down at the pavement as we set off, avoiding the cracks in it. 'Is this for exercise or something?'

'What? No. Do you never just walk places?'

He shakes his head. 'Walking is how you get somewhere – why wouldn't you just fast-forward to the destination?'

He comes with me on a walk anyway. When we get to the park, it's busy. Neon running trainers glaze by. We watch a cute kid with chubby fists throwing bread to the ducks. A woman with cherry-red hair and a chest the mocha brown of sunbeds waves at him.

'Hello, lovey,' she says, walking over to us, her hand resting on his shoulder. 'How's your mother? I've still got that hose I need to bring over.' They talk for a while. I stand slightly behind him, tapping my trainers into a shallow puddle.

'Sorry about that,' the delivery man says when she's gone.

'It's fine,' I say.

He didn't need to apologise. I like it when stuff like this happens when I'm with him. It's proof of how rooted he is in this place. All of him tied up in streets that he knows, that he learned to ride a bike on, in trees he's pissed on, in the men who nod on their way past. He knows this ground so well, it's solid beneath his feet when he stands on it. I think it's what makes him so confident, so at ease with the world, as if the reason it was there was to give him something to rest on. I feel I stand on that same ground when I'm with him. As though it were correcting the statelessness I felt when Joe left. A woman without a country.

We sit on a bench and the sun is so bright I have to put a hand over my eyes to see anything but glaring white. He knocks my hand down, leans over and kisses me with those always-closed lips. 'Shall we go back to yours then?'

We never go for a walk again.

'He sounds nice,' Mum says on the phone when I tell her about the delivery man. 'It's good that you're having a bit of fun.' She's in a charity shop looking for designer clothes she can resell on eBay.

'No, but, I actually like him,' I say, and then I tell her about all the things I like. How he puts mugs in the dishwasher without me having to ask, is saving up to go on holiday to Japan.

'That's lovely,' she says, but I can tell she's not really listening because her voice has that strained tone it gets when she's using her chin to hold the phone on her shoulder. I can hear the snapping of clothes hangers hitting each other.

'Sorry that he's not a lawyer,' I say sarcastically.

'What?' Mum yells, moving the phone back into her hand. 'It just didn't sound like you have much in common, is all. More of a rebound type of thing.'

'A rebound?' I snap. 'Is it because he's a delivery man?'

I'm not actually annoyed with her. I'm annoyed because I know he will stop coming over soon. I wanted to feel for a moment that he might stay.

He would think I was so weird if he knew I mentioned him on the phone to my mum.

'Are you about?' the delivery man texts.

'Wanna go to the pub?' I say.

'It's raining, though.'

'But it will be raining on your way to mine?' I point out. 'We can sit inside.'

'Dunno, would rather just come to yours.'

'I suppose we could watch a film.'

An hour or so later we're on the sofa together watching *Planet Earth*. A family of elephants struggles to feed themselves on the savannah where a lack of rain means all that's left of the grass is withered twigs. A baby tries to suck from its mother's dry teat, but she's too thin to provide any milk. Eventually the baby collapses on the cracked ground. The mother tries to nudge her up, but she's too weak. In the distance their family marches further and further out of sight, but instinct means the mother won't abandon her young. I want to feel this sadness with the delivery man, but he's on his phone. Then he's leaning over me, his hand rubbing over the crotch of my leggings.

I can't be bothered to try to make him care about the programme.

'Shall we just go to my room?'

'Sure.'

We're lying down in bed together and he's pressing into me. But then he starts moving his hand between my legs and moves it in time with his hips. In a matter of seconds a thick, tarry wave rushes over me. My face crumples inwards. My back arches. A moan escapes from deep in the pink of my body. Not the *ah-ah-ahs* that drift off from the top of my throat. Afterwards I'm twitching on the bed. Roadkill. The central nervous system of the fox on the road slowly shutting down.

'You just made me come,' I say, almost as a question.

'Isn't that the point?'

Not with the lack of effort you usually put in, I think. But I don't say.

'I've got to go,' he announces afterwards. 'My sister says she's at the station and I don't like her walking on her own at this time.'

'No worries,' I say, not bothering to ask how he'd

know she was there now without looking at his phone to check the time or for a message.

'Bye,' he says.

'Bye.'

It feels like he's always saying bye. The hellos feel less frequent even though they happen at the same rate.

One time the delivery man does actually stay over. He makes a big thing of it, walking into my room and announcing, 'I brought my stuff,' as though he were waiting for me to stick a big gold star on his behaviour chart. 'Shall I just put it down here?' he asks, gesturing towards the sports bag in his hand.

'Yeah, wherever,' I say. He goes to the toilet and I look at the stuff poking out of it. I can see his washbag. It's strange thinking of him as someone who brushes his teeth, eats dinner. Like when you see a teacher at the supermarket and it's odd because you didn't realise that they existed outside of the classroom. When he comes back we watch YouTube videos on the bed. He keeps shifting positions, checking his phone. I can tell he doesn't want to be here, but he is because he thinks this is what women want and he likes me, sort of, so he's decided to try to make me happy. It's actually quite adorable. I haven't told him that I'm going through a break-up. I wonder if he'll see the traces of another man here. The big socks. The razor blades in the bathroom. I'd like to tell him about it because then he'd know I was wanted elsewhere. Wanted so much that someone used to stay here with me every night, only ever making one excuse to leave.

I can't sleep with him here. All the objects in the room feel like they're staring at me, as though they are toys waiting for me to shut my eyes so they can come alive.

'Sleep well?' I ask him in the morning.

He yawns so hard it makes him shudder. 'Really well, thanks.' My legs are on top of the duvet and he leans down and looks at my feet, takes my toe, the bendy one that curls towards the one in front of it in a C shape. 'It looks like a little cashew nut,' he says, and he holds it with such gentle consideration that for a moment I wonder what would happen if we liked each other enough to stick around to see what it takes to make each other really happy.

I'd buy him tickets to see Arsenal because he's supported them ever since he could walk but has never gone inside the Emirates Stadium. I'd bring his mum orchids because they're most women's favourite flowers and I'd help her scratch the fat off pans at the end of the meal. He'd drive me to McDonald's when I'm hungover to get breakfast muffins to take away and I'd feed him his chips while he held onto the wheel. When he reversed, he'd put his hand behind my seat in that way that's so inexplicably hot it makes your crotch turn to pudding. He'd go to put a cashew-nut emoji by my name but find that there isn't one, so instead would use the croissant one because they look very similar.

But chances are I would never take him to Arsenal, and I would never meet his mum. There were too many things I liked that he didn't. I couldn't see the world how he saw it.

'I would stay, but I have to go because my mum says our aunty's coming around later and she needs help in the kitchen.'

'No worries.'

'Bye.'

'Bye.'

And he's gone again, at least until I call him back for another distraction.

12

'Read it back to me again,' says Ruchira, glugging from her water bottle. We're in her bed because last night I was too drunk to make it back to mine.

'I'm really sad. I know this isn't really about me at all. Are you going out tonight? Can I speak to you?'

It's a text from Joe and neither of us knows what the right thing to say is.

'What if he says something you don't want to hear?' she asks. 'What if he tells you he's not in love with you anymore? That he wants someone else?'

'That would be shit,' I say.

Together we scroll through a pizza takeaway menu and draft out different replies.

'How about . . .' Ruchira takes my phone in her hands and I watch as her long navy nails click against the screen. She passes it back so I can read it. 'I'm seeing someone tonight so it's probably best if we don't speak.'

'I'm only seeing my brother,' I say.

'He doesn't know that.' She smiles.

I press send and he replies almost instantly. 'Are you seeing them all night? Could we talk after you see them?' Then a few minutes later another text comes through. 'I'm not trying to pry if it's a date or anything. I just really want to speak.'

The doorbell rings. Ruchira goes to collect the pizza. 'I suppose he wants "closure",' I say as she walks back into the room. I'm making sarcastic air quotes in the air even though it's not a quote.

'What does closure even mean?' asks Ruchira, ripping the foil off a pot of garlic sauce.

I google it and read out the answer: 'Closure is getting an understanding as to exactly why a relationship ended and no longer feeling emotional attachment or pain associated with the relationship. It allows you to move on and establish new and healthy bonds.'

She starts talking but there's too much dough in her mouth so she speed-chews to tell me what she's thinking. 'I think a lot of the time closure is just people trying to appease their own guilt. He can explain himself – why he dumped you on the side of the *road* – and then walk away feeling like everything's tied up all neatly in a bow. Meanwhile, you've just been reminded of how much you like him. You're doing so much better now – do you really want to risk all that?'

'Yeah, you're right.'

'You don't need to go all the way back there. You don't need to know why he made this dumb decision. You just need to know that it was dumb.'

'Yeah.'

'You're going to go, though, aren't you?'

'Yeah.'

I laugh, and then she laughs so much it turns into a cough. She bowls over her stomach and I slap her back a few times until the coughing softens. She wipes the water from her eyes. Takes a deep breath.

'There's no right or wrong way to do this,' she says. 'If you go and see him and it makes you feel worse, don't beat yourself up for going. Like, if you're just going to keep thinking, *Oh, maybe I should see him, maybe I shouldn't,* just go and then the decision is made for you and if it's the wrong one you're gonna be sad anyway for like a year so it doesn't really matter.' She takes up the last slice of pizza, orange oil glistening over it like volcanic lava. She folds it in half so she can fit more of it into her mouth. 'Just don't sleep with him.'

'Yeah.'

'Oh Jesus, you're going to try to do that as well, aren't you?'

'Yeah,' I say, and we're both laughing again.

I'm holding my breath when I walk out of the station. I can't actually look at him; I worry that if I do I might not be able to hold myself up, deflating like a punctured car tyre. Instead, I divert my eyes to the cashpoint behind him, the hot chocolate he holds out towards me.

'You didn't need to get me that,' I tell him.

'I know. Just thought you might like it.'

I sip from the cup and it sears a little rectangle into my lip. It's only October but today it's cold enough that clouds of grey steam puff out of me when I breathe. And yet my forehead is slick with sweat. I go to take off my coat and struggle with passing the hot chocolate between my hands. 'Let me,' he says.

'I can do it,' I tell him, but it's already in his hand and the coat comes off much more easily with his help.

'How have you been?' he asks as we start walking towards Regent's Park.

'Not good. You?'

'Not good.'

'How's your sister?'

'Yeah, she's all right. The dog's still a nightmare.'

The conversation carries on like this for a while. Stiff, as though we never really knew each other. *It's me,* I want to say. *It's Annie,* like when families kneel at the beds of their relatives with dementia. *Can you hear me?*

We turn into the park and follow the long concrete path bordered on the other side of the road by huge custard-tart-coloured mansions with big shiny sports cars parked outside. I dare myself to look over at him. He's different. His tan is deeper than before. The colour of hardwood floors, or the hero in westerns. He's put on some muscle. His arms press into the sides of his jacket. But most of him is exactly the same and I'm sad because I realise how much of that sameness I forgot. The way he scratches his nose when he feels tense. His hands that can't be fully straightened out. The snowflakes that gathered around my image of him are starting to melt.

'Fuck, why am I crying?' I say, embarrassment burning me up on the inside like a radiator. 'I promised myself I wouldn't cry.'

'You can cry if you want to cry.'

'I don't want to,' I say, looking up to the sky and blinking. I hold a finger underneath each eye ready to catch any tears before they run lines through my make-up. There's silence for a while after that and I promise myself I won't break it, but then, without asking, my mouth is opening again.

'I just don't get it,' I say, snapping a branch off a tree and tearing off its leaves, dividing each one into smaller and smaller pieces, scattering them over the grass.

'I mean, I'm not sure I do either,' he says. 'I just know I need to be on my own.'

'Why, though?' I ask, shouting.

'We were so co-dependent, it wasn't healthy. We were always trying to fix each other's problems. Then we'd get angry when we couldn't.'

I've heard of co-dependence only once before. Joe told me about two of his friends that broke up for that reason. 'But that's what a relationship is!' we laughed. 'You trust someone so much that you depend on each other!' That's why Joe was the first person I rang when I was upset, why I felt sad when he felt sad, why he would proofread my writing while I made him dinner to say thank you. We spent a lot of time together, but that's because time felt better spent with him.

'That doesn't sound like a problem,' I tell him.

'Well, for me it is a problem.'

'Do you know how hard it is to find what we had? We like the same films, we like the same music, we have the same politics, we both fancy each other so much.' The words pour out of me as though someone has turned a tap on. 'No one will ever know you like I do. That phase in uni when you would eat an entire packet of double chocolate cookies every night. When you would hang out with that annoying guy called Ralph even though you didn't like him just because he had no friends and you didn't want him to be lonely. Do you remember how many library fines we both racked up just because we were too lazy to bring the books back? We're both always losing things – phones, IDs, wallets. Other people won't understand that, you know? They'll find it annoying. They'll ask you to change it. I love all of you, even the parts that are mistakes, and I'm sorry if towards the end I punished you for those mistakes because now I regret it so much. I've never met anyone else who has what we had with their partner.'

'Me neither,' he says, kicking a Diet Coke can that's squashed down flat along the concrete path. 'I know I'll never love anyone as much as I love you. That's not the point.'

We reach the can and he kicks it again. This time it hits a bin and stops. I let out a long breath.

'What?' he asks.

'I promised myself I wouldn't do that,' I say.

'Do what?'

'Rant.'

'I liked the rant,' he says, looking back at me, and I see that there's something twinkling like fireflies in the back of his blue-green eyes.

'Good,' I tell him. 'Because I've been rehearsing it in the shower for weeks. The shampoo bottles have been giving me pointers on my delivery.'

He looks in his pockets for his tobacco. 'You're funny. I forgot how funny you are.'

We walk past the ponds where ducks dip their noses into the inky brown water and scream as they flap their wings, fighting for the big pieces of bread that people have thrown in.

'I've been cooking a lot,' he says as a kid wearing little red wellies runs through the gap in between us. 'I bought a pasta maker. I make a really good cacio e pepe.'

'I'm sure the ladies love it.'

'They do,' he says, joking, and I punch him in the arm hard enough to leave a bruise. 'Maybe I'll make it for you one day.'

'Oh, so now we've broken up, you want to cook for me?'

'Don't start,' he says, smiling. He's quiet for a moment but then he keeps on talking. 'I am sorry, Annie. You did so much for me, picking my clothes off the floor, reminding me to take the bins out. I'm sorry I didn't appreciate it at the time.'

'No, I'm sorry,' I say. 'None of that stuff matters. I was freelance. I had more time for housework. You came back from work tired. I should have just done it rather than making such a big deal out of everything.'

'I just keep thinking of when we went to that exhibition,' he says, looking over at me, his gaze boiling on my cheek. 'The one at the Royal Academy of Klimt and Schiele? I was in a mood because we were late and it was busy.' I remember the day he's talking about; he was shoulder-barging people, scrolling on his phone on the bench in the middle of the room. 'I would kill to go there with you now.'

'Well, I would kill to take the bins out for you.'

'I would kill to not let you,' he says.

A dog comes over with a ball in its mouth and he picks up the ball and sends it spinning far away into the distance.

'We both made so many mistakes,' he says. 'I wish I could do it all over again.'

I think for a moment about these mistakes. How quickly I made them. How easy they were to make. I stopped making an effort, always walking around the house with Sudocrem on my spots. Carrying on talking about my work even when he was trying to relax so that falling asleep would come easy. I was so secure in this love, I thought that he would forgive me for each and every one of those mistakes, but soon they all piled up and there were too many of them and all these tiny ones were enough for him to say, 'I want to be on my own.'

After her husband left her for another woman, Sharon Olds cursed herself for the arrogance with which she sleepwalked into his departure. In her poetry collection *Stag's Leap* she writes, 'I did not work not to lose him, and I lost him.'

There were mistakes from Joe and from me, but the very act of not seeing this coming, of not believing it could happen, is a mistake all on its own.

Seeing Joe now after he's decided it's over, there's no margin for error. Each action I take is pivotal. If I leaned in and kissed him, he would run. If I don't do enough by the end of this, we'll just say 'bye' and it will really be a 'bye' – a pleasant one with more rounded edges than the one by the side of the road, but a 'bye' all the same.

'My granny is poorly,' I say when he's finished talking about the new job he's got, looking down at my feet as I do.

'I'm so sorry,' he says, and I feel a twinge of something rotten in me. I think it's because I enjoyed making him feel bad for not being there to stop what's hurting me. For using Granny as a tool for something.

'She's the loveliest woman. Are you OK?' Joe leans over and puts his hand on mine and squeezes it hard enough that my fingers bunch up into a claw. 'You know you can still ring me if you want to talk about that stuff. I've not gone anywhere.'

We move through the rose garden where pinks and yellows border each other in neatly dug-out rows. We stand by the water fountain, look down at the rusting coins in the bottom and think of all the wishes that cleave to them. *Let that bet come through. Please say those exam results turn out well.*

'They haven't been great,' he says about some of our mutual friends. 'They've obviously been supporting you, which is fair because I did this, but that doesn't mean I'm not hurting.'

I'm drinking from my bottle, but then I start coughing on it when some of the water goes down the wrong way.

'It's true,' he says.

'No, I believe you,' I tell him. 'It's just, every time I messaged them wanting to hang out and they said they were busy I assumed they were ignoring me because they were hanging out with you. I thought you were the one they picked.'

Hearing this stuff makes me feel less alone. How funny that the best person to help you through a break-up is most likely the one who did it to you. Only they know what really happened, just like how your siblings are the only people who know how fucked up your upbringing was and therefore the only ones you can tolerate passing judgement on it.

We walk through the playing fields. Far away in the middle of the grass teenagers in neon tabards play football, their watching dads blowing on their hands, rubbing their fingers together.

'The most embarrassing thing happened the other day,' I say. 'I went to get some jeans taken in at this seamstress place on Seven Sisters Road and the guy was like, "Put them on for me," and I did and then he pulled out the waistband to see where they needed to be taken in, and these jeans are, like, waay too big for me so the waistband came right out and he looked horrified.'

Joe nodded, looked over to me to watch me deliver the final punchline. 'I realised I'd forgotten to wear knickers 'cause I just wore trackies to the place, you know? So he saw my whole arse crack. I hope he didn't think I was some weird flasher.'

'You're funny,' he says again.

I told the delivery man the same story last week, but he carried on looking at the football, even though he'd said it wasn't an important match. I tried to get his attention in other ways – asked roaming questions like, 'Who is that player?' 'Which kit do you like the best?' – but when he answered those questions they didn't turn into new questions, they knocked up against dead ends. It was fun learning each other's stories at first, but when we try to invent new ones we find that we have such different ideas about what makes a good story.

We're walking and he pulls me by the sleeve of my coat to the side because behind me are two people I didn't realise were trying to pass. I stumble slightly from the force of his tug, climbing over his feet, holding his arm for a moment to regain my balance. And in this exchange of arms and legs I can feel something warming up between us, the air softening like putty, the edges of our bodies blurring so that we're turning into two parts of the same thing.

The path curves around the river, brown water lapping gently against an orange buoy. A swan looks white, but if you look closely it's yellowing, discoloured. There's a patch of grass with a good view of all the water and

I sit down on it. Joe does too, which is weird because it's muddy and he always takes good care of his clothes, putting T-shirts in the wash with handfuls of whitener, his long coat laid over both of our knees in a taxi so that it doesn't crease. I lie back, letting my coat ride up so my belly is out. I look up, the sun peeking through the greyness like a blade, shining warm on my skin. He puts his palm flat against it. 'You've lost so much weight,' he says, a finger moving down the line that leads from my chest down to my belly button.

'Yeah, I've not been eating that much.'

'But I love your tummy,' he says, and he leans down and buries his face in what's left of it. His nose is cold but I don't flinch. Instead, I move my finger up and down the outside of his ear where the blonde fur of his hair has been singed away from too much box dye. I lean down and kiss the thin skin there.

'Stop,' he says, sitting back up, tugging grass from the soil and throwing it into the air. 'You're making it difficult.'

He looks over at me and I can see in his eyes that he's terrified, of me, and of the screws that come loose when he's around me. I can feel something slipping out of his hands. I know now what was sparkling in the back of those blue-green eyes: it was how much he still loves me. He turns away, but it's too late for distraction now that we've touched. I feel like I'm getting bigger, huge, a monster with tentacles bursting out over the whole river. Did he really think it would be so easy to walk away? I move over and sit on him and his body is propped up on his arms so our faces are close. I nudge at his nose. Breathe into his ear. Put my lips on his and at first his don't move, but then they start to kiss me back, and we're pressing hard, disappearing down each other's throats. His hands are under my top. He gasps. His neck rolls back. His mouth drops open.

'Annie,' he says, and something in him gives way, breaks off, floats away down the river, joins up with the Thames, finds its way out to sea. With one hand he unbuttons my jeans and slides his hand down into my underwear.

'I've missed you.'

We drink, we kiss, we drink, we kiss. 'You need to eat,' he says, and we walk to the pizza restaurant over the road. When our order arrives I realise that for the first time in a long time I'm actually starving. But I like it when he tells me what to do so I eat the crusts slowly, lazily, a kid who knows there's no pudding without eating the green vegetables.

'Good,' he says when I've finished, and from those words I can see that part of him is enjoying what losing him has done to me. The havoc it's wreaked on my body. He loves how much I love him. I am a vessel for him to see his own perfection. What Virginia Woolf meant when she said women are looking glasses that reflect the image of man back at twice their natural size. This shouldn't be something I want, but I want anything that brings him closer to me.

When I go to the toilet I send him a picture of my ass, bending over in a black thong. He looks weak when I come back. Drooping over like a plant that's been over-watered. 'Can we get the bill?' he asks.

On the way out he playfully slaps my ass and I scream-laugh in response. An old couple who have been eyeing us all evening pinch their lips disapprovingly. I bet they think we're in the first flushes of love. Really, this is a haggard love. One that's been torn apart and patched back together. It's pushing at its stitches. It's busting out at the seams.

We get back to mine and Moll catches me walking out of the kitchen with two wine glasses in my hand. 'I'm not saying anything,' she announces, hands held up as though to prove she's unarmed. She's actually saying quite a lot.

The sex is the best sex because it possesses the perfect alchemy of getting with someone who knows you so well they can sense exactly where you want to be touched, but also they've been gone for long enough that their body has all the newness and sparkle of a stranger. We do it so many times that by the end everything is swollen and puffy. He touches me again and I say, 'I can't,' but then somehow I want it again and my mouth is filled with pillow so I don't scream out.

'I want to hear you,' he says, so I'm loud, dribbling, making sure Moll has to put headphones in. I remember now what I forgot before. That to have power you have to have someone to be powerful over. That's what I am for him. I bend so that he can climb on my back and stand taller. In that way I make the power. Really, it is mine. If I said no, there would be nothing. No one would ascend and we would both be crawling around on the floor. But I want him to be tall, so I think about becoming the carpet he sinks his toes into. The table he rests his feet on. Everything is a yes. I am one enormous big fat walking yes. Shame or embarrassment – 'I don't think I can do that' – becomes me doing that very thing on a plate. I stretch out, I open up. I fit more of him in my mouth than I ever have before. I spit and gag. I roll over. He says, 'Jump,' and I say, 'How high?' and together we reach the stars.

It's supposed to be humiliating, what I've done, letting the one who said he didn't want me have all of me – so much that he's literally inside my body. In 'The Glass Essay', Anne Carson sees sleeping with her ex for the last time in these degrading terms.

> *when I found myself*
> *thrusting my little burning red backside like a*
> *baboon*
> *at a man who no longer cherished me.*

She admits she was appalled by this action, but I don't see it that way. I gave to him, but in doing so I feel I took from him the peace of thinking he made the right decision. I was a trap that lured him in. A habit he couldn't give up.

'I missed that sound,' he says, when we sit in bed together the next morning eating cereal. He used to get so annoyed at the way I'd slurp the milk off the spoon. Tongue smacking against my gums. Sometimes he would complain so much I'd leave the room to eat at the kitchen table. Other times he would put earphones in until I'd finished eating. 'Louder,' he says now. 'Do it louder.'

We used to hate that things never changed, that we had the same arguments about the same mistakes again and again. But now that sameness is a blessing because we can come back after all this time and it's still there. I was so worried about all the mistakes I made, but now I see that they are the most special part. They mean we wanted each other at our worst.

Romantic comedies always build to this climax where one of the characters realises all that they've neglected and how perfect the one they've been ignoring really is. When they run to the airport to stop them from getting on a flight to wherever they're going, they always make a big speech and in this big speech it's always the mistakes that they focus on.

Remember *When Harry Met Sally*? When he tells her, 'I love that you get cold when it's seventy-one degrees out. I love that it takes you an hour and a half to order a sandwich.' Or *Along Came Polly* when Reuben tells Polly, 'Since we have been together I have felt more uncomfortable, out of place, embarrassed, and just physically sick than I have in my entire life,' right before he tells her that he loves her for the first time. Or *10 Things I Hate About You* when Kat reads that poem in front of the class which starts, 'I hate the way you talk to me, and the way you cut your hair. I hate the way you drive my car, I hate it when you stare,' only for the last line to be, 'But mostly I hate the way I don't hate you, not even close, not even a little bit, not even at all.' The bits that are wrong are always the bits that make them want to stay.

We go up to shower and when he gets out he opens the drawer and takes out my moisturiser. 'You can't dump me and still get to use my face stuff.'

'Can't I?' he smiles, a big teacher's-pet smile, one that old ladies would say 'oh, go on then' to.

He used to always steal this stuff and when I told him to stop he would say that he'd buy some more. Sometimes when I was falling asleep I would think about all that white cream melting into his face, how he would warm it up in his hands before putting it onto his face so that most of it would sink into parts of him that didn't even need it. I'd become so mad I wanted to kick him out of the bed, see his face shocked out of sleep.

'What's mine is mine and what's yours is mine,' he says, and I snatch the moisturiser out of his hands. Then he's reaching behind me to get it, but I move it back and forth between each hand, laughing giddily. He tickles me and my body shrinks to one side. I drop it on the floor, some of it splashing across the tiles.

We walk back into the bedroom and he closes the blinds. It's our code that we're going to have sex because our room opens out onto the street and so you have to shut them to stop people walking past the window from seeing. He's used these blinds so many times before and you can see that from the way he touches them, pulling the string slowly because they will slam down at one side, pulling the stiff side by hand. He knows how to move over the bed so that it doesn't make that squeaking noise. The room has been calling out to him, a light-house shining out onto nearby rocks; it missed him, all these empty drawers, and his ship has landed on the shore now and he's walked back onto land and it's like he never left. There's no hurt anymore, no questions, no anger, just two things coming back together, settling back into place. Finding their other set of arms and legs.

'We probably shouldn't tell anyone about this,' he says in the semi-darkness of the bedroom after we both finish, the gaps in the blinds casting yellow stripes over the sides of his face.

'I won't,' I say, putting my leg over his body. 'Everyone will say that it's unfair on me or some shit. But I'm OK, I want this.'

We lie there for a while, red-wine headaches, limbs tangled like ivy crawling up a building, enjoying the process of achieving comfiness again and then – as soon as we do – turning over and trying to get comfy again, as if to stop ourselves from taking for granted what's good. To never get used to something, to feel it afresh every time. Before he leaves he leans down and holds my face in his hands like it's something delicate he's worried about dropping. 'I'm off to the pub to meet Ralph,' he says. 'He's going to think this is jokes.'

'I thought we weren't going to tell anyone?'

'Well, you're going to tell Ruchira, aren't you? And I'll tell Ralph and then that's it.'

He winks at me, pulls up his collar, slips out of the door. I watch the blue of his jacket through the slices of the blinds as it moves along beyond the window.

I ring Mum. 'I thought this might happen,' she says.

13

'So what's actually going on?' Ruchira asks. 'Are you getting back together?' We're in a taxi on the way to the airport for that trip to Lisbon we booked right after the break-up. I haven't spoken to her since Joe and I slept together. I've been messaging him almost constantly and not really doing much else. He wanted to see me again before this trip, but I thought it best to make him wait until I'm back. So he can miss me.

'Not really sure,' I say, picking off my pink nail varnish, all the little shards clinging to my leggings. 'Basically, I think we're just going to sort of go on a date every now and again and see other people and then maybe in a year or so's time, when he's ready for a relationship again, we can go back out.'

'Did he say that?'

'We didn't really speak about it, but that's the impression I got.'

'And this is something that you want?'

'Yeah, I mean – yeah,' I say and then I turn away from her, shut my eyes, enjoy the heating blasting into my face, the gentle mumble of the traffic reports on the radio.

We get off the plane, walk around the city. Point at two cats nuzzled together so close one of their heads looks like it's missing. 'It's us!' we shout. We sit in bars where women with big hoop earrings and long curly hair sing in pained voices about adulterous lovers. In one we end up talking to some guys from Yorkshire about football and whether my home town is posh or not and then they're just off to get cash out but they don't come back and later we see them in another bar, eyes squeezed shut as they suck on lemon wedges after putting away another tequila shot.

'I think they felt intimidated,' we tell ourselves. We buy tacky fridge magnets. We eat fish with buttery potatoes. Chicken and chips. We completely lose track of how much money we owe each other.

The first message from him arrives on day two when me and Ruchira are sitting on a balcony drinking cheap, sugary rosé. I send him a picture and a few seconds later the phone buzzes on my leg.

'You both look lovely,' he says, and the inside of me glows, turns ultraviolet.

I read the message out loud. 'Tell him I say thanks,' says Ruchira, reaching in her bag to get her own phone out, her mouth gathering at the side, screwing shut.

He sends another. 'Don't cry because it's over, smile because it happened.' It's a joke because he would never use a phrase like that.

Ruchira and I go to the shop to buy bread and cheese for breakfast and old women with silver hair and wobbling arms purse their lips into thin cracks when they see what we're wearing.

'You look fit,' Ruchira says. 'That's just the politics of the envious.'

'Did you just quote that thing people use to justify why we shouldn't tax the wealthy?'

'It's early,' she says, chucking some bacon-flavoured crisps into our basket. 'Leave me alone.'

I replied to his last message with a picture of me in the club. The photo is slightly out of focus, my flaws smoothed away in a flurry of movement, lips pulled wider than they really are. He's seen it but he doesn't say anything back.

We go to a convent where they take in blind people. There's a big orange tree in the garden. White tiles patterned with blue vines. Paintings bordered with angels with chubby legs. We sit and the tour guide tells us about Saint Teresa of Ávila and how God would put her into spiritual raptures so intense that she would levitate. Teresa found these displays embarrassing and would ask her sisters to hold her down when they occurred.

'Any questions?' asks the guide.

A man puts his hand up and starts talking before he's chosen. 'A lot of psychiatrists have studied Teresa's accounts of these raptures – it's more than likely that she suffered from a form of temporal lobe epilepsy.'

Ruchira leans over and whispers in my ear. 'Classic case of: it's a statement, not a question.' I bite my lip to stop the laugh but it just travels up from my mouth and comes out of my nose.

* * *

I want to message him again, but I can't because he's not replied. But then this feels like such a childish game. Aren't we beyond all that? If I send another it might even make me look relaxed. As if I'm so casual about the rules of messaging I just send them off when I feel like it. The justification comes easily, its pathway well reinforced from all the times I've used it. 'R U bored of me?' I write, hoping the half-formed words help me to sound less serious.

It's late and I'm trying to sleep but he's still not replied and mosquitoes have bitten up my fingers and all along my feet. It's so itchy when they go that close to the bone and there's not enough space to get a good scratch. I once told Joe about how badly I get bitten when I'm on holiday. 'It's because they've got good taste,' he said, roaring like a tiger and leaning down, lightly digging his teeth into my bum cheek. Maybe I should text him about this now? Perhaps my messages aren't sending because I'm in Portugal? There's blood on me now from all the scratching. I go to the bathroom and run the cold tap over the bites until they turn numb.

Both Ruchira and I hate being in charge so all holiday we take turns to find our way to places. 'Ryan normally does this stuff,' she says.

'Joe did too.'

It's her turn and she says it's the next left, but twenty minutes into our walk it turns out it was actually the next right and it takes us so long to find where we're going I can feel anger tingling in my stomach. She says, 'We're nearly there,' and I want to repeat the sentence back to her and then I want to keep repeating what she says until she asks, 'Why are you repeating what I'm saying?' And then I'll respond, 'Why are you repeating what I'm saying?' 'That's mature.' 'That's mature.' Eventually we find the strip of restaurants we were looking for and go 'Here?' at the first decent-looking one. Her chicken arrives and it doesn't look like it's got any seasoning and my prawns are watery and pale. We don't say much during dinner except 'Yes, it's lovely' to the waiter when he comes over.

'Spoken to Joe?' asks Ruchira the next morning as we do our make-up.

'I feel like you think it's weird that he is messaging less,' I say. 'I know it seems like he's doing that thing where he's slept with me and so now he's losing interest, but he's not. He's only ever liked me more after we've slept together, like when we first went out, he was obsessed after he first got with me. He's just cooling off because when it happened the other night I asked him to take it slow. I said I need space and time to heal and that's what he's giving me and now he's being criticised for doing what I asked – like, it doesn't really seem fair.'

'I literally didn't say that,' Ruchira says. 'I didn't say anything.'

* * *

It's our last day and we sit on a bench looking over the red, blue, lilac, white buildings on the other side of the city moving down a cliff face. We open a paper bag filled with pastel de natas. 'This one could do with a bit more charring on top,' I say because we've eaten so many of these now we're connoisseurs. 'Very creamy, though,' adds Ruchira. We said we were going to go to the beach but neither of us could be bothered to work out which bus we needed to take to get there. Shame, because I liked the idea of stretching my body out next to her. Sand between our toes. Being the one who makes it into the sea first, shouting back, 'It's not cold once you get in!' Burning in our trainers on the walk back. 'Do you remember before we came we were both talking about how many men we were going to get with?'

'Ha,' says Ruchira. 'Ryan keeps sending messages where he sounds really worried I might elope with some hot bartender, and I'm like, wow, if only you knew how much that's not happening.' She crinkles up the paper bag in her hands, throws it into the bin and carries on talking. 'Maybe we could live without men? You know, like in that convent. Those nuns seem to have an all-right time of it.'

I lean over and rest my head on her shoulder. I remember a scene in *Sex and the City* where Charlotte says something similar to her friends: 'Don't laugh at me, but maybe we could be each other's soulmates? And then we could let men be just these great nice guys to have fun with?'

Ruchira and I stand up, the sun breaking through our cheap sunglasses, making us hold our hands up over our eyes. 'We spoke to *some* guys,' I say. 'Remember those ones who ran away from us?'

I love her laugh. It sounds like winning.

I send him a picture of a Leonardo da Vinci quote that was written in the book I'm reading. 'Love is something so ugly that the human race would die out if lovers could see what they were doing.'

The problem with messages is, the more you send them, the more you want to send another one to correct the one you just sent, but then you want to send another one to correct that one too.

When we get to the airport we find out that our flight is delayed. For hours we sit, stiffening up on the tiled floor, eating pots of muesli, looking at couples and guessing when they last had sex. 'I wish I could teleport,' I say, and Ruchira nods. A new gate is announced and we're made to go through security again, but then it turns out they put the wrong gate on the screen so we have to go all the way back through security a third time. 'In forty-five years I've never seen anything like this,' says one woman, shaking her head, wrapping her cardigan more tightly around her middle, narrowing her eyes at different members of the crowd in the hope that they will share in her outrage. Her husband looks at the floor, then back up, like a disappointed football manager watching his team concede another goal.

'Last night,' I say, pointing at the couple, playing the game again. 'Their food arrived without a bread basket and they complained to the manager, and expressing fury at the organisational misdemeanour turned them on so much they had to –'

Ruchira finishes my sentence: 'Go and fuck in the toilets.'

I get a message. It's not him, it's the delivery man asking when I get home. 'Oh God,' I say, passing the phone over to Ruchira so she can see his response to my update on the delayed flight.

Make sure that pussy gets home safe.

'No, stop it!' she screams. 'I'm going to get a stitch. Do you think he knows there's a woman attached to said pussy?'

14

'I've got bed bugs,' I say down the phone to Mum. 'When I was in Lisbon I thought they were mosquito bites but they're not, they're actually bed bugs.'

'Are you sure they're not fleas from the cat?'

'No, they're bed bugs,' I tell her.

'How do you know?'

I know because they bite in straight lines, because they tend to go for your hands, feet, back. I read about them when I'm supposed to be working. They are red because their stomachs are filled with your blood. They lay eggs in the seams of the mattress. If there are brown dots in the bed it's their faeces. I lie in bed brushing my arms because even though I can't see them I can feel them all over me. When I wake up I scan my skin for new bites. Three more on Tuesday. Seven more on Wednesday. You could draw a dot-to-dot over my back with a pen. The ones on my hands have hardened into wart-like lesions. I dig my finger into one and it pops and liquid squirts out. I've itched so much I worry they are infected, that they will scar and I will have mottled red rashes over my hands for the rest of my life. I can't stop, though. I like it when the itch turns to soreness. It feels more bearable then. When I'm drinking a tea I put the boiling base of the mug against one and it feels almost like it's fizzing.

Sometimes they are so itchy I drag my bitten hand across the carpet, my face gooey with pleasure.

'Use Anthisan cream,' Mum tells me, very loudly. 'Don't itch. That will spread the poison through your skin.'

Susan Sontag wrote in her diaries that her mother led her to believe that 'I love you' means 'I don't love anyone else'. I learned this same lesson with you. Though I'm not sure you were trying to teach it to me. Either way, it took me under, stole things from me.

'Please can we hang out? Just one night? You're literally always with him,' I remember Jess asking. She was sitting on my bed in the house we used to share at university. 'Like how we used to.'

'I can't tonight,' I tell her. 'I already told Joe I'd come over later. I'm free on Friday?'

Jess smiled when I walked in on Friday evening. I guess because she couldn't sense how much I now regretted making this plan. I wanted to be where Joe was, eating cereal from other people's cupboards and watching *Twin Peaks* in our friend Nik's room on the big TV. She'd rubbed fake tan into her arms so the whole room smelled like warm biscuits. I helped her with her back, making sure the swampy-brown foam dried evenly into her skin so that when she washed it off there wouldn't be any streaks. I remember telling you once, before we went out, how Jess and I fake-tanned each other, hoping it would make you think of me naked, bring up images of girls having pillow fights like you see in teen movies. Jess told me about the hot Irish guy she'd slept with. *Keeping Up with the Kardashians* hummed in the background.

'I'm gonna head off,' I said.

'You're leaving?'

'Well, I'm just going to sleep at his. I've been here for hours, Jess.'

She'd been slowly tidying the room for a while, putting one item away a minute, but then she became ferocious with it – cups shoved along the wooden dresser, strappy tops lobbed into a pile near the door. She wrapped her hair straighteners up and threw them in the drawer, then slammed it shut with her hip.

'It's fine, you can go,' she said, not looking at me.

'Well, not just yet,' I said and then I stayed there for twenty awkward minutes, the air between us prickling. I enjoyed how much my presence punished us both. *You want me here? Well then, here you go.* Each second proof of how fine I am without him.

I could have stayed – it would have been easy. We'd watch 'How to Twerk' tutorials and laugh at how our necks move instead of our bums. We'd hold each other's wrists, comparing how much pressure we apply when giving blowjobs. We'd restart the squat challenge. I gave up at 80, she made it to 100, but neither of us got up to the 250 a day that you were meant to do. I could have created some boundaries between me and Joe, stopped seeing him every night, focusing instead on my friends, talked to him about how to stop us from becoming what he now calls 'co-dependent'. But I didn't do that. I left and when I walked down the stairs I could hear Jess crying. I felt something dragging through me, a knife from the top of me all the way down to the bottom.

Jess didn't ever get annoyed, she just stopped asking what I was up to. We never got back to how we were before.

Maybe this was my first break-up.

'He still wants to see me!' I say to Moll, walking into her room without knocking. 'He wasn't getting my messages because he broke his phone!'

'Broke his phone?' she asks, unconvinced. 'Did the dog eat his homework too?'

I ignore her and say yes when he says let's get pizza on Friday at a place near his dad's house where he's staying at the minute. I'm so excited I buy a gold glittery halter-neck dress and snake-print over-the-knee boots. I shave everything on my body, rub my skin with salt scrubs and then soak it in coconut-flavoured body moisturiser. I slather Vaseline into my lips and elbows, peel charcoal masks off the bridge of my nose. I put cold spoons on my spots to reduce swelling, ice packs on my eyes to get rid of puffiness. It's when I'm getting another pack out of the fridge that I see his message. 'I may not be free on Friday,' he says – one of his friends is going through something difficult and he's worried about him going through it alone.

My stomach turns as if someone has their hands on it and they're wringing it out like a wet towel. I want to ask him why he's not suggested another day. But I can't do that because to make him want me, I have to make him feel as though he's losing me.

Why is so much of love built out of pretending not to love at all?

I pretend that I don't mind. We talk about Lisbon, the new season of *Succession*. I ask him how he's been. 'I'm great, thanks,' he says. 'Haven't had a drink all weekend! Also had a boxing lesson.'

'I'm sorry I was holding you back so much!' I say. 'Pasta maker, boxing, gym, therapy, job, holidays. I must have been a real nightmare!'

My fingers typed the message quickly, moving fast so that my brain didn't have a chance to stop them from pressing send. It felt good, though, in a bad way. Like smashing a glass against a wall or spitting phlegm out onto the pavement. These past few weeks I've been carefully moulding myself into the shape of something he might want again. I took deep breaths when I was with him to stop myself from crying. I shaded under my cheekbones until they looked bigger. I started taking fucking supplements. But like the Incredible Hulk, the real me is breaking out from under her skin and I can't hold her back.

'Would you rather me say I was miserable?' he replies.

'No.'

'You told me you were well.'

'You dumped me,' I say, and then, realising I'm losing control again, 'Sorry, shouldn't have started talking. Gonna go now.'

'What? Why?' he asks.

'Because you make me crazy.'

'Ditto.'

'This conversation is skewing my head.'

'Same. When I message you I don't look away from my phone,' he says. 'Stay, Annie.'

I feel something breaking in me again. The crazy is a big wave coming and you can't stop the sea; it tingles down my arms, pours out of my thumbs – they won't stop hammering against the screen. I type and type and type and then I delete and retype because my phone keeps changing 'fucking' to 'ducking'.

'My head is so ducking fucking messed up right now,' I tell him. 'I feel like I'm going to be sick. Sometimes I feel better and then I talk to you and it's like I've been hit by a truck. I'm in so much pain again. And ten minutes ago I was happy. Can I see you tomorrow? I'm meant to be doing something but I will cancel those plans. If you don't want to lose me then I suggest you do too because I dunno how much more of this I can take. I don't know what I feel or anything. Like, I don't have a big pronouncement or anything, I just hate all this vague fucking around.'

I ring him and he doesn't pick up. I ring him again and there's nothing but my breath crackling against the speaker. When he finally answers I'm even worse over the phone. I just keep shouting 'Fuck!' and 'When did I start to hate myself so much?' I call him a coward for giving up on us, a fucking coward.

When I wake up in the morning I'm calm again. I focus on how easy it was to win him back two weeks ago on the bank of that river. 'Are you scared to see me because you know it will feel good?' I ask, and then I send him lots of pictures of me. Bending the phone into different angles so different parts of me swell outwards, others gather in. I'm on my knees. He says he's hard. I send him videos. He doesn't do any work even though he's got a deadline. We talk for hours. I win. We make plans to see each other the day after he sees his friend.

15

'You do washing now as well?' I ask as Joe hangs up the billowing pale blue and pink of his dad's work shirts on a drying rack.

'Funny,' he says.

I pull down the hem of my very short lilac dress, stand up off the bar stool and walk towards the window of Joe's dad's London flat. Outside boat propellers cut through the Thames tide so that the air feels wet and heavy. His dad must like water because he's got another flat by the coast and it's so quiet there you can hear the sea as you fall asleep.

'It's nice here, isn't it?' Joe asks.

'Yeah, shame it's not your place.'

He smirks – 'Will be one day' – and then he looks at me with those blue-green eyes. I confront them in a way I couldn't when I saw him for the first time since he ended it, as though we're in court and I'm testifying against the man who hurt my daughter. I try to see if there's anything sparkling in them this time, but he drops his gaze down to his phone before I can see, angles the screen away from my face – almost comically so.

'Who's that?' I ask.

'Not sure you'd want to know.'

I pick up my phone too, scroll for a bit and then laugh at something I read on there that's not funny.

'How's the PT?' he asks, because I lied and told him that's what the delivery man does. It sounds more intimidating.

'Yeah, he's good, says he's gonna give me and Ruchira some free sessions.'

Joe pings the ring on his beer can. 'Well, you'd hope he wouldn't charge you.'

'Are you seeing anyone?'

'Yeah,' he says and then rolls a cigarette, walks towards the balcony to smoke it. 'Nothing serious though. She's a bit older. I've worked out that's the way to go. God, she can put away the wine.'

I sit for a bit, still scrolling. I don't want him to have the satisfaction of knowing I'd prefer to be nearer to him than further away. But it's obvious that's the case, otherwise why would I have come here? Begged him to change his plans? I try to think of a way out of this bind but it's hard to concentrate when the grey gauzy material of the sofa is so itchy against my thighs. I try to rearrange myself, sit cross-legged, then with my legs to the side, hand against the sofa arm, on the cushion, but nothing feels right, like when someone leaves the room right before you have sex and you're lying on the bed trying to look normal when they come back in but your body no longer makes sense to you. I follow him to the outside, but I can't get settled there either. The iron chair I'm sitting on is uneven, with the left side slightly raised up off the stone. I lean to press on it, but it just rises up again when my weight adjusts so that I feel I could become completely unstuck, toppling off the balcony into the water.

He leans over, starts wiping the fabric below my neck that I can't see.

'What is it?'

He ignores me and starts picking at the same spot, until he comes away from it holding a small white feather.

'How's Ruchira?' he asks.

'She's great, Ryan's honestly *so* nice to her. The other day he hired a van and drove it across London to help her move house.'

'I'm glad. God, she dated some right idiots.'

I laugh and as I do something in between us softens for a second. I see the curve in his hands, the ridge in his nose, the things that make him someone I remember. I want to bring up that morning we went for breakfast with Ruchira and she was so hungover she wore sunglasses in the café and managed one sip of orange juice before she started gipping. She told the waitress that she would take her Mediterranean breakfast to go and Joe and I laughed so hard she called us an unbearable combination, 'like chocolate and toothpaste'. I know if I did we might be able to find our way back to each other, to who we used to be. But I can't bear to show him how much I still need him. That's why I take Ryan's kindness and sharpen it into something that can hurt.

'Ryan made us sushi the other day, it was so good.'

'If only you'd gone out with Ryan!'

'I know!' I say. 'Us three went to see that new Kanye film together, *Jesus Is King*.'

'At the IMAX?'

'Yeah,' I say.

'At 10 a.m.?'

'Yeah.'

'I was there.'

'Who with?'

'I'm not sure you want to know.'

He said that before. And I said it too when Joe asked where a mark on my leg was from. He repeats it later on when I ask who the girl he's seeing is. I will say it again when he asks what gym the delivery man goes to. 'I'm not sure you want to know.' We pretend it's a kindness, that we're stopping each other from hearing things that might hurt the other, but really it's a way of showing that there are parts of us that are out of reach now, where before they got everything. We call it 'setting boundaries', making 'ground rules' to ensure whatever it is that we are doing is easier. It's what polyamorous people do, those in open relationships; it's what people do to reduce harm. But we like creating these boundaries a little too much, watching the bricks being cemented on top of one another, rising up higher and higher until we stand on either side of a very high wall.

I go to get another beer and when I'm at the fridge I see his shadow bending up diagonally across the kitchen cabinets. *He's behind you*, I think, as if narrating my own horror movie. I turn around and look at him. The hairs on his shaved head like the first scattering of snow. His top clings to his stomach so you can see the outline of his abs. I want him to open up his big mouth like a wolf and devour me until there's nothing left except the stains I'd leave on his T-shirt.

Eat me up, my love, or else I'm going to eat you up.

Love turns us all into cannibals, or that's what French feminist Hélène Cixous says in her essay 'Love of the Wolf'. We want the other to swallow us up into them so we no longer know who we are.

> *Want me down to the marrow . . .*
> *Sign my death with your teeth.*
> *We love, we fall into the jaws of the fire.*
> *We can't escape it.*

For Cixous, excitement comes in at the boundary between wanting to be eaten and wanting to survive. This is the tension, the thrill of love.

When we lean forward to kiss each other we keep stopping before we get there. Neither of us wants to make that admission. I'm not sure how much I can bear his lips, how much of me would disappear into them, down his throat. How it would feel to continue to live in the world through him, how much of me would be left if he spat me back out. So I turn around before we reach each other, push my ass into him and he pushes me back, towards the wall, my face sideways against the cold of the plaster. He pulls my underwear down to my ankles. His mouth is between my legs. It feels so good that my knees buckle but I hate that it feels good because that means he's made her feel this good too. I don't want to be a 'yes' for him anymore, the chair he rests his feet on, but I like it when I am. I like it when he stands all over me. 'Stand up straight,' he says, because I'm sinking down the wall, but I don't because I want him to tell me to do something again. I think about stopping but I can't, like those bites on my hand I'm always scratching. I hope I've brought the bed bugs here on my clothes. That the eggs will sink into his dad's furniture and hatch in there and the woman he sleeps with will get them too, think sleeping with him gave her a funny rash.

He moves so he's on the sofa and I sit on him, arching my back right around like a scorpion's tail. I scratch at his back so that I can take traces of him home under my fingernails like a murderer too careless to wear gloves. I bite onto my thumb and I'm rocking back and forth. His chest is mottled with red patches from where blood has rushed upwards from desire. I'm turning inside out, warming up, I open up like a flower, he loves me, he loves me not. I turn to him and each of my petals fall off because I thought love was fullness but right now it feels like an obliteration, like burning out into nothing – white heat, purple flames and then it's gone.

At the end our bodies fall off each other like dead things where normally he'd hold me on top of him and say, 'Stay.' We shrink away into different corners of the room and look at the mess we've made twisted up in the sofa cushions. I try to distract him from it, crawling closer, tracing lines into his back with my forefinger. 'We're weird, aren't we?' I say.

'Fucking weird.'

I can feel him drawing away. I try to say things that will bring him back. 'You've got nice eyes,' I tell him and a tiny snort comes out of his nostrils. I try to find his face but it's facing the other way, flat against the sofa arm, his jaw slightly distended, one arm lolling towards the floor. 'Wanna get dinner?' I ask after a while. 'Or maybe we could cook? Watch a film? Or nothing, we could do nothing?'

He sits up quickly and puts his underwear on. Leans down and starts to pick up some coins that must have exploded out of his jeans, fluffs the pillows, readjusts the rug to where it's supposed to sit, straightening up all the lines we pushed diagonal. But then it's like he's too exhausted to tidy and he flops back onto the sofa. 'I don't think I can do this,' he says. 'I don't think this is good.' He runs a hand over his head and looks over at the other side of the river. 'I want to be on my own and the other night when you were annoyed at me for bailing on Friday, like, it freaked me out a bit. I can't have someone relying on me right now.'

I'm sure there's something I could say to stop this but I can't find it. I feel those two things in my chest snapping again, drifting apart. I don't cry, though. I'm hardened behind those walls we set around each other. All I manage is: 'If you do this, you know you'll never see me again.'

He looks embarrassed when he nods. I get dressed slowly, just in case I hear a 'wait', but there's just him picking up those coins, clinking them against each other at the bottom of his pocket. I turn around at the door and see him with his wrists pressed up hard against his eyes.

16

It was near the end of third year and you had come over to mine. Jess lived somewhere else now, but Yla was still there and three other lovely women.

'Hello, ladies,' you said as you walked in, letting your rucksack slip off your shoulders, leaning into the living room where my housemates were watching *Ex on the Beach* with their dressing-gown hoods up. 'You're all looking wonderful this morning – sorry, afternoon.'

'We do leave the house, I promise,' laughed Sabrina, because they were always on the sofa when he came over, deep grooves built into the cushions from long days of missing lectures.

'Sure,' you said. 'I'm going to make a tea, does anyone else want one?'

'Yes, please,' we all replied in sing-song unison and you rolled your eyes.

When the ads came on, Sabrina turned to me, her feet in fluffy socks raised up on the three-legged coffee table. 'You're so lucky. Tell me he's got some mates he can set me up with?'

I was fixing my hair into a bun, pulling out strands so that it looked messy. I smiled at her. 'Trust me, he's not always so perfect.'

Hearing me, you walked back into the room, curled

a hand around your ear as if you were trying to amplify the sound. 'Sorry, what was that? Sorry, can you repeat that? Sabrina, shall you and I couple up instead?'

I laughed, shoving you. 'It might be fun if said boyfriend wasn't flirting with my mates.' You slapped the bit of my bum that was hanging over the sofa arm with the plastic spatula you were holding.

They were parts we played, a comedy skit: weary girlfriend, irresponsible boyfriend. We enjoyed performing these roles because they weren't real yet. We were just learning how to be in a relationship by copying what we saw everywhere else, like kids playing Mummies and Daddies at nursery. I liked complaining that you were always playing FIFA. I liked how the boys laughed when you answered the phone to me in a baby voice. I liked going on a girls' night when you went on a boys' night. I liked making fun of you with your sister, her saying, 'I'll sort him out,' when you were annoying. I liked it when you would complain about how long it took me to get ready or how much room I was already taking up in your wardrobe. I liked rolling my eyes at you, I liked it when male friends said, 'You look nice,' to me and you said, 'Easy, pal.' I liked it when people at graduation asked, 'What's next for you then?' because I got to say, 'I'm moving to London with my *boyfriend*.'

I buy pest spray and a pest-defensive mattress cover off Amazon. I hoover the bed, focusing on the seams. It doesn't matter, the bed bugs keep biting me. Mum works with a guy whose younger brother is a pest killer and he gives her a discount so I only have to pay £100 instead of £250 to get my room aerated. Afterwards I won't be allowed to go in there for twenty-four hours and I'll have to wash all of my clothes at 140 degrees. I decide not to wash Joe's clothes. I can't bear the humiliation of putting them in the machine, my knees needling against the laminate floor. I won't tell him about them either. I'll just stuff his things in bin bags and put them in the under-stairs cupboard. I tell him to come and get his stuff by the end of the week.

The pest guy walks around the room in white overalls and a plastic visor, sniffing the air. 'Are you sure it isn't fleas?' he asks. 'You have a cat, right?'

The delivery man only comes over two or three more times after I get back from Lisbon. It ends when I ask him if he wants to go on a double date with Ruchira and Ryan.

'I think we want different things here,' he says.

'It doesn't mean anything, it's just meant to be fun,' I tell him, but it's too late.

He never replies.

When you met my parents you had slicked-back hair and a comb in your pocket to keep it in place. 'Can't wait to flirt with your mum,' you joked as we walked down to the station to meet them.

'She's not that kind of mum,' I told you.

They shook hands and kissed cheeks. We walked into the restaurant and you said, 'Table for four, please,' and then as soon as we sat down: 'Can we have some tap water for the table?' You were saying all the things Dad usually said and I could tell it was making him uneasy.

'I don't like fancy full Englishes,' said Dad when his all-day breakfast arrived. 'They're never quite the same.'

'The sausages are better, though,' you said.

'I'm not sure about that,' said Dad, even though he always buys posh sausages from the butcher. Mum had two sips of wine, then said she was hammered. She asked loads of questions about house prices in Newcastle.

It felt a bit like a parents' evening. 'Annie's always doing her reading,' you said.

'Now I wasn't expecting to hear that,' said my parents.

'How did you get on?' asked our friend Ali when we got back to yours.

'Smashed it, mate,' you said.

'He seems really nice,' said Mum. 'Dangerously good-looking.'

For the first few years my dad only referred to you by your full name, as though you were a celebrity. He was always asking me if you said anything about him after you spent time together. He wanted reassurance that he'd said the right thing, even though it's the boyfriend who's meant to get nervous.

They always liked you. You stayed at my house in Leeds during the summer holidays. My dad's a Man United supporter and to wind him up you would make purposefully stupid comments about the game, calling players the wrong names or giving them the wrong positions. Like, 'Ah, Marcus Rashford, great defender.' You bought him a Man City annual for Christmas and my dad laughed so much he nearly choked.

'Where did you get him from?' Dad laughed. 'Do they have a returns policy?'

You mentioned Dad recently when we sat on the banks of that river. Said you missed him, said: 'I bet he won't like any of your boyfriends as much as he liked me.'

And I said: 'He still likes you,' and you nodded, the words seeming to coat your skin, make you sit up straighter.

17

'I'm so angry I am having to do this,' begins my message. It's been nearly three months since he ended it and one week since he ended it again and Joe still hasn't collected his stuff, even though I've asked him to multiple times. 'This is not a storage facility. It's not nice having to see your things in my room. I don't want to be reminded of you, it hurts. All you need to do is order a big Uber to your dad's house, it won't take all weekend.'

'Regarding my stuff . . .' begins his response. 'I can try and grab it over the weekend but I'm not sure whether I'll be able to. I'm not sure I have that much, though? Maybe a picture and a few books?'

I march into the kitchen where Moll's making food, hold the messages in front of her while she carries on chopping up peppers. 'I mean, he dumped *me* and he's not sure if he has *time* to get the stuff out of my room?' I say. 'What else could he be doing? Am I really that far down his priority list? Does he have any respect for me at all?'

She nods, reaches up into her cupboard, knocks over the rice in there. 'Fuck,' she whispers, moving onto her tiptoes to scrape the grains off into her hands.

'If he'd just organised this himself I wouldn't have to have this worry,' I carry on, following her as she moves over to the pan. 'I literally feel *sick* now, I get so anxious for when he's going to message and when he does I get this rushing excitement and then I open it and I feel shit again.'

She nods, crushing garlic under her knife, picking all the skin off it. 'I told you what I think before, Annie. He doesn't respect you.'

The writer Zora Neale Hurston once wrote, 'If you're silent about your pain, they'll kill you and say you enjoyed it.'

She was referring to much more serious pains than losing a boyfriend, but the logic still applies.

Mum rings me before I finish typing a reply that begins, 'Who the fuck says "regarding" in a text message?'

'You all right, lovey? I saw I missed your call.'

'I'm honestly just going to burn his shit at this point. I'm going to pile it up in the garden and burn it.'

'Don't do that,' says Mum, her voice wobbling. 'He's not worth it. He'll just tell himself that you're crazy and it will justify the reasons he has in his head for leaving. The best revenge is silence, that will show him.'

'He's not worth it,' that's what they always say. But why do so many things seem to be worth more than women's anger?

Still, when I go back and open the half-written message, I can't quite gather myself to send it. The words feel as though they didn't come from me, but a stranger, one that I'm not sure I want to be. It reminds me of something someone once told me about the mirrors they always have behind pub bars. Apparently, if you're shouting at a member of staff, seeing what you look like when you're doing it can help defuse angry customers. There's a disconnect from who they think they are and what they're seeing, and it encourages them to calm down, apologise, turn into the reflection they want to be. I delete the words and start again.

'I said the end of next week and you said that was fine,' the new message begins. 'I didn't want to have to speak to you again and now I can't concentrate on my work. I just didn't want to have to talk to you again. It hurts so much.'

'I'm sorry you're still in pain and this is difficult for you,' he replies. 'I'm sorry that I still have my stuff in the house. I should have moved it earlier. I'm not trying to ignore this stuff. I'll ask for a day off this Friday so I can get it?'

'Yeah, just lemme know what time and I'll get out of the house.'

'I know you won't be there, obviously. I just need a key under the doormat.'

I read over what he's just said again.

'*You won't be there*, obviously.'

'*I'm sorry this is difficult for* you.'

I hate these messages. The way he tries to take control of what's happening when I'm the one saying he needs to take it away. Anger simmers at the edges of my vision like heat lines. I feel powder on the end of my tongue from the filling I've been grinding down with my jaw. I pick up my phone and throw it at the wall, but Moll doesn't even look up from her video game so I storm out, knocking over the drying rack covered in clothes on the way and enjoy hearing her shout, 'What happened?' after me.

For a while I remembered only the good: the sharp hiccupping sound of his laugh; looking across a busy room and nodding at him and both of us knowing that it's time to leave the party. But now all I see is the bad: damp towels on the carpet; cancelling that holiday in Venice because he didn't get enough of his dissertation done; late arrivals; the wave of air as a door slams.

Love and hate are so close together some think they are two parts of the same feeling. Freud said that the first example of this comes when we are babies, sucking from our mother's breast, then needlessly biting at it until it's sore.

At this point hate sustains me. I need it in order to persuade myself to keep moving through this world, to remind my lungs to breathe. So much of the ending was passively letting things happen; hate pushes me off my seat and says, *Show him what you're made of.* So when he tells me, 'I will be at the house at about 3.30/4. Danny has told me there will be keys under the brick?' I go into my room and lay out tiny dresses that could only be worn on nights out. I make it messy as well, hoping he'll think I'm living an interesting life. I'm building a trap, like I'm setting someone up for a crime. I take the bin bags filled with his belongings out from under the stairs and lay them in the room, hope he's insulted to see everything he owns bagged up in what's used to take out rubbish. Although perhaps it would have been better if it was strewn everywhere, then he'd have to linger in the place where we fought, made up, loved, laughed, where we promised to make a home.

We hadn't really planned to live together; I don't really know why we did. But you turned up at the flat I used to live in off Caledonian Road with a bigger bag than normal and you never left. It wasn't a nice room; there were spiderwebs criss-crossing the ceiling, flyers and posters blu-tacked onto the wall that kept falling off with a loud slapping sound. I was scared of you living here because I worried it might make us imperfect too. Things did change, but not for the worse. Our love sank to that deeper place where there's no mystery and you know what the other person is thinking even when their back is turned. It was like having a favourite coat that you want to wear every single day because it's better than all of your other coats. It was like having your best friend there all the time.

I was working at a pub and when it crept past midnight and we called last orders I would shove all the trays in the dishwasher, cling-film the taps, run around with a mop, never stopping to lean against the bar or to have a drink on the house because I wanted to get back before you fell asleep. I'd walk up the stairs and see a line of yellow light under our door and I would feel so pleased because it meant I could probably persuade you to watch an episode of something before we went to sleep. I'd get in with you, the mattress sinking down at my side so I rolled towards the wall. 'Why do you get the good side?' I'd ask.

'Because it's my side.'

And even though it was annoying because it was my side first, I would put my cheek against your hot skin, my limbs heavy, my head unravelling from remembering long orders like, *'One Heineken, two Stellas, three gin and tonics – two with cucumber, one with lime – and can you get me a straw?'* (Even though the straws were always right in front of them.) And you'd stroke my head and say, 'You should get paid more,' about the £8 an hour and, 'I would have smacked him if I was there,' about my boss who dropped ice cubes down barmaids' tops.

And my life would start to seem all right, nice even, because when I told you things they seemed to rest more lightly on my shoulders because you held them on yours too. Then in the morning we'd sit in bed together with laptops propped on our knees, you doing reading on phenomenology for your master's course, me emailing people for internships, copying and pasting the same 'I would be so grateful if you would consider me' to editor after editor, even though I knew none of them would reply. And I'd be frustrated and headachy but then some-one would respond to my email with someone else to email or you would think of a line of argument for your essay, which I didn't understand but I'd say, 'So good, baby!' And we'd be so happy for each other, for the dreams we wanted for ourselves as much as each other. We weren't playing at boyfriend and girlfriend anymore; we really had become that.

I used to hate the feeling of walking into the house after being on holiday. I'd come back in with my mum and dad and it would be a bit cold and Mum would go to put the heating on and Dad would head off to the shops to get milk for breakfast and my brother would go on his Xbox. And I'd sit there on the stairs or leaning against the landing wall, or some other place I never usually sat, and nothing would feel quite the same as when we left it. As though we were in the wrong house – one that looked like our house but wasn't our house. Or like someone had come in and moved everything and tried to put it back in the exact same spot. I get the same feeling when I walk back into our room. He's taken those two bin bags and above the fireplace there's a big gap where that sketch of Joan of Arc was propped up. Apart from that, not much has changed. The crinkles in the duvet are still there, the smears on the mirror. Yet everything feels different, like it did when we came back from holiday. He's really gone. Perhaps he already had, but I only notice it now.

The realisation comes to me calmly. There's nothing of him left to rail against in this room. The dialogue between us has been broken. I walk into the living room because there is one thing I kept. I hid them down the back of the sofa so that he couldn't take them. A pair of Adidas tracksuit bottoms, size 12–13 from the kids' section. Orange smudges all over them from when they were wiped with hair bleach. White paint splattered from when he got paid £100 a day to paint that office building. He wore them almost every day. Now I do. I like how they look on me. He never asks where they went.

FOG

18

We'd been living together for a few months and it was so hot outside that the whole of London smelled like warm sewage and barbecues. The World Cup was on and England was doing so well that everyone made a collective decision that it was acceptable to be patriotic until the final. Some fans trashed up an IKEA when we beat Sweden. I went to see a game at the pub with little England flags on my cheeks. Watched a guy in a full Gucci tracksuit kissing his hand and then slapping it against the part of the projector where Harry Kane's body appeared.

We woke up late and caught up on two episodes of *Love Island* and then we headed out into the day. My red hair was now a brown-to-blonde dip dye and you'd shaved your rat's tail off and bleached the rest. And with these new hairstyles we both looked almost like grown-ups. Dried sweat and denim cut-offs meant that my thighs caught and rubbed together until there was a patch of raw skin. I could feel wetness where my sunglasses rested on my nose. Burn on my shoulders. We went into a corner shop to get a drink and I leaned as close as possible into the cold air humming out of the fridges. There were so many colourful drinks cans piled on top of each other trying to catch the sleepy eyes of people like us, fuchsia pink and desert orange and cherry red.

There was something so dizzying about this amount of choice, but when taken out and studied in isolation each can looked slightly disappointing. You picked up a watermelon and strawberry one, I pointed at the Coca-Cola and mango one and said, 'Pass us the –' then I meant to say 'bottle' but my voice wobbled so I pronounced it like 'bowtle'.

'Bowtle,' you repeated in a more exaggerated way so that you sounded like a Dutch person speaking English, and something about your highlighting of my minor fuck-up was hilariously funny in that way some things just are, like when a person falls over or asks a dumb question. So I laughed, big and brash, and so uncontrollable that I nearly snot-rocketed onto the floor.

'Easy, love,' you said, pretending not to know me and shaking your head at the other people in the shop. 'Dunno what's wrong with her.' Then you turned to me again and said, 'It's just a boWTLE,' except this time with so much comic exaggeration it no longer felt like a word and it made me think about how words are just sounds that don't convey anything until you apply meaning to them and all this made it so that for a while the world seemed entirely surreal and because of this I was laughing so much I was bent over my middle, holding my stomach, because the laughter was giving me a stitch.

I always found you so funny, but what I found funniest changed over time. At first it was long-drawn-out

explanations of why such and such a person was a hyp-
ocrite or why such and such a film made no sense or
contradicted itself. But now I could see the conceit in
those stories, the cogs turning as you worked out how
to make them cut. Knowing the effort that went into
them took away the blind spontaneity, the surprise. So
that by this time it was the silly things that really made
me laugh, so ridiculous they shook me out of the pre-
scribed movements of our everyday interactions. Getting
your balls out somewhere inappropriate like in a lift
and waiting for me to realise or the way you used to say,
'Maybe go up a gear, mate,' when someone slowly cycled
past us while aggressively pedalling on the flat road.

I could find your lips with my eyes closed. Finish your
sentences. Know what kind of mood you were in from
the rhythm when you walked up the stairs. We could eat
a meal in complete silence and I would still sense that
the woman on the other table talking about the students
moving into her area was annoying you. At dinner parties when you started telling a story I would jump in to
give prompts every now and again because I knew the
important details that were needed to get the laughs.
There were no surprises, so much so that when you told
me that on Friday lunch you treat yourself to a meal at
an Italian restaurant near the office I didn't believe you
because it felt like if that really happened, I would already know about it.

The end of surprises sounds like a sad thing, but it
wasn't because even if you know exactly how a person

will react to everything, hopefully in your mind the way they react to stuff is a way you admire. There's a security in that, waiting for the inevitable and the inevitable always being a pleasure. Love sits there like a scaffolding and frees you up to think about other things. I hung out with friends and didn't answer the phone when you asked where I was. I left the office later.

When I finished laughing in that corner shop there was a long outpouring of breath as all the tension left me. 'Was that a good one?' you asked of your joke, and when I nodded you repeated again: 'Bowtle.'

But this time your impression didn't have the same effect on me. Instead, my laugh was small, obedient, not spontaneous.

'Did I kill it?' you asked and I told you yes, but I didn't mind because I thought it was sweet that you wanted to make me laugh so much that you would keep on trying a joke until it stopped working. You must have really liked hearing my laughter. I wonder what it sounded like to you. Like heaven? Like rain on the window when you know you don't have to leave the house that day?

I know you weren't embarrassed by me fake laughing because I don't think we had the capacity to be embarrassed in front of each other anymore, having seen so much of that other half from every possible angle. But you pretended to be, hiding behind one of the aisles like a shy child, refusing to look at me when I grabbed your arm.

'Try one more time!' I said.

'No, I ruined it,' you replied, moving further away still, to the cans of soup and the boxes of cereal. You were acting a bit like a child now and I liked this too because it was like I could see what made you into who you were now.

And then I said, '*Please*, I really, really want you to say it again, *please*.'

'Bowtle,' you said with a big grin.

And this time it was my turn to be funny. 'Fuck me, that was fucking hilarious! Fucking Bill Bailey, you are! When are you off to Wembley?'

Just as easily as our relationship reached that place without surprises, the end of it has too. Heartbreak is like a chronic illness I have learned to live with. Knowing which recipes will taste like a Thursday night in with him, what songs will remind me of how we used to dance in the blue of the oven light until the neighbours told us to turn the music down. I have mantras to repeat to myself when it gets bad. *He's not having as much fun as you think he is. You only miss him this badly right now because of hormones.* There are certain procedures I continue to follow, like looking over at a friend's phone to see if the person who just messaged is him, and if so, is he talking like a happy person? Like a person with a new girlfriend? Rarely do I get that gut-punch sensation now that it's November; instead, the feeling of loss has come down around me like a cloud, one that people would look up at and say, 'Doesn't look as though the weather's going to turn.'

You'd think in these circumstances I'd think about him less, but at this point he's on my mind almost constantly, like this bit of food stuck in my teeth that I can't get out, that is giving me a headache from the way I curl my tongue around to try to get at it. I imagine this is because when humans experience grief they can't process the pain all in one go. It comes in waves. That's why there's denial at first, then guilt, then anger and bargaining, and then there's depression when you finally start to work through what happened.

I wonder if perhaps he had seasonal depression. He dumped me in August and during that same month the year before he became quite distant from me. Maybe he finds the end of summer sad, and rather than dealing with those emotions he transferred the negative feeling onto me, because getting rid of me was a quick way of changing up his life. And Freud is always talking about mothers so maybe it's something to do with that. I bend every narrative to suit the one that suggests he still wants me, scrolling down the list of people who have watched my Instagram story to see if he has, because if so then I can tell myself that he hasn't quite let me go because he still wants to see what I'm up to. If he hasn't that doesn't really matter either because I'll just pretend that he can't watch my story as it will make him miss me too much. 'Why did he do it?' I ask people, but I never like their answers.

'I feel so aimless nowadays,' I tell my friend Hannah.

'What do you mean?'

I try to explain the sensation but it's difficult. How many times I go to have a bath, or for a walk, and stop halfway through; turning off the hot tap or pulling the laces back out of my shoes. I can't stop thinking about how there's no one there to know that I've gone for a bath, or for a walk, and as a result the act of doing one of those things, anything, starts to feel completely pointless. So I turn off the tap or I take off my shoes and curl up at the bottom of the bed, held in a sort of paralysis where all I can do is slide my thumb up and down the screen of my phone.

'You can tell me about that stuff instead,' she says.

'I know, but it's different with a partner, isn't it? I'm not exactly gonna ring you every time I see a nice tree or have a friendly interaction with a bus driver. I told Joe all that stuff because we were together all the time. I didn't worry about boring him.'

Actually, the fear of boring my friends to death isn't the only reason I don't talk about these tiny offshoots of experience anymore. I told Joe about my day in this much detail because he was another part of me, and if that other part of me didn't know what I was doing it felt like only a fraction of an experience. A large part of the enjoyment of doing something was telling him about what happened after it happened, the minutiae of it: thick hot air as the Tube was held at a red signal, me dropping my lighter when I tried to pass it to the man asking for it. I lived life all over again through him and learned each action's merit through the response it pulled from his body.

Hannah looks at me, puts down a forkful of lemony chicken and, almost as if she's seen these thoughts flicker across my brown eyes, says: 'Annie, you need to be able to enjoy things just for yourself.'

I dab a grain of rice with my finger and bite down on it with my two front teeth until it's powdery on the end of my tongue. Jerk my head back. 'You're not going to tell me to date myself, are you?'

'Well,' she says, grinning, picking up a chicken bone and tearing off the last bits of meat. 'Yes, I am.'

My eyes widen in mock terror.

'I'm just saying I reckon you'd be happier in relationships, and in life, if you centred yourself more. Then you won't have to rely on someone else for quite so much of your happiness. You'll walk because you want to walk, not because he says a walk will be a nice thing. You can feel full with your own experiences and then you probably won't even feel like you want a boyfriend.'

I get what Hannah means because every self-help book regurgitates a version of this argument. 'You are the prize, the sun, moon and the stars. Not him or anyone else,' begins the chapter 'It Won't Work Unless You Are Number One!' from *New York Times* bestseller *It's Called a Breakup Because It's Broken*. 'You have to learn how to love yourself, like yourself, and put yourself first before you will ever find the healthy, loving, and lasting relationship you're looking for.'

The chapter ends with the authors telling the reader to draw the hottest picture of themselves along with a

'Superfox Breakup Warrior Crest'. I'm not sure what that means. They don't really explain either.

I hate this modern way of viewing love. It's like you've got to be so fucking perfect before you can enter into anything serious. What happens if you've got depression or body dysmorphia? Are you not allowed to accept love? Do you have to ride it out on your own until you've overcome your issues? Even if they last a lifetime? And what if love from another allows you to love yourself? Like how Joe helped me love how my belly spills over my jeans or the way that I wear a lot of make-up? Does it have to come from you first otherwise you'll always require too much reassurance from an external source? Everyone seems to think Joe and I were damaged because we relied on each other, but isn't that what made us close? What do these people want to see? Just two fully formed individuals who never ask each other for anything? Who are so self-sufficient that they only spend time together when they want to have fun, and if they need help they have to go to therapy, because *lord forbid* you ask your partner for support. They're probably the type of person who will say something cold like, 'I'm not in a position to receive this information right now,' and then bitch to their friends about how their boyfriend was demanding too much emotional labour when they're trying to work.

It's all 'he's holding you back', as if relationships were valued only for how they help you better yourself. How they helped you ditch your phone addiction or speak to you in Spanish so that you pick the language back up again. Love isn't a night class, though, is it? It shouldn't just be about self-optimisation. 'Be your own best friend,' they say, as if satisfaction means overcoming the feeling of loneliness, because apparently this emotion is not a logical result of the fact that humans are social animals but a defect that can be eliminated if you spend enough time focusing on hobbies. What's the logical end point of this self-sufficient ideal? The happy couple floating around in separate micro-climates that one of them cultivated through a start-up business they launched straight after graduating from Cambridge? Why bother being in a relationship at all if it looks like this one? Why not just go it alone? Eat, Pray, Bath-bomb your way to romantic ecstasy?

In a better mood I might not have had so many angry thoughts in response to Hannah's suggestion. I might have even jotted down some of her comments on my phone notes. Asked her if she knew any books or films that touched on these concepts. She might have recommended bell hooks's *All About Love*, particularly the passage where hooks questions why we deny ourselves what we ask for from other people.

'One of the best guides to how to be self-loving is to give ourselves the love we are often dreaming about receiving from others,' writes bell. 'There was a time when I felt lousy about my over-forty body, saw myself as too fat, too this, or too that. Yet I fantasized about finding a lover who would give me the gift of being loved as I am. It is silly, isn't it, that I would dream of someone else offering to me the acceptance and affirmation I was withholding from myself. This is a moment when the affirmation "You can never love anybody if you are unable to love yourself" made clear sense.'

I just wasn't ready to hear all this yet, but I found hook's book later on when I was. I realised in that moment that Hannah was right: my lack of agency in so many aspects of my life meant that I expected Joe to create meaning for me, and that pressure was frustrating for him a lot of the time. Why should I wait for someone to tell me my baths are a good idea, that a walk is a nice thing to do, that I'm beautiful? I don't need to wait for someone else's approval, I can do things for myself and feel fuller all on my own.

19

The summer heatwave carried on over June and then into July. The grass turned yellow, then brown. We tried to buy a fan, but they had all sold out. In the flat, the first one we moved into together right after university, flies buzzed around the fruit bowl because there were mouldy plums in there that no one would take responsibility for. The kitchen was such an ugly room. The linoleum floor peeling away at the corners. The oven and the wall it grew out of oozing with this yellow sticky stuff that reminded me of tree sap but was really grime, the sort you'd have to burn the flat down to get rid of. Moll's cat Io slunk towards the opened window and I picked her up and chucked her slouching, long body out into the hall-way because she wasn't allowed outside. She snapped up straight when she hit the ground and walked as if on high stilettos up the stairs.

'Sorry you're having to do this,' I said, looking at the straw-coloured strands at the bottom of my hair. The two of us were sitting at the table, one on the office chair we found on the side of the road, the other on the stool with the missing leg.

'It's fine,' you told me with a tight smile. I knew it wasn't really fine because when I asked you to look at my article you said you really couldn't tonight but would make time on your next lunch break, but then I said, 'It needs to be tonight because it's actually in for tomorrow and I can't tell if it makes any sense at all because none of the words look like words anymore but just a big wall of symbols and the backs of my eyes sting and what if I wake up and with my fresh eyes see that it's all complete nonsense?' Then you said, 'OK, go and get the laptop,' your fingertips pressed hard into your temples. That's when I said thank you for the first time that evening, and as it got later, I said it about twelve more times because I thought that me saying those words might make up for the fact that you were having to spend your only two hours of free time before you had to shower and lay work clothes out and eat and pack a lunch ready for work doing even more work. Work that wasn't even for you, but for me.

You leaned on your fist so heavily that the skin on your cheek was crumpled up to your eye, half closing it. You started a new line for me, rewrote the sentences, and under your fingertips they started to sing a much better song. Words hardened down into arguments, as if you read my thoughts and thought them out of me better. Sometimes I'd look at them and think, *I would never say that in that way*, but I would leave it how you rewrote it because I trusted your way of talking more than I trusted my own. I bit at the tough skin around my nails. You patted my thigh. 'We're getting there.'

Moll walked into the room with that tropical, beery weed smell clinging to her princess pyjamas after playing video games for hours in the small Harry Potter-sized understairs cupboard she smoked in because Danny didn't like her doing it in the room anymore.

'What you guys up to?' she asked, opening and slamming each cupboard as she tried to find the Disney *Moana* mug that was the only thing she would drink out of.

You ignored her question, leaning so close to the screen that the white page was reflected in the dark of your retinas.

I could tell you hated that about her, her loudness. You came from a quiet house where people nodded when they walked past you and she one where they shouted up several floors, 'WHAT WAS THE NAME OF THAT FILM WE WATCHED THE OTHER NIGHT, LOVE?' You probably thought her noise inconsiderate. She probably thought it rude not to speak to someone when you entered a room. You both seemed to think the other was being unreasonable and oftentimes one of you was, but you both had such different definitions of what was reasonable.

'He's looking over my article,' I said, providing a small answer in the hope she'd leave the room before your mood started to dip.

'Nice, what's it about?'

I mumbled, 'Just this thing.' She left the door open on the way out.

When we were in bed together later, I drew messages on your back with my fingertips that I don't think you were bothering to try to read. Y-O-U-R-E T-H-E B-E-S-T. The plastic blinds rattled against the glass window. I turned over under the sheet. 'I can't always do that, you know,' you said. 'It's not fair to demand that I do things if I don't want to do them.'

'I know,' I said. 'It's just that everything is better after you look at it and it was a really important piece and I really want them to commission me again.'

But I did keep expecting you to do things that you didn't want to do. I can see the evidence in our email history. I would send you stuff and you'd edit it while pretending to be liaising with clients.

In one I sent you two different intro options.

'2nd one is better! Let's have a lil work on it tonight at home. It's realllllly good though! Really funny!!!!! Luv u.'

To another you replied: 'Tiny changes. But overall, REALLY GOOD!'

You started expecting me to do things for you too. Put the bins out, hang up the washing you didn't have time to lay out. And gradually between us both, all the thank-yous faded out and turned into 'but you promised', 'but I made dinner', like love was a contract filled with IOUs that the other would be charged interest on if they didn't fulfill.

I don't live in that flat anymore, I live in a house in Tottenham. We moved into it nearly a year ago. It was big enough and cheap enough that we could turn the tiny upstairs box room that no one wanted into an office and still only pay £542 a month, or £271 a month because we shared a room. Me and Moll's boyfriend Danny work in here together now, or rather try to work. For such a skinny person, he manages to make more noise than a fucking elephant. I can't concentrate when he's around me because his breathing is heavy and strained as though he's permanently coming. He takes a call and I spin my chair around and glare at him. He puts two fingers up but the call isn't two minutes, it's six, and I know because I stare at the clock as he talks, excited that his reasoning has once again proved false. I try to type but then he's turning on the light, even though it's bright enough in the room for it to make no difference. I turn it off again on the way back from the toilet. He's turned it on again by the time I return.

I know it's not actually Danny's fault I can't work, which is difficult to admit because I feel like there should be consequences for his annoyingness. I'm struggling because Joe's not looking over my shoulders saying, '*You need to signpost more. Delete those metaphors.*' This isn't the way it's supposed to go. I'm supposed to sit in front of the screen and realise I could write all along and that I never needed his help. The words running out of me like they're bleeding out of pricks at the ends of my fingers. Instead, I feel like one of those baby birds you see on nature programmes where there's no opportunity to practise before they leave the nest; they just have to fly out and hope they stay up.

20

England reached the World Cup semi-finals and to celebrate Mayor of London Sadiq Khan organised for a huge screen to be erected in Hyde Park. Before half-time Kieran Trippier scored, making us 1–0 up. So many people threw their pints in the air that the liquid spray looked like smoke rising off their backs, as though the crowd was caught in one of the wildfires that was stretching across the country's scrubland. I watched the reaction on TV in an airconditioned pub on the other side of the city. We ended up losing and the camera focused on puffy-cheeked toddlers crying into their dads' football shirts, everyone's heads bowed as if leaving the funeral of a dictator.

After that, summer didn't feel like something anyone wanted anymore. On *Love Island* everyone coupled up with people they actually liked so there wasn't any drama. Just people with good teeth describing how excited they were for their new man to meet their family. We spoke of swimming in the Hampstead Heath ponds but there was always an hour-long queue. Ice-cream vans were charging £3 for a 99 Flake. People either moaned about the heat or moaned about those who were moaning about the heat. The grass wore away until the ground was just soil, more grey than brown. It was like we were

watching the planet dying in real time. People kept faint-
ing on the Tube from heat exhaustion. The bees were
dying because there weren't any plants left alive.

I opened the door to let you into the flat because, although you lived with me, we never got you a set of keys
cut. You kissed me quickly and started to go in, but then
Io weaved between your legs and ran outside onto the
little patch of concrete at the front.

'Fuck,' you said, stepping out, looking for her behind
the bins. I pointed at where she stood two doors down, tail
licking the air, yellow eyes flashing. We tried to corner her,
but she darted in another direction. She wanted to stay out
in the smell of burning concrete and other cats' piss.

'Moll should just let her out anyway,' you said, shaking your head. 'This is so fucking dumb.'

Io is named after Jupiter's third moon, the most vol-
canically active in the solar system. She often lived up to
her name, chasing flies around rooms and jumping from
surface to surface in a way that didn't make you think
of her as a pet. She dipped out of her hiding place now
and trotted along just ahead of us, as if she knew that
the closer we got to her, the more frustrating it would be
when she ducked under the metal fence of a neighbour's
garden.

'Io!' you called with lullaby softness, tension rattling
through the end of your speech from the annoyance
of having to plead with something you're meant to be
superior to. A bunch of teenagers on BMXs streamed
down the road, hands in their pockets as they steered

the bikes without holding on, nonchalantly turning the pedals because sometimes going slow looks much cooler than going fast. Under their gaze I felt at once really young and really old. We stopped for a moment because it was embarrassing to chase an animal in front of them. But then it seemed ridiculous that we were changing our behaviour to save face in front of teenagers. *Stupid runt of the litter with those stupid ginger speckles,* I thought when I saw Io's face from inside a bush. *You know the only reason Moll bought you is because she knew no one else was going to buy you.*

'Fuck this,' you said, walking back to the house and returning with one of my cans of tuna. You laid it open on the ground and we pretended to walk off. And when we turned around there she was, flakes of pink in her little sharp teeth. We carried her back inside the house. You stomped up the stairs, muttering under your breath. I hated the cat for ruining your morning, and Moll for buying the cat, and me for wanting to move in with Moll, and London for being so filled with traffic that it's dangerous for a cat to be outside, and I hated all the things you hated because I felt your feelings right down in me as if they were mine in the first place and not things that had come from you.

With someone else I might not have minded having to catch the cat. It might have been funny that she kept running away.

Empathy is defined as the ability to sense someone else's emotions. The way I felt went one step further: I didn't just sense your feelings, they became my feelings too. As though I was an empath but only for you. Or as if we were cars connected by jump leads. I never felt like this before you. I used only to care about people's moods in so much as they affected my own. I felt bad when people were skint because it meant they wouldn't be able to come to the festival with me. I was happy when they got a boyfriend because there would be male friends I'd probably fancy. But your happiness didn't have to serve my own. When we were in the flat and Moll had the TV up so loud it mumbled through the wall, it would be me who would get up and tell her to turn it down, who bought a door stopper, who said, *'I'm sick of asking – can you shut up? He's got work in the morning,'* because if you couldn't sleep, I couldn't either and I felt it was my fault that I'd brought you somewhere you didn't want to be.

'I know you really loved him – sorry, love him,' Moll says to me now as I watch her unload her shopping into the fridge. 'But it wasn't healthy to be so involved with each other.'

I jump up and sit on the grey worktop and enjoy the feeling of youth that comes from having my feet dangling so far away from the ground. Moll carries on talking, slightly out of breath as she does so because there's a lot of shopping and it's a struggle to make room in the fridge. 'When one of you was upset, the other would try to fix it because you felt responsible for their mood and when it didn't work that thing became your fault, or his fault, or whichever way round it was.' Moll looks up at me, a slight gloss over her face from speed-walking in the cold and then coming into a house beaming with central heating. 'Sorry, tell me to shut up if you don't want to hear this,' she says.

'No, carry on,' I tell her, and it surprises me that I genuinely want to hear her diagnosis of the situation. I don't usually want to hear people's opinions because the only thing I can bear to believe is that he's made a huge mistake. Why would I want to hear what was wrong when it's already too late? Explanations amount to criticisms of a relationship I was desperate to stay in. But as I near four months away from him my body has become habituated to a world without him in it. When I hear his name there's no sting, it just feels a bit jarring, as though I've been hit on the funny bone. The sensation is mild enough that my body can work through what's happened to it.

'What were you going to say?' I ask.

'Me and Danny, like, if he's annoyed, he's just annoyed. I let him watch those shit documentaries he likes called *Russia's Ten Toughest Prisons* and when I'm in a mood I just go and play video games and he knows to give me a minute and we comfort each other if the other one asks for a hug or whatever, but we don't think it's our job to sort anything out. You must have been so tired, weighed down by the moods of two people. I reckon he was freaked out by how much he needed you the same as how much you needed him.'

She goes to walk out of the door but stops by the frame and turns back to look at me.

'I was watching my little sister play the other day. She had this snail and she was holding onto it really tightly – she was like, *Snail, snail, snail,* named it Ronny, made it a bed of leaves, said she was going to find him a friend, but the whole time she was holding onto him so tightly and eventually, when she let him go, I saw that she'd crushed his shell.'

She doesn't say why she brings up this story, but I get her. Love made us grip so tightly that we broke it; each other too.

It's funny because I no longer feel responsible for his happiness. I don't even want him to be happy at all. I love it when people say things to me like, 'He will regret this decision for the rest of his life,' or 'You're doing so much better than him.' I can be glad that this happened so long as he isn't OK.

Now I wish him everything I used to want to protect him from. Badly faded haircuts, dinner parties where the host didn't make enough food, house parties where the speakers overheat, corked wine, broken flints on lighters, allergies, getting the arm of his bag caught on the stair's handrail so that he'd miss his train by a few seconds, the pedals of a bike swinging around and whacking him on the bony bit of his front leg.

Does that mean my love for him is dying?

Or maybe, and more likely, I still see my happiness as entirely tied up with his feelings, even though they aren't supposed to have anything to do with mine anymore.

* * *

The pavement was warm under my worn-out Converses and as we walked past the local leisure centre a chlorine smell wafted out and I wished I could spend the afternoon languishing in the shallow end of one of its big turquoise pools. I don't even remember what the song was now, I just know that I put the headphone in your ear and you joked that you'd listen to it if I promised to stop going on about it. It had been in my head for weeks. I tried not to play it too much because I didn't want to get sick of it. And when I did give myself permission to listen to it, I made sure I gave it my full concentration. Starting it from the beginning if the bus announcer spoke over a good bit.

'Yeah, it's all right,' you said, passing the earphone back only just halfway through.

'Well, I like it,' I said defiantly. I saw a gap in the stream of cars and crossed the road without nudging you to do the same, waited at the other side, hoping my smooth negotiation of traffic might emasculate you in some way. I was annoyed by what I knew was coming. After your dismissal it never sounded quite the same. I noticed the predictable lyrics, the unimaginative beat. I couldn't remember a single reason why I liked it, and now I can't even remember the song at all. This happened with everything we experienced together. Things glowed under your approval, turned invisible without it. Films I thought were dull and meandering became experimental interrogations of surveillance and paranoia. I started liking plain clothes with clean lines because that's what you preferred. It was never something you asked for. I disappeared all on my own.

In *The Second Sex*, Simone de Beauvoir describes the way women lose their identities when they fall in love with men.

> The centre of the world is no longer where she is but where her beloved is; all roads leave from and lead to his house. She uses his words and repeats his gestures, adopts his manias and tics. 'I *am* Heathcliff,' says Catherine in *Wuthering Heights*; this is the cry of all women in love; she is another incarnation of the beloved, his reflection, his double: she is *he*. She lets her own world flounder in contingence. She lives in his universe.

The reason the woman in love acts this way, identifying with all of the man's values and actions, according to de Beauvoir, is because she sees it as a route out of subjugation. Women cannot walk down the street without being shouted at, they are interrupted when they are talking. Men can actualise themselves in the world in ways that she cannot and, seeing this, the woman seeks to transcend her social status by merging with him. This is what love is, obliterating yourself into this more powerful being. With that she waves goodbye to her identity, to all the things that made her, in order to become part of his value.

In this way it didn't matter to me that I lost myself. That my backbone broke at every challenge. That my tongue was so often bitten. Because I wasn't in myself any longer, I was a parasite riding on his shoulders. All I cared about was his success, his rightness. Yes, I was hidden, but in many ways I felt like I was exactly where I was always meant to be, where women are meant to stand. It's like Little Dog asks in Ocean Vuong's *On Earth We're Briefly Gorgeous*: 'Why did I feel more complete while reaching for him, my hand midair?'

We're not that into Chinese takeaways. I think we're going to the Fullback because we don't like that you can't sit down at the Roebuck. We, we, we, we.

Earlier on I mentioned a study which found that people in love adjust their breathing and movement in order to match that of their partners. But I missed out that it is usually the woman who adjusts to the man. He stays the same.

I gave him my arms and my legs and he ran away with them and I don't know how to get them back.

We moved to the house in Tottenham together. We thought it was perfect. It had that little office room with a big bay window looking out onto the garden we told ourselves we'd have barbecues on, soft-close cupboards, a powerful showerhead. I was lying on the bed and you'd set my hairdryer down so that it blew through the neckline of your white T-shirt because you only put it in the wash an hour before and you needed to leave soon.

I was saying, 'Don't come complaining to me when the heating bill's huge,' and as a joke you put your middle finger right in my face because we'd worked out that one could defuse anger by pressing all the energy of it into a ha-ha-ha. I pulled down my phone screen but there were no messages. 'I just don't get why I can't come,' I said with a sigh.

You were rummaging through the sock drawer, sipping from your beer. 'Because it's just the boys tonight. I wouldn't come on a girls' night, would I?'

I could have left it there and I did think about doing that. I could have heated leftovers for you in the microwave so that they were ready for when you finished getting dressed. I could have told you your aftershave smelled nice and done something cute like block your path out of the door and say you could only pass if you kissed me. Been the sort of girlfriend I always thought I would be, growing up. But I didn't do any of that nice stuff. Instead, I said: 'But they're my friends too. There are no other girls in the group. It's not a night out with the boys, it's just a night without me.'

Your shoulders dropped.

'You've got your own mates, Annie.'

'Who?'

'Ruchira, Georgie, Moll, Amy?'

'They're busy tonight.'

To smooth out the creases of your jeans you raised them up in your arms and then dropped them down fast so that they smacked in the air. I heard lighters and lip balms rolling around drawers as you searched for your deodorant. The effort of getting ready to leave meant you were too distracted to think of good comebacks. You used to be the best at arguing, but I was getting better, laying out a road map of my thoughts before saying them as though I was planning an essay. Imagining responses to various objections you might make. I did it because I really thought I was right, but often I wished I wasn't. Then I could just apologise and change rather than working to persuade you around to my point of view.

'They used to treat me as their friend anyway until I became just "Joe's girlfriend". Then they stopped inviting me out and just expected you to bring me along, except now you don't even do that because apparently my presence is a burden or something.'

You snapped your face around to me, your cheeks slightly flushed. 'Do you *really* have to bring this up now?'

'And you never introduce me to your home friends either.'

When you're this angry you're not just angry about the one thing, but every argument you've ever had comes back into sharp focus so that's all you see. I brought up his home friends because I couldn't stop thinking of an incident only a week before. We were in the pub and this girl turned around at the bar and wrapped her arms up over his shoulders. She wasn't wearing any make-up except for some bright-blue smudges over her eyes. Everything she wore clashed but in a hot way. Her green eyes shut as though in seeing him there was too much joy to look upon. 'It's been *so* long.'

I stood slightly behind him, his face covering over mine so I became a half-moon. I waited for the 'this is my girlfriend, Annie' but it didn't come. Instead, there was just them talking about some mutual friend's festival and next to me endless streams of bodies saying 'sorry, sorry' as they bumped past me on the way to the smoking area. I felt like a kid at a wedding clinging onto their mum's leg.

'Why didn't you introduce me?' I asked after she'd walked off into the smoking area.

'Just seemed pointless – we don't hang out anymore anyway.'

It always was a plausible reason. *'I thought you were talking to Jess. I don't even like her. I wanted to keep the conversation short.'* And most of the time I chose to believe him, but occasionally I thought my worst fear really might be true: that he was embarrassed of me. In the moments when I lay on our bed waiting for him to leave for that night out I felt I knew this for certain.

'He definitely wasn't embarrassed of you,' Moll says when I ask her about it now as we cook dinner together in the kitchen. 'I think he loved that you were different from the people he grew up with. Wearing tight dresses and, I know you're like the least Leeds person ever, but you still probably seemed it to him. I just think he liked having a part of his life separate from you.'

It made sense. I was so tied up in him. He would look for a T-shirt and it would turn out I was wearing it. He took a holiday from work and he knew he had to dedicate a sizeable amount of that time off to me. He would start watching a TV series and I would say, 'Wait for me to catch up, I want to watch that too.' And the only exception were these childhood friends he sometimes hung out with, for birthdays, the occasional dinner. They were something I never brushed up against so hanging out with them must have felt like an escape from me. In keeping me away from them I guess he could feel that at least one aspect of his life was free.

He wanted to go to places alone. But that seemed unfair given that those places I used to visit without him didn't really exist for me anymore. I felt it right that I follow him everywhere. I couldn't bear that he was keeping something back. When a man isn't including the woman who loves him, 'everything he sees, he steals', says Simone de Beauvoir, so much so that the woman in love becomes jealous of sleep as the man travels to a place she's trapped outside of. I suppose it's my fault for giving it all over to him in the first place. I felt he owed me all of him like he had all of me.

This is a problem so many women face. That of trying to make men care as much as they do. You see it in season two of *Sex and the City* when Carrie calls Big a dick for saying he was moving to Paris. To make up for it she turns up at his apartment in a beret with a big McDonald's order and tells him they can make it work.

They can have phone sex or, if things get bad, she can just move there and write her column from Paris.

He brushes his chin, looks at the floor. Tries to make her agree that she'd be moving to Paris for herself, rather than for him.

'Well, why would I move to Paris if it wasn't for you?'

'I'm just saying, don't uproot your life and expect anything.'

Big sees Carrie as an addition to his life rather than the whole of it, one element added to so many other things he owns, like his very clean apartment and his important job, and the thought of her becoming more than that terrifies him. He doesn't even like it when she leaves a toothbrush at his or a spare pair of knickers. His love is made of brief intersections; nothing sticks. This bit is the good bit because Carrie decides she is fucking sick of it, and to make sure he knows that she throws the bag of McDonald's against the wall so hard that mayo splatters all over his TV screen.

He tries to tell her it's just about work, but she corrects him. 'This is about us getting closer and you getting so freaked out you have to put an ocean between us.' She looks him right in the eyes and asks: 'Why is it so hard for you to factor me into your life in any real way?'

21

The landlord tells us he won't be renewing our contract on the house in Tottenham because he wants to sell the place. Apparently that was always the plan, he was just waiting for the market to become even more of a seller's one. It makes sense now why he was so cagey about the condition of the property. Coming over for inspections once a month. Writing on one of the reports 'garden overgrown', 'pictures hammered into walls' and even 'toilet soiled' as though that wasn't the precise purpose of a toilet.

I'm sad because I like it here. The PT at the local gym fist-bumps me and calls me a 'little meathead' because I'm pretty strong. Yesim at the corner shop tells me to give him the rest tomorrow when I've not got enough change. My roots have sunk down into the soil. I feel almost permanent. But the area still reminds me of Joe, even if he and his stuff have gone. Memories cling to the red bricks of the terraces, the neon shop fronts. I see him walking down the highroad with me past the outdoor markets where watermelon quarters are wrapped up in cling film and bright green apples catch the sun. A man leaning in his ear to ask if he smokes weed. Fresh starts and all that. Most of my friends live in South. So when Moll asks me if I want to stick with her and Danny and find somewhere else in North, maybe more North-east, like someone on a property programme, I say, 'Now just feels like the right time to move on.'

Moll nods, says: 'Don't worry, if I was you, I wouldn't want to live with a couple either.'

It's weird thinking about not living with her. We've been together so long I know how she likes to live down to the smallest details. How she doesn't eat all day and then just has one ginormous meal like a pizza and eight chicken wings and that's how she gets her daily 2,000 calories, or how randomly she'll prepare some ornate Japanese feast for herself, copied from an extremely complicated food blog, as if there were only two options for eating: all the effort or none at all. Walking back from the supermarket with a stolen trolley having told everyone staring at her to fuck off.

I can't tell if she's upset or not. She scratches her nose. Puts a YouTuber on the TV that she likes. She does look a bit disappointed. I'm not sure if I would have decided the same thing if it wasn't for one of the many talks about my future we'd had. Unknowingly she pushed me towards an end which didn't serve her needs, only mine.

It's not like we promised each other we'd live together forever. I guess I just assumed that would be what happened, at least until I moved into a flat with Joe. She might be relieved it's coming to an end earlier than we thought. Our relationship has become difficult. We used to argue about each other's boyfriends through each other because they never seemed able to sort out their own problems without our help. She would tell me Joe hadn't done his weekly cleaning and I'd defend him by saying how busy he'd been at work, then she'd tell me she wouldn't have lived with busy people if she knew it meant she'd have to do all the cleaning, so then I'd do his cleaning for him, banging cupboards, making as much angry noise as possible, and when she reassured me it could wait until he had time, I'd mutter, 'Honestly, it's fine, it's fine.'

And I'd always be calling her boyfriend Danny entitled. When I was doing my washing up he'd say: 'Excuse me, can I just . . .' and I'd move to the side thinking he was just going to fill a glass of water or rinse out a cup, but then I'd realise he was actually just doing his plates because presumably he thought it was more important for him to finish them off than it was for me to do mine. She'd say he didn't realise how close to finishing I was. I'd say he had no manners.

When I saw her I also saw Danny. When she saw me she also saw Joe. And we bore the weight of our other halves' flaws. Women are never just women, they're the men they prop up and save.

I go onto SpareRoom and look at all these beige boxes scattered across the city, trying to decipher what makes one better than the other. Who the flatmates are, based on their limited descriptions of themselves. It's difficult when almost everyone mentions how much they like roasts and lists 'going out with friends' as a hobby.

'Love to play the occasional board game together or beers in the garden. We also respect each other's privacy and have our own friendship circles' = these guys only talk when it's time to complain about whichever flatmate keeps using the 'it's soaking' excuse instead of doing the washing up.

A man saying 'females only' = you'll have to sleep with a chair under the door handle every night.

'Love travelling and meeting new people. We all pitch in with the cooking and do yoga together on Sundays and there's lots of communal space in the house if you work from home or like socialising of an evening' = at least two members of the house are currently sleeping together. When you've finished work they'll ask you lots of questions about your day that you can't be bothered to answer.

I hear that Facebook is a better place to find somewhere. It's competitive, though. When someone posts on a housing group there's about 47 people commenting asking to look at the place. I message one poster and, after introducing myself, say: 'Ahhh I'd love to have a beer on that balcony!'

A week later I see her repost on another page. 'Have been struggling to find anyone who's our sort of person. Looking for a fun, interesting girl to join the flat.'

I wonder what I did wrong. I hope she didn't think I was like, *Ooooh, alcohol is so rebellious* or something because I just meant it would be nice to sit up on the balcony they've got when it's sunny. I don't think beer is a *thing*.

When I do make it to house viewings I find that they're a lot like dating in a way. You end up modulating yourself into the sort of person you think they'd want you to be.

'I'm clean . . . yeah, but not, like, anally . . . I mean, I tidy up after myself, you know? . . . No, sorry, I didn't mean it like that . . . if there's a general mess I'll help out because sometimes it builds up and you don't know whose it is and someone's just got to do it . . . Yes, I like parties . . . Yeah, that's fine that this is not a party house . . . I don't want to party in my own house . . . No, I won't be coming home late . . . much . . . yes, I'm a freelancer . . . Your landlord needs someone in full-time employment? OK, no worries, thanks, nice to meet you, yep, thanks, bye, bye . . . bye.'

I get three nos before I quit trying to move into other people's houses and decide I'll find my own with other people. There's a guy posting on one of the Facebook groups saying that he and his friend were looking for two more people to move into a place they found in Camberwell. I look at his profile. He seems fun. There's a picture of him pressing his face into a shower curtain so that all of his features smush downwards and lose their shape. Another of him running into the sea naked on Boxing Day. The one with the most likes shows him in a floral-patterned silky dressing gown with an expensive-looking lilac-coloured guitar draped over his shoulders. We arrange to meet for drinks at a pub near his office after he finishes work.

He's hairy; it's dirty blond and hanging in a loose bun on the back of his head; it's wiry and dense, poking up over the collar of his beige knitted jumper. He's got an accent – not a posh one, a farmer one. I can tell without checking that he's got a bad half-sleeve tattoo of a dream catcher or something, maybe a wolf. At his worst I imagine he might have worn a Native American headdress at a festival. At his best I imagine him stealing a car when he was a teenager and joyriding in it until it ran out of petrol. He leans over the bar and orders a cider. I ask for a gin and tonic and he pays even though rounds don't really work when one drink is much more expensive than the other.

We talk about the house, how childish cleaning rotas are, the importance of a living room, but mostly we talk about other things. What it was like for him growing up in the middle of nowhere. How I managed to get through the whole of school without ever learning to tell the time on an analogue clock. He says he feels weird at the moment because he's coming off antidepressants. They were working, he just didn't like the idea of being on them.

'I get you,' I say. 'I don't take paracetamol when I've got a headache because I don't like the idea that I can't feel what my body is going through. Like, it's not gone, but I can pretend it has.' Then I laugh. 'Sorry, *so* not the same thing.'

He smiles. 'Yeah, mental health is just code for "extremely bad headache".' But then generously he tries to understand me. 'It's like I want to stop the headache rather than just stopping me feeling the headache.'

He has the easy charm that the best man at a wedding always does. My laughter fills up the room all the way from the garish patterned carpet to the pictures of old rich men on the walls, all the way round to the bar where there's a man in a suit who I swear is listening in to our conversation. We move to sit on a table next to a sofa and sink down into the battered brown leather with matching tired sighs. I imagine he grew up without a TV. His mum probably thought they give people cancer or something. He tells me he doesn't really work in publishing like he said over Facebook. Or he does, but not in the way he led me to believe. The company he works for publishes textbooks for A-level students. He says it's fucking boring and he's thinking of doing a creative writing course. I try to say hating your job is anti-capitalist without being so extra as to call it anti-capitalist. Tell him that 'society has convinced us that our only value comes from what we produce. Not caring about what you make is kind of cool, I think. There's something so desperate and needy about ambition. Like you're searching for this approval from somewhere. I want a lazy person with lots of money,' I half joke. 'A guy who's not really posh. Maybe he robbed a bank or something.' I'm not quite sure how we ended up talking about my hypothetical future boyfriend.

The barmaid tells us it's last orders. He says two more, please. Finds his wallet, taps his card, says he doesn't need a receipt. I enjoy watching his languid movements. Never hurrying. I bet he's been a life model before. I imagine a slim but naturally muscled, sinuous body sloping in an awkwardly elegant pose over different props like one of those melting Dalí clocks. Then I imagine all the bad things that have been done to that body. Lighters pressed into the skin. Eating nothing but Pot Noodles on camp-sites. Maybe he's a vegan, though. One who eats lots of hearty lentil stews. I quote my favourite statistic at him, which is that only one guy has gone down on me since my ex-boyfriend. He says that's the best bit of sex. I say, 'I do feel bad for them, though, men. With casual sex all the onus is on them to do everything. Make the first move, get on top, finish. With women it's like everything you do is seen as a bonus. If you get on top, people think you're wild or something. And women will tell all their friends what happened after.'

He tells me I sound like a men's rights activist and then I laugh and then he laughs. He has surprisingly nice teeth.

The next day he messages me saying he had a fun night. 'Yeah me too!' I reply, 'I know I've just met you, but I think we should take our relationship to the next step and move in together.'

'I was thinking the exact same thing,' he says, and then there's those three small dots as he writes his reply. They disappear for a moment as he deletes whatever he typed out. I guess he's wondering whether it's OK to say whatever it is that he's thinking. Then they're back, one by one fading along the screen until there's a loud ping as he presses send. 'In all seriousness tho . . . it felt like we were on a fucking date.'

I don't take it seriously at first, thinking about what he's said only in terms of how I can mould it into an anecdote to tell others about. *The guy from the Facebook group who drinks kombucha who I didn't get to move in with because why do men have to sexualise everything?* But then I remember how I was behaving. Flipping my hair to one side when we were talking. Trying to sit straight against the too-soft sofa cushions because I didn't want to look like I have bad posture. I fancied him. I just didn't realise that I did because he wasn't my type. If he came up on an app I would have seen the long hair and the battered lace-up boots and scrolled right past, thinking, *I don't want to be with someone who stinks of incense and who probably thinks it makes him look clever if he pretends not to know who Kim Kardashian is.* Maybe the reason we had such a good date is because I didn't know it was one, so I was honest. I was actually myself. I argued back. I said what I meant. I let my body wander where it wanted to. I came jumping out from between my lips. I felt full from underneath the walls of my skin.

'It did lol' I say, trying to be casual. Then we talk for a while about how hungover we are. How shit the weather is. After twenty minutes or so he says, 'I'm off now, need to get in the shower.' This is where the conversation starts to get weird.

I ask, 'As if you're choosing hygiene over me. Can you not shower and text at the same time?'

'That's difficult because I have to shave.'

'Is this how you flirt? By telling women about how much care you take when shaving your dick?'

'Yeah, I make them picture me shaving my pubes and texting at the same time. I want them to know that I'm both great at multitasking and also silky-smooth down there.' Another message comes through seconds later to clarify, 'I actually meant I was going to shave my beard, or trim it, before you think I'm actually really strange.'

But I ignore the truth and carry on taking the piss. 'There's a person out in the world who's into smooth multitaskers.'

'You're speaking to him right now, girl,' he says. 'Joking . . . I wouldn't possibly be flirting with my potential future rentee.'

'Absolutely not, unless that meant I got a discount??'

'Would you like it if I was your landlord? Is that what you're into??'

'Yeah, millennial-underpaid-overworked-housing-crisis roleplay really gets me going,' I tell him.

'Stop, you're making me so hard.'

'£500 a month for a studio flat.'

'Don't stop,' he says.

'Bills included.'

'Fuck, I'm coming.'

'There's a garden and the neighbour's a deaf woman so no noise complaints.'

'That took me over the edge,' he says.

'Thanks for indulging my kink,' I say. Then I'm being serious again, telling him I've got to go because my dinner is ready but that I look forward to when we get to live together.

'I'm a bit nervous, though,' he replies. 'It's going to be difficult living with someone I find so attractive.'

I turn over that last phrase in my head before I fall asleep, as though it were a spell I'm casting. It's going to be difficult living with someone I find so attractive. I think about him sneaking into my room when everyone else is sleeping. I think about him doing stuff to me that I didn't even know I wanted people to do to me. He kind of repulses me but in a hot way.

He messages me later in the week and we arrange to go out together on Friday. I don't plan ahead what I'm going to wear and I don't tell friends about him because he doesn't seem like a legitimate option. Mum asks to see a picture when I tell her about him. 'Wow, he's handsome,' she says when it loads up. 'Very Extinction Rebellion.'

'Looks like Poldark,' said my uncle, because my mum showed him the picture for some reason. It's a bit weird that she showed him, but I think she's just excited because she's becoming more and more desperate for me to find someone new. The other day she said to me, 'Dev Patel is only twenty-nine!' as if the only thing stopping me from getting with Dev Patel is our age gap.

Back before we broke up, me and Joe had a holiday to Berlin booked and in the run-up to it everyone kept saying things like, 'How are you feeling about it?' because there's always something slightly ominous about holidays; people say they're 'make or break' and we'd been arguing more than usual. Conflict wove its way into the fabric of our relationship so that even normal conversations were made up of comebacks and criticisms and 'how many times do we have to go through this?'.

But I didn't need to impose any kind of narrative onto the situation. It turned out to be the best week of my life. We walked around parks with your hand in my jeans pocket, we slept in until 2 p.m. without guilt. I remember one night when we were out, I took half a pill and then I took more of it because it didn't seem like it was doing anything and then all at once it felt like a rainbow was beaming out of my chest. 'Are you OK?' you said, your arm over my leg the whole time. I nodded, said I felt like I was melting into the pavement but not in a bad way, in a really comfy way. You nudged my drooping eyelid so it went back into the right position. I don't know how long we sat there for, but my sight gradually returned in waves until I clicked back into reality and could carry on the conversation we had started hours earlier about our Airbnb host, Laila. Before coming out we'd been sitting with her in the kitchen as she slurped up gooey brown noodles out of a takeaway box and she was telling us about how she got caught on the subway without a ticket.

'I gave my mum's address in Cork,' she sighed, her chopsticks elegantly holding a sugar snap pea right by her head. 'She keeps asking me about all these red stamped letters. I just tell her it's a scam. I'm not paying it. I'm literally *never* going to pay.'

I turned to you then on that pavement and shook my head. 'How could you live like that, knowing that the fine is going up and up? What if they find her?'

Then we spoke about how funny it was that there's a Toys 'R' Us on Karl Marx Street and about the guy we met from Atlanta who plugged his own speakers into the bar and was drowning out the ambient techno with his own trap music. At how we thought he was cool because he told us about how he and his ex-girlfriend used to go to the famous Atlanta strip club Queen of Diamonds with 1,000 dollars each to throw, until he said he worked for Apple. Eventually we managed to stop talking and got into a taxi, which was taking us to another club.

I was still pretty fucked so as the car sped down a dual carriageway I held your hand and it felt like holding onto a buoy in the ocean, like something important I had to grip onto when the tide hit. You must have felt it too because there was clamminess there that neither of us flinched away from. Out of the window the tarmac looked like a big black sea and I imagined we were on a speedboat but then got freaked out when it started to feel too much like one. I tried to think of a way to explain what was running through my head but it seemed too difficult, so I just shut my mouth. 'Just here is good,' you said even though it was still a while to go yet. I was relieved that you did the talking.

There were no windows in the club so when we walked outside at 10 a.m. into the light it felt as though we were passing through the gates of heaven. And even though everything was weak, my mind was blaring with the energy of a toddler who'd drunk too many Coca-Colas, because apparently, when you haven't slept, your body releases a huge adrenaline shot to keep it going. I was starving but my stomach was cramped up like a fist. You insisted we eat something. I tried to order, but rather than saying, 'Chicken sheesh, garlic sauce but no chilli,' I mumbled something completely nonsensical.

'Who are Drake's best mates?' you whispered in my ear and I laughed so much I had to walk out of the shop and wait for you on the street because the loudness of it was annoying the other customers.

In that kebab shop past and future collided between us through a language that no one else understood the logic of. There's no other person you could say that to who would enjoy or understand it. So saying it was almost the same as saying I only need you. And it did feel like that was all that mattered for the whole of the holiday. We fantasised about moving there forever – a new flat, new friends, new jobs, only us staying the same.

I have a theory that in life, when it comes to the important stuff – family, friends, work and love – you can't have them all going well at the same time. Sometimes you get one of these aspects in line, sometimes three, but one of them always needs more attention. Your mum says you don't call enough, you have the dread every

Sunday of going back to the office, your friend says you never come out anymore, you're not having sex. Going to Berlin for a week removed all the other distractions so all that was left to focus on was love. In these conditions we were great at it. Maybe if we'd been able to stay on holiday forever, things really might have worked out between us. Maybe it wasn't a problem with us so much as the lives we were leading. Maybe if we'd had a bit more help we could have sorted it out.

I think this again when I'm listening to the relationship therapist Esther Perel's podcast *Where Should We Begin?* The thirty-minute-long episodes are recorded therapy sessions with real couples facing problems. Perel is so good at diagnosing their issues and giving them the tools to deal with them that it feels as though any couple could make it work with her help. I have listened to her so often that sometimes I can almost hear her voice in my head. What would've happened if we'd have had a session with Perel?

I can imagine him starting off with a complaint. 'You get so stressed about work and you wind yourself up into this teary state and I feel like I have to sacrifice my evening to make you better but I can't always be there to do that. It's the same with how you want to come with me to every event I go to. You rely on me so much. I feel suffocated.'

I'd sigh. 'Oh, and you don't rely on me?'

'Not in the same way.'

'What about last week when Moll was keeping you up by playing the TV too loud? Why was I the one who had to go ask her to turn it down? You make me feel so guilty when you can't sleep as if it's my fault. And you're always asking me to come sit with you when you shower and to chat with you while you cook. I'm not a fucking podcast you can have on in the background.'

Perel would presumably interject here, pointing out what we can't see ourselves.

'What's happening here is your two selves have fused together. This makes you feel secure but also trapped. Now Joe's self would like to free itself to a certain extent, without triggering the abandonment issues [because everyone in therapy seems to have abandonment issues] which you both have.'

In response to Perel's analysis I'd laugh. 'What's so funny?' she'd ask, sensing an insecurity in me. 'This is a very painful situation, and often when things are painful we use humour to distract ourselves and everyone around us so that we can avoid processing it. You're trying to push what's hurting to the side, but it only means that I see it clearer.'

Eventually the tensions between us would begin to thaw. At that point a separate recording of Perel made after the session would provide an overview of her findings where she'd say something like:

'One of the main struggles of relationships is learning how to find the right balance between connection and independence. What do we share and what do I need just for myself? Where is the "I" and where is the "we"? How close is too close? Often in relationships one person clings on tighter than the other. They are afraid they will lose their partner. Meanwhile the partner fears they have lost something infinitely more serious: who they really are.'

Back at the session, Perel would turn to Joe and say, 'Initially you might have liked that Annie was so involved in your life; it helped you overcome some of the rejections you felt in the past, but now it's making you seek that freedom, break away from it. Oddly, it's her who's made you strive for independence, but it is her who is keeping you from attaining it too.'

To improve the terms of our relationship, Perel would propose an experiment where we pick one night a week where we're not allowed to ask each other for anything. 'The point is those are your nights to locate the "I" away from the "we". They will help you feel like an individual again, one who still has access to the shared whole.'

At the end of the hour he'd say he loves helping me but sometimes it's like there's nothing left afterwards for himself, and he'd be crying while he said it because most of these episodes end with one or both people crying.

What if we could have spent the rest of our lives on holiday? What if we had a therapist to help us through our issues? What if, what if, what if. Knowing what went wrong between us doesn't make me feel better. It encourages the small, noisy part of myself that's always saying I should have tried harder.

22

It's the day I'm scheduled to meet the Extinction Rebellion guy again and I've forgotten why I agreed to this. It's cold enough that all the moisture has frozen on the surface of cars, walls, lampposts, so that everything glitters. Kids pretend to smoke because there's steam coming out of their mouths when they breathe. I want to barricade myself inside my room, light lots of candles and watch their yellow light flickering up against the walls while I carry on playing the game of *what if* with my memories of Joe. But I pull the duvet off and get on the bus because I said half-seven and so that's what I have to do. I feel trapped by this man, as if he's taken me hostage by my own morals.

I thought he'd be late, but he's already at the bar when I get there. He wraps his arms around me and my face rests comfy against the navy woolly jumper he wears, one with holes on one arm that he pokes a thumb through. I imagine Joe saying something snotty about his appearance, like, *'Does he think he's a pirate or something?'* He's also wearing Docs and Joe hates it when men wear Docs. *But he is actually quite hot*, I think, half telling myself.

We sit down and drink lots of cheap, vinegary red wine and for hours we talk and talk and talk and all the talking pours out of both of us like someone has stabbed a paddling pool and let it all drain out. He moves from the stool opposite and sits next to me and we stop talking and start kissing, and I normally put my hand in a guy's hair when I kiss them but this time I don't know how to do that without it getting all tangled up in knots. He kisses with a lot more tongue than other guys do and it slides right over mine and makes me feel all prickly on the inside. Our heads angle left and then right. He pushes into me and then retreats so that I can do the same, hard and soft, the red leather seating squeaking as I sink further down into it, unsure whether I'm about to flop off it and onto the floor. I can hear the building pant of my own breath. His hand slides around my waist. Squeezes into it like a stress ball. I'm so into it that I don't even notice who he's talking about when he pulls away and says, 'We should probably stop kissing soon, they're about to come over and tell us this is a respectable establishment.'

I look over at the table next to us where two women with statement earrings and trouser suits are sitting either side of a half-eaten cheese board. I'm drunk and confrontational so I stare back until they snap their gazes away. When he leans in to kiss me again I see that there's purple varnish on his teeth from the wine.

For a little while I forget about all the *what ifs* because this man is proving that some things are just good and there's no way they could have been otherwise. Me and him in this pub on this cold day – there's nothing about it that couldn't work. Even if I got out of bed on the wrong side and wore the wrong outfit and spilled wine on his jumper, the night would still end up as nice as it is right now. Yes, we might never exist beyond pubs like this, bedrooms like the one I imagine he has, but then that's OK. *What now?* is all I think of; *What now?* as he leans into the curve in my neck, the slight scratch of his stubble against me.

Friends and family do so much to get you through break-ups. Listen as you cry into the phone. Order a curry to your Wetherspoon's table to guarantee you eat something. But then there are these strangers who come along and help you in ways the ones close to you never could. And they're never thanked because, for whatever reason, it would be too intense for them to know the depth of the pain they tugged you away from. So they do their invisible labour quietly, unknowingly pulling you from a darkness they can't even see. It's unfair that our closest friends work so hard to help us and then a man like this can do it without even trying. While acting in ways that still benefit his own interests. Just speaking to him, watching his eyes glance down to my chest and his face breaking open into a smile when I catch him, just that is enough to make me feel, if only for a little while, that it might be right Joe and I ended.

'I feel like we'd have really good sex,' he says, wiping away the wet from his bottom lip. Normally I'd hate that kind of pressure levelled on an encounter because it sets you up to disappoint and I do better when I'm proving something wrong. It makes me worried that I might forget what to do, like where your legs go when you're on top or how to move your hips. But right now, I know what he says to be true.

It's not a particularly nice reason why. It's because this ugly part of myself thinks I can do better than him. He doesn't look like the man I want to end up with, so there's a recklessness to our interactions. I'm more forward, flirtatious. In bed I might actually direct him to what I wanted. If I made a weird grunting noise or my teeth came out from under my lips when giving head, it wouldn't matter to me because losing him is something I would need to happen at some point anyway. But then maybe that's precisely why it would be bad for it to end, because I only feel comfortable around people I'm not scared will leave. Maybe I shouldn't lose those people I want to lose. Perhaps my relationships would work better that way.

He is going to come home with me, but at the last minute he says something weird about having to let in the cleaner in the morning. I'm a bit confused as to why he doesn't then just ask me to come back to his, but I don't say anything. Just tell him, 'Yeah, I'm free,' when he asks if we could do something tomorrow instead.

I'm not surprised when he doesn't get in contact the following day. That kind of optimistic planning of seeing each other so soon afterwards is the sort of thing you do when drunk. But when he doesn't get in contact the following night I text him and ask what he's doing next week.

'I'm about on Thursday?'

I say yes, but then Thursday comes and he says, 'Hey, just remembered I have to see a friend tonight after work, but I'll meet you after at about 8?'

It's so obvious he'll have two pints with his mate and then bail on me when it's too late and I've already got all my make-up on so I suggest the weekend instead. He says yes but then never messages me.

'Sorry, it turned out to be a heavy one,' he says eventually. 'How about Wednesday?'

But when Wednesday comes, he once again says he has to meet someone first. I'm sick of waiting now so I say it's fine. He promises it will literally just be a couple of pints. But then when I'm about to start getting ready he says, 'Oh sorry, it won't be until 9 because he's not free until 7:30.'

'Why are you so slack?' I ask, perhaps too aggressively. 'What are you doing next week?'

He doesn't reply.

I'm so annoyed that I let that ukulele-loving prick talk his way into making me like him. I'm not in so deep that it actually hurts that it's over. I mean, I bet he's dated at least one white person with dreads. Probably has a sticker over his webcam camera. Probably would try to convince me to wear less make-up if we went out. He looks like he'll get old and start fangirling Julian Assange. I didn't want him anyway, I tell myself. I'm just annoyed that his mismanagement of his schedule meant I spent a number of nights staring at my phone waiting for him to reply when I could have been out having fun. I have no idea what happened, and when people ask I can't explain it because he looked at me like he really fancied me.

What if I wasn't so forward, maybe he would have felt like he needed to work for me more? What if I hadn't said that weird insensitive thing about paracetamol? What if he didn't like the way my kisses left lip gloss all over him? I thought he would get rid of my *what ifs* but he just brought me more of them.

23

I did think about not going when Joe's friend Rupert invited me to the night he's putting on in Tottenham. 'You should come,' he said, which I interpreted as, 'Obviously don't come, that would be weird.' The 'should' makes the statement sound hypothetical, rather than assertive, in the way a 'you're coming, right?' would be. A bit like when you ask people a question and they say, 'Sure,' and it's like, sure as in yes? Or sure as in *sure, if you want to take what I said that way.* I imagine Rupert wants Joe to have fun without having to worry about whether or not to say hello to me. Predicting that at some point in the night I'll do something weird like drag him out into the smoking area and repeatedly shout, 'I literally don't even care!' even though he'll be able to tell I do because I'll be saying all this through tears.

I get annoyed at this imagined thought process of Rupert. For days afterwards I argue with it, tell it, *Why should I continue to prioritise someone else's happiness above my own when we're not even together anymore? Did you know that he's more cut up about the break-up than me? You should have seen him when we saw each other last time – he was all like, 'I love you, baby.' I hate this narrative that I'm the desperate one or something, which I think is pretty sexist actually, that I'm just here pining for Joe when I'm out here focusing on work and friends, and so if I came to your night, I wouldn't make an issue of it, I would just be dancing and enjoying the music. Yes, I do know who Floating Points is. And I have a really good outfit to wear – these black leather trousers and a slightly see-through white crop top and a good push-up bra, which I'll carry everything in because there'll be no room for it in the tiny – but adorable – bag that will be over my arm.*

When I tell Mum that I've bought a ticket she isn't pleased. 'You'll miss your train if you go,' she says over the phone, because the club is open until 6 a.m. and the train I'm due to get home for Christmas is three hours later. 'And you won't be able to book another one so you'll be stuck in London and we can't just come and pick you up, you know, because it will be snowing and my car is awful in the snow.'

'I'll make the train, Mum, I'm good at functioning when I'm hungover.'

'You're so going to miss it,' she says again.

'Right, you're annoying me now, bye, love you.'

Just before I hang up, she shouts: 'And for heaven's sake, don't go home with him!'

Since it's December now, the sky is always dark. Not black, because it never is here; it's more like a muted petrol blue. Light pollution means the atmosphere reflects the light of high-rises and street lights back onto themselves. As though the arrogant city saw the stars and thought it could do better, so it made up its own solar system, one so powerful it never lets it be night. My friends Adham and Georges have agreed to come with me to Rupert's so I head over to theirs for pre-drinks. On the way tiny flakes of snow fall on my nose, carpeting the pavement in a white fuzz that will soon disappear. The street is quiet; it's that odd transitional time when everyone's preparing for the night rather than inhabiting it. A kebab-shop owner installs a fresh doner for the evening shift, pale-brown meat revolving on the spit. I'm nervous that the eyes of one of the men I pass will leer up and down at my body until it feels like it's no longer mine but his, but when none do I feel slightly deflated because when you spend your whole life being stared at, as young women do, when no one's looking you wonder if you mean anything at all.

'Hello, mate,' says Adham, wrapping his arms around me as a gust of central heating breaks against my face. I follow him inside the little pebble-dash house. I love this place. Pictures of Yuri Gagarin, the first man in space, are all over the walls as a result of some in-joke no one's ever explained to me. There's a large golden moose in the kitchen, Free Palestine and ACAB posters, newspaper clippings made into collages, colourful baubles dangling from ribbons glued to the ceiling, a garden with a mouldering pumpkin from the Halloween party that happened months ago, emptied red-wine bottles and lots of people – ones who they met in bars, on language training courses, who cycle over and stay over for unspecified periods of time on one of the slightly damp-smelling sofas, because this place becomes a home to anything that enters it, including me, who once met them in a smoking area and made it here because they really did mean it when they said we should hang out.

One of the housemates, Rudy, has organised a dinner party for some guys he went to school with and they're at that point in the evening when all of the food has gone and they're scraping off the burnt bits at the side of the pans, arms over the backs of their neighbour's chair, hands rubbing the skin under their T-shirts. It's a nice time to walk in because I'm full of energy, having not spoken to anyone all day, and they have no fight left in them so I tell them a long story about the awful Hinge date I went on where the guy made me sit through a twelve-minute video of him and his friend on ket before telling me that he tweeted in the wake of the Manchester attacks at an Ariana Grande concert, 'That's why I listen to drum and bass, because they drop bangers, not bombs.' I get a strange sense of pride from saying that I'm going somewhere my ex-boyfriend will be because part of me still gains self-esteem from my proximity to a man, even if it's one I'm no longer with.

'Don't you have work in the morning, Adham?' asks one of the guys.

Adham laughs. Scratches his forehead. 'Yeah, but Annie needs moral support.'

Inside the club I buy a round and carry the flimsy plastic cups high above heads to the corner of the dance floor we're sticking to. Lasers scan the crowd like searchlights and I see Joe in every face that's lit up, all teeth and eyeballs from the terror of having a good time. There's the slap of a wet torso behind me as someone pushes their way to the front. Cheers roll through the bodies when a song drops and people shout into phone receivers, 'Where are you? I'm at the bottom left near the pillar,' then type out texts that definitely don't make sense.

I see my friend Henry, making sure to talk to him for a little while before asking: 'Is Joe here yet?'

'Haven't seen him,' he shouts into my ear. 'He's bringing his new bird, I think.' For a moment it feels as though a big hot hand is pressing into my chest. But I don't let on how I'm feeling, just nod slowly. And in hiding my feelings on the outside, on the inside they gradually disappear to some other place, a dark corner they will crawl out of when I have more time to think about them.

For the rest of the night every woman I see I kind of hate because it could be her, and even if it's not, my mind wonders how bad it would be if it was. A group of girls in front of us keep tying their hair up and down and there's something so hot about the long, thin backs of their necks when they're wearing a ponytail and then again when they shake the hair out of its tie so that it's all wild like a big cat's and then again when they're grabbing it all up with frustrated hands. All of them oozing sex even though the only skin of theirs you can see is a tiny slice of tummy when their raised hands pull their tops up slightly. Most of them have gaps in their teeth, are rather gawky in that cute Bambi sort of way. They look like what Ruchira and I used to call slash girls: model/ activist/floor manager in a trendy retail shop.

There's no one more beautiful than the woman who has taken a man from you. You want to possess her because in doing so you would possess what he possesses and be closer to him again. Perhaps if I slept with her it would resolve all the feelings of jealousy because then I'd have taken what took him from me.

'She's really sound,' said Henry at the end of our conversation about Joe's new girl. 'You'd like her.'

I never do get to see her, though, because she and Joe never arrive. I spend a lot of the night wondering what they're doing instead. Is she washing his back for him in the shower? Is he making her fresh pasta with his pasta maker? He hasn't come because of me. There's some slightly satisfying cosmic retribution in that. I get to enjoy this night. I'm the taker.

When Adham leaves at the end of the night I find Rupert sitting on a bench outside with his girlfriend, Eliza, and two friends. 'Do you want some beer?' I ask, and I hand him my bottle, and as he takes it he sucks his cheeks in and raises one eyebrow so that he looks like he's in a beer ad or something, and with most people it wouldn't be that funny but with him it is because he's so spot-on at making faces. 'We're all right, aren't we, Annie?' he asks, patting my leg. 'We're still mates?'

And I nod with a big smile on my face.

'I really appreciate you coming tonight.'

So many times, I've sat next to Rupert at Joe's birthday parties, heard him do funny accents in the background of phone calls to Joe, watched the long-drawn-out impersonations they did of characters on the fighting video game *Tekken*. 'Psych,' they'd repeat as a hand came against the other's neck. And I've always found him completely ridiculously hilarious, but Joe was always the reason we spent time together and that seems silly now because seeing him is making me smile.

We get in a taxi and I look out of the window and focus on not being sick, burping out the trapped air and thinking about the cold wind hitting my face. I look at my watch and I've got two hours and twelve minutes before I have to get up and go to the train station. I thought tonight's love story would be Joe watching me as some hot guy whispered in my ear, but really it wasn't much to do with him at all. Instead, it was Adham coming out even though he had work in the morning and seeing Rupert and realising people still like me even though I'm not Joe's girlfriend anymore and how if people say, 'You should come,' I will do unapologetically because it probably does mean they want me to be there. Those people I knew when I was with him haven't gone anywhere and they don't like me any less now that I'm not joined to him. In fact, maybe they like me more because they see me more clearly, as if I'm in full daylight and not something standing behind someone else.

In the morning I wake up with snot filling my nose and the faint memory of waking up an hour earlier and turning off my alarm. I snap upright, grab my phone, see that I've got twenty minutes before my train leaves and for a short, optimistic time pretend to myself that I can still make it, pulling my weak body down the street with a big sports bag whacking into the backs of my calves. But then I stop, lean against a wall until the itchy out-of-breath feeling in my lungs has gone, tell myself how much I fucking hate myself and spend £75 on another ticket.

When you wake up next to someone every day for years you stop perceiving them in an objective way. You can't tell what they are because you've looked at them for so long, in the same way that a word stops sounding like a word when you repeat it too many times. The closer you get to them the more they turn into this blurry extension of yourself, which is neither beautiful nor ugly, but just a thing that exists beyond measure. Their qualities are invisible to you now and it's hard to desire something that you cannot gauge.

He could walk into our bedroom dripping wet with a white towel tied around his waist, tanned skin smelling of tree bark and pepper, looking like he came straight from that 2009 era of Burberry. He probably did walk in like that loads of times, but I stopped seeing him do it. Asked him if he could pass me my phone charger. Fell asleep.

He'd kiss me and I'd roll over onto all fours. 'But it's not hot for me like that,' he'd say. And I'd reply, 'But this is how I want it,' and it didn't feel good or bad, but like trying to tickle yourself and realising that the lack of surprise meant it didn't work.

This is the central paradox of love: it longs for closeness but the more you achieve it, the less you value what you're attaching yourself to. Esther Perel discusses this issue in her book, *Mating in Captivity*.

> Love rests on two pillars: surrender and autonomy.
> Our need for togetherness exists alongside our
> need for separateness. One does not exist without
> the other. With too much distance, there can be no
> connection.

She goes on to say that the paradox is that if we merge too much, we eradicate the sense of two separate individuals who remain intrigued with and longing to connect with each other. If there is no distance to transcend then there is, essentially, no one to connect with anymore. So, as alien as it may sound to us, remaining separate and individual is a condition for connection. Perel calls this 'the essential paradox of intimacy and sex'.

I had become Joe and he had become me. There was no gap between self and other. There was just this being with four arms and four legs. And I only wanted to get closer to him, not seeing that this closeness was pushing each of us further and further away.

We were out at one of those pubs that gets a dance floor at night and we were drunk because there was a £10 card limit so you ended up getting two drinks instead of one. The toilets stank of shit. Girls with dirty-blonde hair and bruised knees danced around piles of coats and bags like they were casting spells over a fire. I kept screaming at the DJ to play Lemar's '50/50' and he kept saying he'd never heard of it because it was a slightly gentler way of telling me to fuck off. I hadn't seen you in a while and, when I turned to look for you, saw that you were leaning against the back of one of those red-leather chesterfield sofas talking with a girl I didn't recognise. You said something and she smiled and touched your arm.

'It is what it is,' I said to Ali, who was out with us, because that's what they say on *Love Island* when the person they like has moved on to someone else. Then I explained the logic of that joke to Jonny and Phoebe and Scott because I was the sort of drunk where you think even the most average of anecdotes is hilarious and requires greater elaboration if someone doesn't get it. Still, no one laughed that much. Perhaps they thought I was jealous, and in some ways I was, but I was also enjoying having some distance from you. The opening up of a gap that I could jump across, not knowing what lay on the other side. The girl's finger circled the top of her pint glass and for a second I caught her eyes and without asking jumped into those same eyes so that I could look at you anew. The way your muscles pushed through your skinny footballer frame, how you talked in that well-spoken but not too posh way that actors use in interviews. I fancied you all over again, like I was

meeting you for the first time in the lift for the Philosophy Department, trying to push the nervous waver out
of my voice. I wondered if either of you was imagining
what it would be like to have sex with the other, and even
if you weren't I did it for you, taking over both of your
bodies in my mind and moving you around like pup-
pets. I stopped the dream before anything was resolved,
before you were lying together in bed, her head resting
on a knot of skinny arms, Maybelline mascara dripping
down her eyes, with the sudden thirst for water and the
slight giggle when everything's back to normal and the
pink bubble of desire has been popped and what you
said five minutes ago seems unimaginable.

And at that moment, I felt the paradox of love, long
before I heard Esther Perel's definition of it. This sense
of unease that no matter how hard I try I will never
truly be satisfied. Everything in the world is so at odds
with itself and humans need all these unhappy contra-
dictions in order to exist. No one likes getting out of
bed, but if you never did, you'd be sad. Exercise feels
awful but improves your mood. Love makes you want
security, but when you get it, it's boring.

You walked back over to our table at the pub, put your
arm over my shoulder and said: 'How weird, I used to be
really good friends with that girl's brother.'

'I love you,' I told you, almost tearing up with how
much I was feeling it, how much I had ignored it. 'Like, I
don't think you'll ever understand how much I love you.'

'Where did that come from?' you smiled, distracted

now by the way Ali was pointing at a pint that belonged
to you.

It came all the way from her eyes.

'I'm so nervous I'm going to fucking shit myself,' says
Vicky as we near the entrance of the club. It's Christmas
Eve and pretty much everyone from school is going to
this club in the centre of Leeds. She's nervous because
loads of the populars will be there. The sort who used
to call her 'Leslie' – because back then 'lesbian' was still
seen as an insult – and me 'Leslie's Best Friend' – because
apparently I was too forgettable to have my own nick-
name. Our reliance on each other in school was so strong
that when she was off sick I used to hide in a cubicle in
the science-block toilets with my feet off the floor.

'They're humans now, not teenagers,' I reassure her as
we follow our friend Marisa past the bouncer and down
the steps into the basement.

Inside, guys who used to call me 'Annie no tits' kiss
me on both cheeks and ask me how work's going, how
my brother is. One of them, who's got his own plumb-
ing business, shows me pictures of his daughter in his
wallet. With their stubble and tired eyes, they all look
like actual men. The passage of time written into the
lines on their foreheads. They buy tequila shots and offer
out cigarettes because money comes more easily to them
now and they like people to see them spending it. They
look you right in the eye when you're talking and wear
Lyle & Scott polo shirts and big shiny watches on their

oversized, veiny forearms. I remember when they were dwarfed by the huge rucksacks on their backs, when they had spider legs and fluffy blond duckling hair that never lay flat no matter how much gel they slicked onto it. I spent so many hours with this version of them, five days a week, 8 a.m. to 3.30 p.m. for so many years, it's cemented down into my brain so deep that it's always a surprise to see them as they are now, no matter how long they've been a man. I wonder if they see my present or my past? What sits in front? Can they see the ways time has pushed and pulled my body into different shapes? Where I used to be straight up and down, now I've got hips. The contraceptive pill made my boobs go up to a D. My make-up is properly blended over my face instead of one flat plane of beige. One of them, called Mikey, puts a hand on the curve of my back: 'You're looking well.' Vicky's standing two paces behind him with her eyes popping out of her head, pointing at him as if I don't notice what's happening. She spends the whole night telling him and some other guy that I'm interested so that they follow me around the club and it's only the next morning when she rings me for gossip that I realise that's why they wouldn't leave me alone.

But there's only one man I'm interested in tonight and that's Josh, the guy standing by the bar, the one I texted a few hours after the break-up. I look over at him and he's scrunching his nose up because a song has come on that he likes, his tongue curled up over his top lip. He sees someone he knows and pushes them off him, picks them up in his big arms. They know him from when our schools would play football against one another. I never watched the games, but I heard he was good, really good. Head down and one finger raised towards the sky when he pinged another ball into the corner of the net. I dance like Josh is always watching, and at one point, just after twelve, he really is. I can feel his eyes on me without even turning around to check, but temptation means I have to and when I do our gazes click together like two parts of flatpack furniture. He mouths 'Annie Lord', then, 'I didn't know you were going to be here.' I shrug and he laughs. I feel completely naked under the stare of his dark-brown eyes, so aware of the way my skin seeps through the mesh holes in my dress that my cheeks burn red like they used to when our boss in the pub would watch me trying to carry three hot plates at once, when Josh would throw bits of scrunched-up receipts at my head while I looked at what we needed to stock up the fridge with. I give him a small wave, think about how much I fucking hate the way I just waved. And then someone's on him again, grabbing him by his shoulders and shaking him forwards and back.

The girls I'm with are off to the toilet. All our hands conjoin and pull through the crowd. Someone once said to me that when women do this it reminds them of clowns getting out of clown cars because the string always goes on for so much longer than you expect it to, and I laugh at this now because I'm reminded of its truth. It's chaos once we get inside. Vicky's taken some girl's phone out of her hand and is telling her boyfriend, 'She'll speak to you when she's ready,' despite having little to no understanding of why they broke up. Marisa's trying to teach someone how to twerk and in doing so has ripped the seam of her dress. The girl standing by the dryers turns around. 'You're Annie, right?' she asks. I'm wondering what I've done wrong but then she says, 'You know, I've heard Josh talking about you before?'

I can tell right away that this information is far too powerful for me not to do something stupid with it. I want to ask her a thousand questions, but I don't know her well enough, so I just say, 'Does he actually?' and then focus on keeping my hand steady as I draw liner outside the lines of my lips. Feel excitement shuddering through me like an allergic reaction.

It's 5 a.m. and the Uber pulls up and all the girls are tiptoeing over to it, heels in hand, singing 'We Found Love' by Rihanna in croaky end-of-night voices. 'Come on, you slag!' shouts our friend Aaron in my direction, and I'm about to get in and accept that mine and Josh's brief catch-up as I ordered a drink was probably the best I was going to get given that it was so busy tonight, but then he's walking up to me in his big North Face jacket with that smirk on his face, which always makes you feel as though he knows something you don't. The girls pull away because they can tell there's no way I'm coming with them now. Neither of us say anything. He looks down at me and I look up.

I feel small and girlish next to him, like his height allows me to become one of those fragile women I always wanted to be. If I don't get him then his coat would do, the feeling of being wrapped up in something that smells like him.

'You coming home with me then or what?'

Before I've fully processed what he's just said, a 'YES' jumps out of my throat. Almost as if each letter was alive, or the word were an insect with wings that's just broken out of my throat and landed on his neck.

'Really?' he asks, his head jolting back in surprise. A tenseness wriggling through his features. He's trying not to let me see it but it's clear even on a street this dark. He looks over at a friend walking off in the other direction. 'Yeah, see you on Friday, mate.'

He sees another friend, asks, 'You off to get food?' and when said friend nods, he turns and follows, escaping.

I know that I should have been softer in response to his question. Raised an eyebrow and said something dismissive like, 'You're going to have to try harder than that,' or made up an imaginary boyfriend for him to be jealous of. Because Josh likes me, but only when he feels as though he won't be able to get me. Sex is a game to a lot of men, and they want to feel like they've won something. A game without rules or conflict isn't a game at all. He wants to struggle for it because then the value of what he's struggling for goes up. Like how shares on the stock market are worth more when people are competing for them. Or how a Champions League trophy is worth more to the team who didn't look like they'd make it. I can only imagine this is what happened with the Extinction Rebellion guy back in London too. That I was so keen to go back with him that the appeal of it faded until he made up that cleaner excuse and then that friend he was drinking pints with until he wasn't speaking to me at all. I know I should be annoyed at this sexist construct that requires women to dampen their desires in order to appease men. And I know I should walk away from Josh thinking, *Fuck you, why did you ask then if you wanted me to say no?* But right now, I don't care that it's backward for me to act in this way. I'm just annoyed that I'm too drunk to have been able to sense that I should have. And I know I should order an Uber home but I don't, I follow him to the chippy, clinging onto what that girl said to me in the bathroom as though it were a prophecy, aware that the flaws of this night won't be able to be fixed but knowing that I will spend the rest of it trying to undo them because he's the sort of man I go absolutely mad for.

'Do you want a bite of my battered sausage?' asks some guy on another table, holding it towards me like a baton, and I'm guessing from the lurid sound of his voice that they're making some sort of half-baked penis joke. For once I'm thankful for his disrespect because Josh will see it, see I'm wanted, when so many of my actions are of someone no one would want – standing up and dropping my bronzer on the floor so that it smashes over the tiles, mud on my feet from walking in the street.

Josh doesn't seem to notice. I catch him in the corner of my eye walking up to the counter and picking up his order. While he's faced away from me I try to sort myself out, pull my tits further out of my bra. *Come on*, I think, trying to drag myself out of the quicksand my mind has sunk into. It takes me longer than you'd hope to realise Josh has actually taken his food and left the takeaway.

I hear from someone else in the chippy that he's gone to this guy who went to my school's house for an after-party. I should order an Uber home but I don't because this friend of theirs called Larry says he'll wingman me if I come. Promises that all I need to do is play hard to get. I look him in the eye as he pushes the last bit of his chips into his mouth, licks gravy off his thumb. 'I think he knows he's already got me, though.'

'It doesn't matter,' Larry reassures me. 'I'll make you seem mysterious and that.'

We pull up in the middle of the suburbs. As we walk towards the door Larry asks why did I bother wearing a see-through dress if I was gonna wear granny pants? Which is dumb because the 'granny pants' are actually very nicely cut and if I wore a thong it would have looked too much. I bookmark this comment, thinking it might be a funny, self-deprecating way of gesturing towards my ass later on. But then we walk into the house and I real-ise there isn't going to be a later on because I've made a really big mistake in coming. It's less an afterparty than some housemates and their friends winding down for

sleep. On the long grey corner sofa sit loads of the football team from my school drinking beer with their arms
wrapped around their girlfriends, most of whom are in
tracksuit bottoms now, make-up off, with their hands
in packets of Doritos. Josh is not even conscious; he's
dozing on the other sofa with his puffer jacket blanketed
over his top half.

That is until Larry chants: 'Annie's here because she
wants some dick!'

I stay for an hour or so, smiling into conversations I'm
not a part of. I don't say bye to anyone when I decide to
leave, just pretend to be going to the toilet and then walk
outside. I can see the Uber approaching from a few doors
down and I'm about to walk towards it, but then Josh is
here again, half running, half walking towards me.

'Naah, stay,' he tells me, pulling my arm towards him
so that I boomerang back towards his chest.

'But no one's even talking to me,' I say, letting myself
be tugged towards the house and back onto the sofa.

Josh's head is on my lap. Larry notices and gives me
a big thumbs-up. I stroke Josh's shoulder and each time
I brush my hand over him I wonder, *Does he think this
is shit? Is this annoying him?* Think about how strange
it is that so much of human touch is driven by intuition
alone with no awareness of what the other person actually feels, only what you think would feel nice. I suppose
that's what makes it so intimate, touching someone how
you would like to be touched, as though their body had
become the same thing as yours.

Soon he's shut his eyes and I don't know why I came in again if the only thing I would become was a place for him to sleep. Granted, it's an improvement from before when I was just dead weight; at least now I'm functional. In the same way that the kitchen island with that curving marble top is, or those lovely exposed light bulbs, which drop low from the ceiling. I can imagine all my friends from London asking the price of this place and saying, 'Seven hundred a month? I pay that for a room,' because they love to make London the yardstick of legitimacy for everything. I could say all this to Josh, we could laugh about how some people down South actually think I have an accent, about whether he still plays football and is his mum feeling any better? But I guess he's probably scared of what allowances I will make if he gives me that level of attention. Perhaps I'd turn wild with it, take it in my teeth and run, so he just lies there with his eyes shut until he says, 'Wanna order an Uber?'

We get in the car and he slots his hands in between my legs. Without saying anything he leans over to me and kisses me on my collar bone and there's the warmth of his tongue and the skim of his lips and I feel like I've melted down into the car seat. A small, cramped grunt comes out of me. As if he's punched me in the gut, not kissed me, or filled me up with so much feeling that some of it had to escape out of my mouth otherwise I might explode. I want more from him, which is perhaps why he doesn't give it to me, just says, 'Here's fine, mate,' when we get to the turning to his parents' house and then waves at me as he walks towards their door. 'Maybe see you in London?'

And in this non-committal question, he once again escapes me. Love is closeness, desire requires distance, and I am so, so far away from getting Josh, always have been. It's hard to say how much I actually like him and how much I like the untraversable gap he places between us because of what it promises.

I know I should say something equally vague like, 'Yeah, see you around,' in answer to his comment about London, but he's tied me all up in knots – confused, delicious knots that form this impossible puzzle I long to solve – and that temptation means I embarrass myself trying. So instead, I shout: 'No, you won't, though!'

It turns out to be the truth. I don't see him again for months. I speak to him a few times over the phone because I develop a tendency to ring him when I'm drunk.

When I tell the story of this night back to people at parties, they say, 'What's wrong with this guy? He's leading you on.' But this obsession helps even though it hurts because it distracts me from the bigger pain of Joe. Like how when I got a tattoo on my foot I dug my sharpest nail into the palm of my other hand in order to distract from the sting of the needle going into my toe. As if by spreading out pain over two different areas it becomes diluted.

24

I'm back in London after Christmas and I'm climbing two steps at a time up the escalator stairs out of the Tube station because I'm late to meet my brother and cousin for dinner. I told them to order for me because I won't be there for another fifteen minutes, which really means twenty, but I shaved a few minutes off because I know that's when lateness tips into the unacceptable. The Christmas lights are already down but the street is twinkling with the red and yellow of car brake lights. The air smells slightly of burning and everyone looks at the floor as if they've already seen enough Januarys. I walk past the roasted peanut guy, left down a back street, and that's when I see him: Joe and a girl who must be *the* girl.

A part of me feels it's my fault this has happened, as if by looking for him everywhere I've somehow managed to summon his appearance. But then I remember I'm near where he works and it's a Thursday, so of course he's going out for a drink. Didn't he say she loves a drink? She's smaller than I imagined and she's wearing a big shearling coat, Dr Martens, not much make-up, has pale skin, dark hair, and on her head is a big fluffy black hat. He looks the same even though he's let his hair grow out into its natural ashy brown colour. But he's moving differently, leaning back in the air as though it were holding him up, one leg swinging gently after the other. He's relaxed, meandering, where I'm used to seeing him rush, stepping away from me to nip around bollards and bike racks, bumping shoulders with those who didn't move around him, his skinny legs carving up the pavement. He's walking like he used to walk when he'd been at his dad's place by the seaside for long periods. Relaxed as though his spine were made of velvet. I follow them, even when they turn in the opposite direction from where I'm meant to be going. I wonder if I should call out, but then I'm cautious of disturbing a scene it oddly feels like I shouldn't make myself a part of. One that's calmer than my presence would allow. I turn back, running, holding my boobs up with a makeshift bra made of my arms, because I'm really late now and because suddenly I have all this energy roaring through me like a fire.

'How're you feeling about it?' asks my brother when I tell him, filling my glass up with the red wine they ordered. My answer is probably not one he expected.

'Actually better.'

When you imagine your ex with someone else you don't believe they exist in this world but in a sepia-toned one where they're non-stop kissing and laughing under fresh white sheets, a big bay window in the corner of the room that the sun pours through until the whole room is golden. But they didn't look like that, they looked like everyone else. Enjoying that there was just one day left before the weekend. Trying to find a pub where they can get a seat. Joe and his new girlfriend don't exist outside the realms of experience, they're just people.

'I'm sure she's *nice*,' I say when I ring Vicky a few days after bumping into them. My mature attitude has now faded to the point where I'm dying to be told I'm prettier than her.

'Yeah, but she's not *you*,' says Vicky. 'Is she?' a conclusion she comes to based on the blurry outline of a woman in the background of a single screenshot my friend took of Joe's Instagram story from yesterday.

And then, without knowing who this woman is, together me and Vicky turn her into something that I can tolerate. Decide she's the sort who never dyes her hair because she's worried about damaging it, who says, 'Can we talk about something else?' when people bring up something controversial at the dinner table, who gets a thrill when she manages to incorporate the red pepper that's just about to go off into the recipe she's following. I bet she thinks she's political because she posts infographics on her Instagram stories. I bet she washes her hands after she wanks. And I bet other things that in my opinion make an uptight and dull person.

'I just think I was too *much* for him,' I say, and Vicky agrees, and we slip into the comfortable grooves of a conversation we have had many times.

We tell ourselves stories in order to live, that's what Joan Didion said in her iconic book of essays *The White Album*: 'The naked woman on the ledge outside the window on the sixteenth floor is a victim of accidie or the naked woman is an exhibitionist, and it would be interesting to know which.' Didion argues that we don't just see images, we also interpret the sight of them, choosing the option that best fits with our view of the world, and this allows us to keep on living. 'We live entirely, especially if we are writers, by the imposition of a narrative line upon disparate images, by the "ideas" with which we have learned to freeze the shifting phantasmagoria which is our actual experience.'

I am still able to tell myself stories and the one I'm writing with Vicky is that Joe wants a boring girl now because he loved me too much. That's the most workable of the choices. It's what allows me to carry on with my day. There are friends I could have gone to who would have chosen a different story. Who would say, 'Maybe you guys weren't good for each other?' or 'Him liking her doesn't take anything from how he felt about you.' But I didn't go to them because we have different friends for different things and I didn't want to confront this interpretation of events. Instead, I went to Vicky who I knew would go low with me so I had someone to accompany me in my awfulness.

I'm not the only woman who's chosen this particular story. In Russian poet Marina Tsvetaeva's 1924 poem 'An Attempt at Jealousy' – which many believe was written about one of her many unsuccessful love affairs – the narrator asks her lover how it is with that simpler woman he picked above her. What it's like living with a postcard where before he stood on Sinai? How is it living with cheap goods? Kissing plaster dust? Lying in a shallow pit?

> *How's your life with a tourist*
> *on Earth? Her rib (do you love her?)*
> *is it to your liking?*

A rib because that's what the first woman, Eve, was made of, Adam's rib, and what kind of woman lets a man take that from her? One who gets on her knees and rolls over like a dog. Really, if you think about it there's no logical reason why a woman would be 'too much' for a man. What would it be like to be with a woman who was genuinely too much? Wouldn't it just be luxurious?

But this explanation works well for me because it allows me to escape accountability. I can't cope with the idea that something might have been wrong with me. Women aren't good at taking criticism. Perhaps because we're not allowed to be anything but perfect in order to be valued. Men can be all types of wrong and still be wanted. You see them in films blowing up buildings and punching people in the face, but we're still cheering them on. Women say I'm sick of doing all the housework and they're a bitch. They sleep with too many men and in the next scene they're left dangling from a rope. It had to be his problem because we know what it meant if it was mine.

'Sorry, but I think you're much prettier than her,' says Vicky at the end of our phone call.

I smile. 'Don't say sorry. My feminism doesn't include women that date men I've gone out with.'

Jonny invites me over for dinner and when I get there he takes me into the living room where his flatmate Rupert, whose club night I went to, is cuddling on the sofa with Eliza. They're hungover and it's like the whole room is coated with the feeling; it lines all the surfaces, the big fireplace, the white netted curtains, the tiny TV where Jason Bourne is launched backwards after an explosion has gone off in his face. Just standing in here, I feel like I am breathing in the fumes of sleep as though it's being hotboxed behind the closed door.

'What've you been up to?' Rupert asks, his eyes sinking shut.

'Bumped into Joe and the girl he's seeing,' I say, and then tell them both about the other night when I followed them through that back street.

'Ah, shit,' Rupert says, sitting up as though it would be impolite to hear this information in a casual position. 'Man, I bet that was bad.'

'It was, but then she was wearing this really shit hat, so that made it much easier.'

Jonny shouts from the kitchen that the food's nearly ready and it's only as I'm leaving the living room and saying, 'See you in a bit,' to Rupert and Eliza and walking into the brightly lit kitchen with the empty cupboards and the washing-up liquid bottle filled with bubbles from repeatedly being diluted with water that I realise how embarrassing that story is. I hadn't really registered how Rupert winced slightly when I said what I said and his encouraging nod, which meant not that he agreed with me that she wears a shit hat, but that he felt sorry for me. I was clearly so desperate to feel superior that I would dump on her in case it would help. Rupert's probably going to see her this weekend; they probably really get on. He probably jokes with her, 'Don't let him get away with that,' when Joe is doing embarrassing stuff like taking a video of himself downing a pint. He's probably already met her and knows she's not boring like I made out but rather the sort of girl who jumps through the Tube doors even if she knows they're about to shut, eats three custard doughnuts even though she's lactose intolerant, pushes to the front of the crowd at festivals and smiles even when the hot liquid that slaps her leg was probably piss, works outside in the sun even if it means she can barely see her laptop screen, who lives in a way that's too much, because I know that's what he wants from a woman, because he used to want that from me.

The air feels heavy as I'm walking to the gym. The sky is a washed-out grey and the trees are bare, and winter is fading out into that non-season whose only purpose is waiting for summer. I'm walking down Turnpike Lane high street with all its key cutters and those furniture shops that always have a closing-down sale on. I'm on the phone to Mum half listening as she tells me about starting the beginners' running guide Couch to 5k for the third time. I'm relieved when she's finished because I only rang to talk about the shit hat comment and Rupert's reaction to it.

She sighs and then there's silence down the phone line for a moment before she starts talking about her best friend, Barbara. 'When we were in our twenties, she had this really bad break-up.' Mum laughs at what she's about to say. 'In the flat we had this beanbag and whenever one of us was upset about a guy we'd say, "Let's go to the beanbag," and we'd sob into it for hours. Anyway, she'd been desperately upset about this ex of hers for months and she never looked happy anymore and she was always saying, "I want to die, I want to die," and I remember one day her mum had heard this so many times she was actually starting to take these cries seriously. So her mum asked Barbara, "You're not really going to do anything silly, are you?" and when Barbara heard this she was shocked because she knew her break-up was nowhere near that bad and could never be that bad. She went back to work, we stopped going to the beanbag and she found someone else.'

'And?' I say, leaning on the wall outside the gym now, watching as women weighed down by bags-for-life wait for others to pass so they can step around the big puddle taking up the pavement.

'What I'm trying to say is, there comes a point where you just have to snap out of it. Maybe it's time for you to do the same? Your friends are going to be bored of you soon if he's all you're going on about.'

I'm ready to dismiss what Mum's saying but then I think about it for a moment. I've been spending so much time recently processing what happened and why and it feels as though I'm making progress unpacking it all – why he wants her and not me, whether or not our co-dependency issues could have been sorted. But I'm beginning to understand that even if I crack the code, it would still be over, there's still no back we could return to. I used to find it frustrating that when it comes to the universe you can't change what has already happened. But right now, this fact starts to feel kind of reassuring as it shows there's no point endlessly contemplating tactics for sorting it all out because you couldn't fix it even if you tried.

A few days later, the Extinction Rebellion guy sends me a message at 4 a.m. 'How's it feel to have made it into 2020? Sorry I went fully MIA, it's complicated but I can explain. To make up for it here's a pic of me (with a tactical crop lol). Am quite sad I never got to actually get my hands on those great-looking boobs of yours.'

There he is. A hairy chest. The top few inches of his dick visible. Faded swallow tattoos. I'm tempted to respond but then I think of how he bailed on nine dates. How he could have just explained why he needed to go off the radar initially so he didn't waste my time. So I leave him on Read. And then again when he sends a wave. It feels delicious and new, rejecting someone who rejected me so many times. Like breaking beyond a barrier of possibility. Like when you do that trust exercise where you fall backwards into the arms of your colleagues, or squeeze through the hole in the cave it looks like there's no chance of you fitting through.

No one is in when I get home, which never happens. There's always Moll and Danny and me asking each other to turn things down, saying, 'Sorry, excuse me, sorry,' while we push each other out of the way to get to our pans on the hob. But tonight, when I open the door, there's no one but the cat clawing the wiry carpet, mewing at a door she wants me to open. I ignore her and walk up to the bathroom and run a bath, turn off the light and sink down, down, down underneath the water until it covers me over.

When I surface in the rare quiet I see all my thoughts from a distance, as if they were sitting at the end of a long corridor – *That email I need to send, I didn't say happy Mother's Day, I need to hang that coat up before it loses its shape* – and they thin out slowly until I can barely see them and all that's left is darkness and the water and lots of tiny sensations that the calm allows me to notice where usually I wouldn't: sweat trickling down the back of my neck; steam rising off my arms, milky white, into the air; the distant wail of sirens; the Bulgarian family that live next door laughing in their gazebo; the plastic smell of strawberry-scented candles; salt on my top lip. Alongside all of these, that other thought, the big one that never leaves me – that he has gone and found someone else – stops feeling like a problem and instead becomes a sensation, just like all the other hundreds and thousands of sensations I have had and will have.

Instead of being the defining feeling that dictates my life, heartbreak starts to become something ordinary that I just have to endure, a sensation like those others – granted, one I will have to endure for longer, but no more or less exceptional.

Mum told me I needed to get over it and I thought I already had when I left his house that second time, or when he came and got his stuff, but I'm understanding there's not one 'over'. Nothing snaps into place in a moment. There are just lots of small 'overs' where gradually you start to understand that you won't be how you used to be anymore, and maybe that's OK because maybe the new you will be all right too.

After the bath I lie on my bed all twisted up in a towel, not moving, not even to grab my phone, and it's not even like I'm thinking about not picking up my phone; my mind has just drifted off somewhere else where phones don't ask to be looked at. Time passes. I'm not sure how much of it and I don't know why, but there's this flicker of realisation where I come back down into myself and snap upright and as I do I see myself in the mirror that sits over the fireplace, all strawberry pink and puffy, and I smile at my reflection as if saying hello. I never confront myself like this. Sometimes it happens when I'm drunk and I'm in the toilet, talking myself through the motions to try to stop myself from doing something stupid, like,

*Yeah, use that toilet roll. I get it's a bit gross that it's
damp at one end but it's probably better than getting wee
in your knickers, and when you get back out there try
to drink some more water and be nice to Hannah cause
you were a bit short with her last time she made a joke.*
And it's through this inner dialogue that you become
conscious of yourself as someone you can talk to and
have a relationship with. I look at her now in that mirror
and she's me and I am her, and although we're the same
thing I see that we can talk to each other even if I will
always know what's coming because she, her, me, is the
only thing I can count on to be there for the whole of my
life. And in the towel now, with coldness starting to prick
up all the hairs on my arms, and the sheets dark with
damp, I experience another 'over', and this time it's a
promise, to keep on being nice to her. To order expensive
takeaways, and go on walks, and watch films that are difficult to understand, because this life could be gorgeous
if only I gave myself permission to allow it.

I take out the drawer at the bottom of the fridge and
empty the greenish-yellow water. I rub white vinegar on
the walls' Blu-tack stains. I pull stray hairs from carpets
and wipe away ceiling cobwebs. I do all this, not to make
our house nicer to live in, but because we are leaving it
tomorrow. How sad that the only time we give the house
this treatment it'll be someone else who gets to enjoy it.
Moll and Danny are moving into a studio flat and I'm
heading to a friend of a friend's house in South London.

All afternoon I fill holes in the wall with Polyfilla, scrub away the brush marks from backpacks scraping at the paint when heading out of the door and dump rubbish in the neighbour's bins. And all these actions mean that when the landlord sells it on to some happy young couple who were given a deposit when one set of parents downsized, they won't see us here; they'll repaint the light-grey walls a soft ochre, they'll pick up the last fag ends left between the garden paving stones, each year they'll mark in pencil on the walls their kids' heights and think about installing a kitchen island, and the house will become something it never was when we were here: a proper home. You are made to move on through this city so much it's hard to feel like it's ever yours. It's tiring, like when you're a kid in the back of the car asking your parents, 'Are we nearly there yet?' because the destination never seems to arrive.

But I tell myself it's OK because the life we built in this place will always exist somewhere, turning corners in dreams to see Joe in the kitchen smoking out of that window in his tracksuit bottoms that I hid from him, the ones I'm wearing now, or at the table chopping garlic with a podcast on. For us, the house will stay how it was when we were there. In our minds it will always be ours.

I'm in the van on the way to my new place now. We drive over a bridge across the Thames where you can see all the high-rises, St Paul's and the purple glow of the lights on the London Eye, and being so near it all I feel like I'm in a film. If I really was, there would be a roof window and I would open it and stand up out of it with my hands in the air while the soundtrack built to a crescendo, but I'm in real life so I just cross my legs on the car seat, say yes when the driver, Ravi, offers me a cig, lean close to the now-opened window and shut my eyes into the breeze.

'Why are you moving?' Ravi asks.

'Break-up,' I say, deadpan. 'Just think I need a fresh start.'

Then I tell him what went wrong. The way that love can make people want to grip on to each other so tight that they have to pull apart before they hurt each other anymore.

'We had a lot of problems,' I say at the end. 'I dunno, maybe we could have worked them out. He just didn't want to, I suppose.'

Ravi says something but I can't hear because he's holding a Marlboro Light between his lips. 'Sorry, what did you say?' I ask and he takes the cigarette out, flicks its ash out of the thin slice of window he's opened up.

'He wouldn't be him if he didn't do those things,' and then he carries on in a louder, more deliberate tone as if somehow he can tell I don't understand him, even though I said nothing. 'When my wife left me for another man I kept thinking, *If she just stayed and listened to me and gave me another shot to get the romance back,* but the thing is, she wouldn't be her if she did those things. Not wanting to work on our relationship is part of what makes her, just as much as her nice hair was, or the way she walked, or whatever.'

I start talking but Ravi cuts me off. 'If she didn't cheat, she wouldn't be her, she would be someone else. We are the sum of our actions, otherwise what else are we?'

I smile at him. 'Yeah, I guess you're right.'

CONCRETE

25

I ring the doorbell and my new flatmate Hayley comes down to let me in, her pretty pixie face drowning under a bright-red ponytail. She has the sort of genetically blessed mane you can tell has been bleached, brushed when wet, burned with straighteners and still continues to shine right down to her hip bones. Like weeds in a garden – say, dandelions or chickweed – which blossom even after gardeners dig up their roots. She's determined, skinny legs stomping up and down the stairs under flannel pyjamas as she helps me carry boxes she could fit inside if she curled up into child's pose. I can tell she's quietly resentful that she had to peel her tired Sunday-evening body out of the duvet to facilitate my arrival. Still, she's polite in the way service staff are to customers, smiling with her mouth while her eyes stay revealingly still as I say, 'There shouldn't be too much more,' for the thousandth time. Regretting it when twenty minutes later she's still helping me haul boxes filled with high heels I don't wear, and spices like za'atar and celery salt I never use, up the steep staircase.

'See you soon,' she says after I've picked up the final box, slipping through a crack in the door into her attic room. I want to shout at her to come back. She has the lofty teacher-like authority that I gravitate towards, being so easily led myself. I want to ask her whether I should order a takeaway or just leave it. Should I unpack now or can it wait until the morning? I imagine a future together with her dragging me through the crowd in clubs, saying, 'Here's good,' when we get to a spot she likes. Telling me the first top I tried on was definitely the best.

When she's gone I realise how quiet it is inside this place. I try to match its disposition, moving around these walls so carefully I feel as though I might have broken in. I'm worried one of the two other flatmates might walk into the kitchen I'm standing in and scream as I turn around to face them. But there's no sign of anything. Not even the whir of a boiler or the creaking of floorboards as someone moves to turn the main light off. I walk into my room, which I find to be a lot less nice than I remember it. There are maroon-and-yellow striped curtains that genuinely need to be burned. The wood pattern on the linoleum floor is too repetitive to recall anything natural. And the neighbour's garden is impressive only for how many things are dying in it. A blue plastic bag caught up in a knotted brown heap of what I suppose used to be grass.

The room I shared with Joe in the last house was beautiful without even having to try. But I tried nonetheless. Found frames for all our posters. Bought candles shaped like Roman busts that were too pretty to burn. Piled up the books so that their colours faded into one another like the graduations in a sunset.

I don't know at what precise point I became a homemaker. When it became some aesthetic requirement for everything to be ordered and exact. I used to have a floordrobe. Turned socks inside out so I could get a second wear out of them. Being a housewife was a future that didn't belong to me but to my grandma, and her mum and her mum before that; women married to men who didn't even know how to make a cup of tea. But eventually it came for me like it did for them, asking me to bring shiny things back to the nest like a magpie.

I'm not sure what the end goal was. What I thought would happen once our room was finished. Maybe there wasn't an end goal at all. Perhaps it was only the searching that mattered. That's what Marguerite Duras, the French wartime writer, said in her essay on the home.

> The house a woman creates is a Utopia. She can't help it – can't help trying to interest her nearest and dearest not in happiness itself but in the search for it. As if the search were the point of the whole thing, not something to be rejected out of hand because it's too general.

I tried to enlist Joe in this endless project of renewal, but he wasn't interested in taking part. I watched in awe at the way he would come home from work, empty out his pockets onto the bedside table – train tickets, gum packet, a twice-stamped coffee loyalty card – and collapse on the bed without thinking to put that stuff away. It seemed his mind was always too busy thinking about other things. Friday-night plans and a new album to listen to. Why did he get to walk over the world as if so little bothered him? So light he seemed to float. The fact that we didn't have a misting spray for our house plants didn't itch at his bones. I was trying to make his life easier, but I could tell he'd rather have done without the help. I think this while reading the part in *Things I Don't Want to Know*, the first book in Deborah Levy's trilogy of memoirs, where she talks about her compulsion to protect her children.

> Yes, there had been many times I called my daughters back to zip up their coats. All the same, I knew they would rather be cold and free.

I knew he'd rather eat his cereal with water on the occasional morning than have a girlfriend so pathologically dedicated to never running out of milk. But I couldn't let go of these rules. I felt if I did the whole world order would turn upside down.

It's hard to say what happened first. Whether I asked him so many times to do things that he stopped doing them, or whether he never did this stuff and I only started noticing when I was so much more involved in them. But at some point, beginning at the start of our fifth year right up until the end of it, he wasn't just refusing to buy the scented candles I linked to him on Facebook Messenger. He also wasn't picking up milk even when I reminded him, couldn't find a towel unless I physically handed it to him.

You were in the shower when I stormed in, and for a moment all my anger softened because after all I loved you so much my heart felt like a bruise.

'I don't like being this person, you know,' I said, the words catching as they exited my throat, treacle-like, guttural, as though some part of me were already trying to call them back into myself. 'Your socks, you left them on the carpet *again*, and you said you were going to start doing more around the house. But they're lying there. On the floor. What's so hard about picking them up? I would genuinely like it if you explained to me where exactly the difficulty lies.'

Your face was calm, smoothed out. 'Don't speak to me like that.' Your lack of anger more hurtful for the way it showed how little you cared about what I'd just said. And then you turned away from me so that I was stuck staring at the long, deep seam of your back.

I don't want to be this person, I thought again. *I want to be the sort of girlfriend who gives blowjobs and gets high. You made me talk to you like this*, I thought. *I'm not your mother, your maid.*

You rocked back and forth under the water, your two hands clasped over your chest as though in prayer. God, I loved that shower. The jets were so powerful you could feel them untying all the knots in your back. It made me squeal with excitement when we moved in here. I thought a proper shower meant we were grown-ups. That we were hurtling towards a future, whatever that was.

'I'll move them when I'm finished showering,' you said.

You couldn't understand why I could be so upset about an issue that could be so easily fixed. It seemed small to you. Takes two seconds. But these things felt so big to me. And if they were big for me and small to you, then why couldn't you just do them?

The argument ended in the way they often did. With you saying, 'Just stop telling me and then I will,' and me saying, 'OK, fine.' And then two weeks later the socks were still on the floor.

I fall back on my mattress now and look up at the spiderwebs drooping between the different wires of the big light in my new room. Trace the cracks running through the ceiling. I want to make this room nice. A fluffy rug to cover the floor. Devil's ivy trickling down from a pot on the windowsill. It has less of a bite knowing this process of improvement will be at the service of myself and not another who doesn't want it. But more than curating my own space, I want to be free to be messy in it too. To see myself as so important that the place I live comes second to it. What books will I write at that desk? What men will be in that bed? So that the room is serving me rather than me serving it.

Rather than unpacking like I would normally, I do what he would have done. I lie on the bed and think, *That can happen tomorrow, or the next day,* and I don't go to the shop to buy milk. Sometimes self-care is not caring at all.

26

At the beginning of April after a few months of living together, Hayley invites me to her friend Moya's birthday. We arrive at Moya's flat early enough to be the first ones there. The whole place squeaks under our trainers because it's been lined in plastic to prevent carpet stains. While the sofas are being tipped up against the walls to make more room for dancing, Moya takes us to her room where she asks Hayley about a person I don't know yet, then she's nodding while furiously typing out a Twitter thread about how chemical exfoliators are bad for your skin. Moya does this a lot: begins one task and then halfway through is drawn into another thing and then another so that nothing ever quite gets finished. She's pouring herself a rum and Coke, but just before adding the mixer she realises she didn't put a fan next to the speakers to stop them overheating. She's like a Duracell bunny or someone gearing up to go into a boxing match. I'm hardly a shrinking violet, but it's hard to keep up with the cyclone of energy whipping through the room. I feel as though I'm watching her and Hayley talk from behind a window, one that I can see into but they can't see out of. More people arrive and I keep misjudging the breaks in conversation so I end up interrupting them, and then when I'm telling them what I was thinking about I feel as though I've never had a single interesting thought in my life. But Hayley tries her best, gesturing towards me every time someone enters the room to ask: 'Have you met Annie?'

But then I get into a good conversation with someone who went to Newcastle Uni about whether or not it's true that someone kidnapped a cow and brought it into the Castle Leazes accommodation. After that I loosen up and people start asking me if I want to come outside for a cig. Hayley pulls me and her friend Hannah onto the dance floor, her grip small and determined like a baby's, and then I'm screaming Robyn's 'Dancing On My Own' so loud the lyrics feel like they're burning through my lungs like an infection has inflamed them, and afterwards I feel lighter because I must have been carrying something I didn't even know was weighing me down. Every time I walk into another room to get something – say, a cup or my lip gloss – I end up in another conversation and it's always so interesting I forget about the one I was in before. Then I blink and it's 6 a.m. and there's grey light prickling out from behind the clouds, and elsewhere in other flats thin men with important jobs are dressing themselves in breathable Lycra for their morning runs, while on the streets the warm air of a car exhaust hits the calves of girls crossing the road on the way back from their ex-boyfriend's house, and the birds are tweeting because they don't understand that beauty is not something anyone's ready to experience right now.

Hayley and I don't leave, though. We collapse in a knot of women on Moya's bed. Limbs woven together like a big tapestry. And we're all talking, talking, talking and it makes me think about something my mum always says, which is that her favourite thing about women is their ability to chat. The sheer endurance of it is impressive even when taken on its own, but the quality deserves praise too. It's so much more artful than the way men tend to communicate. Instead of short, sharp snippets of banter, making fun of a friend's shit haircut or commenting on the good contact made when they slap the back of the other's 'pan head', everything roams and spirals, turns down unexpected corners. There's no competition, no devil's advocating, because why does anyone need to advocate for the devil? They say, 'I've never thought about that before,' and 'How does that make you feel?' until each sentence layers on top of another like bricks for a house we could all live in. Men say women aren't funny and I think that's because they need a *badum-bum-tish* punchline; they don't see that the humour is riddled through everything we say, so that everyone's always laughing a little bit. Most of the time we talk through the language of experiences, a few too many of them painful, and we find our way to those hurts and tug them out of each other, like following the trail of a map we didn't know was already inside us. Moya yawns, falls back onto me, her compact body smelling like tangerines from the vitamin E cream she methodically rubs into her eczema. And I bask in that satisfying feeling where you know you've cracked someone and I smile because it's warm and golden in the light of her affection. My hands are twisting around one of her sun-tinged curls as her friend Bex tells us about the guy she slept with who wouldn't let her use his phone charger.

I don't know it yet, though part of me can sense it, but I will know these people for long enough that their first impression of me as the blonde girl in the double denim who told that story about Bryan Adams holding her as a baby expands into something three-dimensional. They know I speak before I think, which means I often offend people. Like when I told that girl she looked like an 'ill Victorian school child but in a hot way' and she asked me what the fuck made me think that was an OK thing to say. They send me memes about Geminis because I fit my star sign so accurately, like one of the singer Nor-mani with her face blurred into two images, one cheeky with 'Gemini saying something provocative to be funny' over it, then another, more downcast face with 'Gemini wondering if everyone hates them for what they said' over it. I have so much fun with them I stop looking over the shoulders of people to scan the party for men who might give me attention. We learn to grasp each other's weird theories, like how I say everyone either looks like a pig or a rat. 'Gareth Southgate is a rat, right?' 'Judi Dench – hard to call, but I'd probably go with pig.' We finish each other's sentences because we know when the good bits are. 'Wasn't the cat called Bollinger?' they ask when I'm talking about a fancy dinner party I went to, and, 'Didn't the cat turn out to be a baby tiger?' until the story has been buttressed and blinged into something it never was in the first place. I introduce them to friends I've got already like Ruchira and they're drawn into the group too until it becomes this complex Venn diagram of connections that makes it difficult to answer the question, 'So how do you guys know each other?'

In *All About Love*, bell hooks distinguishes between co-dependency, where excessive reliance on someone else becomes unhealthy, and 'healthy interdependency'. To explain the latter model of love she uses the example of Alcoholics Anonymous, where millions of people find that the community of regular AA meetings creates an environment of healing, support and affirmation. She praises the organisation for providing the 'acceptance, care, knowledge, and responsibility which is love in action'.

I thought love had to come from a boyfriend, but you can find it in friends too. They bolster me and build me up, and being with them is like being in a support group. Like having a bunch of sponsors you can call on when they're needed. That's the main lesson I took from Dolly Alderton's memoir *Everything I Know About Love*. Right at the end of the book Dolly is talking to her best friend Farley about how she's never managed to hold down a long-term relationship.

'I want to know what that feels like,' she says about Farley's past engagement. 'To be truly committed to someone, rather than having one foot out the door.'

'You're too hard on yourself,' Farley replies. 'You can do long-term love. You've done it better than anyone I know.'

'How? My longest relationship was two years ago and that was over when I was twenty-four.'

'I'm talking about you and me,' Farley tells her.

After this conversation Dolly realises she does know what love is. How it was right under her nose the whole time, she just didn't take the time to see it.

I thought about how excited I always am to tell her a good piece of news or get her view when a crisis happens; how she's still my favourite person to go dancing with. How her value increased, the more history we shared together, like a beautiful, precious work of art hanging in my living room. The familiarity and security and sense of calm that her love bathed me in.

When I was younger I always thought friends would be the biggest love story of my life. When we were at school Vicky and I promised each other that when we were sixty we would divorce our husbands, get married and move in with each other, where we presumed we'd continue doing what we liked doing together back then: singing along to Paramore and doing each other's make-up. But somewhere along the way I forgot about this promise to always put my friends first. It's come back to me now. It's funny how often the future is just a return to the past.

* * *

'We should get a drink together sometime xxx'

The girl I was best friends with at university, Jess, mes-saged me because she's just moved to London with her boyfriend. The girl I shared a bed with every night for a month because I found it hard to sleep if I wasn't near her. The one I heard crying into a pillow when I left our girls' night in to go and sleep at Joe's house. A few weeks later we're sitting outside a pub together and it's so windy we have to tuck the menus under a pint glass otherwise they'll blow away. On another table a menu does actually escape and a man runs after the paper as it backflips down the pavement so fast he sheepishly slows his jog to a walk when he realises he's not going to catch it. Jess and I both look different from how we did when we first knew each other, but in a lot of places we've changed in the same ways. No bras because nipples out is cooler than cleavage now. Our long, mauled, split-ended hair shorn into blunt bobs, hers brown, mine now bleach blonde. But she's stopped fake tanning, going for the 'mysterious look' as my mum would call it. You can see her freckles shining through what is a much thinner base of make-up than mine. I've got enough highlighter on to look like I could be made of metal. We manage to feel our way back to an easy familiarity. She picks up my hand to look at my green nail polish. Our legs brush together under the table and neither of us flinches away from the contact, though some part of me feels I would be more comfortable if we did.

She's talking about something completely unrelated when I bring it up. 'I'm really sorry that I dropped you like that when I started going out with Joe,' I say, hurrying. 'I regret it a lot, think about it a lot. I just became so swallowed up by him and that's not an excuse. I know I let it happen. I stopped caring about you and I'm really, really sorry.'

Jess smiles, moves her head to the side as though trying to look at me through different eyes. 'I mean, it's like . . .' She stops, starts again. 'I hadn't ever had a boyfriend back then. I didn't realise what it was like, you know? I should have been more patient with you, given you more time to get him out of your system. You were in love! Of course you wanted to embrace that!'

A waiter comes and collects our pint glasses and we go silent for a moment. I hope when we start talking again we can speak about something else, having got all that out of the way. But she has more to get off her chest.

'He really didn't like me, did he?'

I shrug. 'I dunno, I mean, he was quite –'

Jess cuts in before I can finish. 'Do you remember when I came up for your graduation?'

I shake my head, feeling as though I should be nodding.

'Mine was on a different day but I came up to congratulate everyone. I remember you were wearing that yellow jumpsuit and you still had your red hair. I gave you that present, remember?'

I want to say that part's coming back to me, but I'm not sure if it is or if I'm just dreaming it up in my mind.

'I tried to talk to you, to everyone in the group, but he kept moving to stand in front of me, blocking me out of the circle. I mentioned it to Jamie and he said he didn't like me. I was surprised because I didn't really have anything against him. Thought he was a bit intense or whatever.'

It's so odd to me that I could not recognise her kindness when it was right in front of me, holding out a wrapped present for me to take in my hands.

'I'm sorry,' I say, knowing it's not enough.

Jess shrugs, pulls a strand of hair that's stuck on her T-shirt. 'I don't want you to think –' She takes a deep breath, and she stares at me with those big hazel eyes of hers that made everyone at uni say she looked like Mila Kunis. 'All of my best memories of university are with you. Stealing bagels from Yla's cupboard when we came back from nights out. When we took MD together and filmed ourselves and then got too scared to watch the video back. Do you remember when I wrapped you up in cling film and then threw baked beans at you for that art project?'

'Or when you made a cast of my bum?' I say, lit up again by that same joy of remembering. 'And I had to bend over the sink as you oiled me up. In my head I was like, *Don't get turned on, don't get turned on,* so much that I really did just turn myself on.'

She laughs with that laugh that always sounds a bit exhausted, like a runner folding over themselves trying to get their breath back. I really want her to know that

I'm not that girl anymore, the one who let her down. That if I could turn back time to that night we were supposed to hang out, I wouldn't leave at 10 p.m. to go to his. I would stay with her all night watching YouTube clips about how to give yourself curly hair without using heat. Looking at clothes online neither of us could afford. But I don't have the time to say that and I never will, because we live completely different lives now. We have a few more beers together, but then her next bus is due in three minutes and she can get there if she's quick so she's marching away, waving her hand at me, leaving me with nothing but the past.

27

'You cooking for the Red Army again?' one of my flat-mates jokes when she walks into the kitchen that summer and sees me surrounded by a mound of chopped red peppers.

I raise my eyebrows, say, 'Coming from you?' because I'm not sure she gets to criticise my cooking given that all she eats are Nutri-grain bars, packets of Thai sweet chilli Sensations and vitamin tablets. Though she wasn't laughing at what I'm making so much as the fact that there's enough here to feed a whole family. I batch-cook in this way because it means that the only cooking I have to do each evening is pressing two minutes into the micro-wave. I'm glad I enjoy eating again but I'm also tired by the effort of it. That's why the chicken traybake that I'm making now only has one step: put chicken thighs, onions and peppers on a tray and then cover them in harissa paste before scattering black olives over the top and putting it in the oven for forty-five minutes. And why I never make anything that requires more than one pan. Don't mari-nate, or sauté, or caramelise. It's why I use garlic paste rather than chopping my own and rip open bags of stir-fry vegetable packets into pans. If something goes wrong and it tastes bad it's annoying, because then I have to punishingly make my way through the same meal every night for days on end. Beef stir-fry turned chewy from overcooking. A veggie chilli with way too much cumin.

It wasn't like this when it was his appetite I was filling. After the supermarket I'd go to the market stalls to get okra or date syrup or whatever fancy ingredient I couldn't find on the shelves. There would be a sauce on the side for dipping. I'd fry chicken legs in a pan to get the skin crisp on the outside of the meat before it went in the oven.

I remember when I was younger, maybe twelve or so, watching *The Jonathan Ross Show* with Mum. Teri Hatcher from *Desperate Housewives* was on it to talk about her new book, *Burnt Toast*. She told a story about how when she first had kids, if she burned the toast she would always just scrape off the charred bits and eat the toast, giving her kids the golden, tastier slices. For her this was a good metaphor for her general lack of appreciation of herself, always thinking she deserved less than those around her.

I looked over at my mum and she knocked her head back as though hit in the face with something she didn't like. 'Sounds like she's been smoking too much pot.'

At the time I laughed along because I was still at that age when you think everything your parents say is right. Plus, Teri's words sounded too earnest and American to me. Why was she labouring this metaphor so much? Just bin the toast!

But I feel as though I've been eating burnt toast for a while now. Feeding myself in a way that's functional rather than luxurious because my enjoyment of food doesn't seem worth the time it would take to make it. I think instead of all the things I could do but don't do with that time: washing clothes, replying to emails, doing an ab workout on YouTube.

It's a Friday in July and it's hot enough outside that I can feel sweat rolling down my back. I've been covering shifts at an online newspaper for the past few weeks because freelancing has dried up. The office is so far from my house that I have to leave at a time when you can still see students with mullets and slit eyebrows linking arms on their way home from parties. It's roasting down here on the Underground and it's only getting hotter because the energy from the friction of train brakes and human bodies cannot escape. There aren't enough ventilation shafts so the heat is absorbed by the walls and earth beneath us. Slowly cooking us all up like ingredients in a stew.

Inside the office I stare at the kettle until my eyes gum over and all I see is smudges. I hope it will take longer than usual to boil so I can avoid beginning work for as long as possible. But then there's the click and rush of bubbles and I walk towards my desk, where I've already been sent three news stories to rewrite. In order to not get done for copyright you have to take the story and tell it in a different way. I find the most efficient way is to take the end of a sentence and put it at the beginning.

'*Married at First Sight* star Mark Strayed saved a woman from "drowning" after she was dragged by a strong current while out canoeing' turns into: 'While canoeing, *Married at First Sight* star Mark Strayed saves a woman from "drowning" in a strong current.'

Sometimes I think about the readers, how disappointed they will be by each article they click open. Nothing but an Instagram post written up as an exclusive. The small pop of intrigue swelling and then bursting, searching for something else to fill the space.

At lunchtime everyone eats jacket potatoes they bought from the canteen hunched over their desks. Messaging each other on Slack when they could just lean over and chat to each other, given how near they're sitting. Wrist-support mouse mats and lumbar pillows for bodies breaking from the strain of doing nothing. I head out with Ruchira, who's working in an office down the road. We wander around Boots for forty-five minutes. I buy a nude nail polish from OPI called Maintaining My Sand-ity. Forget to buy the disposable razors I came in to get. Come back to the office and someone put the wrong member of K-pop band on a story and now their fans are doxxing her Twitter account, but it's OK because someone else will have fucked up much worse than her tomorrow. I try to concentrate because now I have a profile to write where I have to try to get an actor to say something juicy about politics or Harvey Weinstein rather than anything remotely to do with the TV series they're promoting.

Later everyone's getting ready to head to the pub where there will be free drinks as some sort of consolation prize for the early-onset arthritis we'll get from sitting at a desk every day. I think of the sour twinge of wine on my tongue. People telling stories of celebrities they met on the job who turned out to be really nice, or the same but they were really rude. Someone saying: 'God, at the moment it just feels like everyone's getting married!' as though that isn't a very normal thing to experience in your early thirties.

'I might actually just go home,' I say to no one in particular.

The idea feels like a revelation and the more time that passes since I said it, the more I realise I want it. Starfished alone over my clean sheets. My laptop playing a slow-paced drama that follows a middle-class family who all fall out on holiday, or something.

Things can happen without you there and you will miss out. But it might give you the strength to be fully there for something else that happens another day.

'What you going to do?' asks one of the editors, wrapping herself up in a long woolly scarf.

'Watch stuff, I think,' I say, feeling out my mood as I speak. 'Might cook something.'

'Make pasta,' she says, walking away from the desk. 'I made ravioli from scratch the other night and it changed my life.'

I press a fork slowly through the big cylinder of ricotta and watch as it crumbles either side of the metal. It's nice stuff, or it should be because I got it at a cheese shop on the way home. One with tasting samples on toothpicks, which I ate with an exaggeratedly confused face so they would think I was weighing up whether or not to purchase. I'm making ravioli like the editor recommended. The recipe asks for mint, and lemon zest, which I never normally bother with because of the way it gets all impossibly stuck inside the grater, but this time I try it, bitter citrus coating the air even when the lemon's back in the fridge. I was hesitant about making the pasta from scratch but it's much easier than I thought. When I'm finished rolling the dough it comes out smooth and thin like a cut of fabric. I keep having to fight against the temptation to rush. To fill this process with more things – say, an educational podcast about space landings or ringing Mum like she asked me to. To start doing two things at once, maybe three if I reorder those bath salts off Amazon I was thinking about. Washing up as I go rather than just leaning over the pan. But each time I stop myself because I read something the other day that convinced me to change how I'm living.

Elizabeth Gilbert's bestseller *Eat Pray Love* follows the author as she travels from Italy to India to Indonesia in an attempt to find herself after a nasty and expensive divorce. There's a scene in the book where she's speaking to her Italian friend called, ridiculously, Luca Spaghetti, about the stereotype that Americans go on holiday and don't know how to relax. She asks him if Italians ever experience this and he laughs so much he nearly crashes his motorbike into a fountain.

'Oh, no!' he said. 'We are the masters of *bel far niente*.'

Which means 'the beauty of doing nothing'. One afternoon, while sitting in a patch of sunlight, reading an Italian newspaper and eating food with her fingers, Gilbert reaches this blissful state. That is until, like it so often does, her guilt alarm goes off and she hears her husband's voice in her head asking if she really ended their marriage just for this – peace and quiet and a couple of sprigs of asparagus.

But these small moments are often what make life worth living. That's what Gilbert realises as she looks up, addresses her ex-husband as if he were sitting on that balcony with her:

> 'First of all,' I said, 'I'm very sorry, but this isn't your business anymore. And secondly, to answer your question . . . *yes*.'

I try to let myself have *bel far niente* too, to not think I have to earn pleasure, but that I just get to pursue it by virtue of breathing in and out. So I load up *A Star Is Born*, which I haven't seen because I always find that when too many people tell me something is good I start feeling as though there's no point in me seeing it, as though I've already witnessed its greatness, or I'm not needed to confirm it. I take the bowl of pasta to bed with me even though that's kind of a disgusting thing to do. And I say to myself that I won't get up and clean these plates when I'm finished with them, or get annoyed at myself if in the morning the room smells of baked things because, like I promised myself on that first night I moved in here, I'm going to try to live in this room like he lived in ours, like it doesn't matter where things land.

Most things that take a long time to make can be enjoyed for a long time too. Like a book with many pages or a big house. But food isn't like that. What takes hours is gone in a moment. Knowing that I took all that time just for a few minutes of pleasure – my pleasure – well, it shows how deserving I think the person eating it is. I've always known how to say I love you with food, and by making this food, and making the effort to do all the parts of the recipe that are normally quite boring and time-consuming, I was saying 'I love you' to myself.

I love you.

I love you.

I love you.

I will try to make sure I do for the rest of my life.

28

'How's Joe?' I ask Jonny when we're out for a drink together as summer is drawing to a close.

He shakes his head. 'Haven't spoken to him in months.
I tried ringing the other day, but he didn't pick up.'

Hearing this doesn't comfort me in the way it might
have once. I don't need Joe's sadness in order to be happy
anymore. I have worked out how to be happy all on my
own.

I almost feel lucky that I got to be the one who was left.
That way I'm allowed to become a hero. I get a dating
column in *Vogue* and people squeeze my arm and say, 'If
he could see you now,' because all of my successes are
proof he made a mistake. If he does well it means he's
stuck up and thinks he's better than me. Friends pick me
for parties over him because I'm the victim of his actions.
I can call him a dick and mention comments he's made
completely out of context in order to get sympathy. Like
when I tell people he said, 'You're almost as good looking as me now,' when I got my hair cut into a bob and I
made out he was being serious and not making a joke. I
can listen to Taylor Swift's 'We Are Never Ever Getting
Back Together' at full volume and know that it's women
like me she's written it for. There's no uncertainty with
me because I had no choice in the relationship ending.

But he had to leave and face the weight of his decision, which means he'll always wonder if it was the right thing to do.

Where is he?

I go to check his Instagram but when I type his name into the search bar his account doesn't come up. I delete the letters and type it out again, knowing already that I spelled it right. I assume he's blocked me, but then a friend says he's deleted all his social media. I feel so powerless, not being able to check on him, like when you're small and someone stretches out their arm and puts their palm on your head so that when you try to fight them you can't reach far enough to hit them with your arms. *I just want to know if he's doing OK*, I think. *I don't hate him anymore.* But you can't argue with 'This page does not exist.'

I go back home to Leeds for a few weeks. Mum and Dad take me to the cinema and then we get back into the car because the restaurant is a bit further out of town. The heating blasts out of the car so hard I can feel it drying out the surface of my skin. In the front Dad chews on boiled sweets and brakes heavily at each set of traffic lights, while Mum clings nervously onto that handle that sits above the doors.

We're heading to my parents' favourite Indian restaurant. Whenever we go for a curry anywhere else my parents always say, 'It's just not the same, is it?' And when they bring other people here they look at them with a slightly cheeky facial expression and say: 'It's a bit rough around the edges.'

To which someone always adds, 'Food's better that way.' Everyone feeling very pleased with themselves at how little they mind the strip lighting. Or the fact that if you look into the kitchen you can often see the chef rubbing off splotches of sauce from the plates with his fingers that he licked seconds earlier.

My dad leans back into his chair and sighs, begins searching the pockets of his green anorak. He likes to cut out reviews from the newspapers so that after the film he can read them with his Cobra. Then he orders for the table because it's a weird thing he does. I don't mind. I get bored deciphering between twenty different slight alterations of the vague description: 'Mild curry fried with onions and spices.' But I remember Joe being aghast that he was denied from adding a lamb rogan josh onto the order because my dad claimed that it would be too greasy.

The food arrives and I tear off some naan and dip it into the bowl of chicken jalfrezi. I'm a messy eater so by the time I'm finished the tablecloth is sodden with stains. I'm lucky I've got away with this for so long. Part of it is my parents not caring for elbows off the table or waiting for everyone else before starting to eat. Another part of it is that Joe let me get away with it too. In fact, he loved the way I ate. Called me a mucky pup. Did funny impressions of the way I hold my knife and fork in my fists like a toddler. So I became grosser around him, my chin sticky with sauce.

It wasn't just eating. When we were together I shifted to encompass him in a thousand tiny ways.

- I realise that you don't need that much toothpaste on the toothbrush.
- That aubergines need a low heat to cook if you want them to taste nice.
- Less stuff in a house looks better than more.
- There's no point spending all day working because after a while it just stops being productive and you'd be better off getting a long, fulfilling rest and then starting up again tomorrow.
- Don't pick spots because you're only pressing dirt into your pores.
- I stop and look at the properties in the estate agent's window.
- I'm politer to my parents.
- Don't try to explain your perspective when you're drunk to another drunk person.
- Even if someone's telling you you're wrong, this might not be the case and they might just be really good at persuading you to see things in a way that benefits them.
- Don't try to fix other people's problems for them.
- I'm not very good at cooking.
- How to write better.
- That I'll never do housework for a man ever again.
- You have to take control sometimes because it doesn't make it easier that you're easy-going, it

makes it tiring for other people to always have to take charge.

Knowing I've learned all these lessons reassures me because I know that even if we've reached the end, I can't ever forget him, because how can you forget something that's in the way you move, talk, breathe?

My mum doesn't like it when I say stuff like this. She thinks it's unfeminist. And I know the better story is the one where you're liberated on your own. But I don't think I would be this way now if it wasn't for him. I was hurt when he left because I didn't know who I was going to be when this person, who contributed so much to my composition as a human, disappeared. What I didn't realise is that he taught me all the lessons and I know them off by heart without him now. So, as much as I'm glad that he made me who I am, I'm glad that I've been left alone to be her too.

29

Mum takes me to see Granny, who is still in hospital. On the way we pass through Roundhay, a place wealthy enough to have a high street filled with 'eateries' and those shops that only sell expensive but useless tat. Love-heart door charms carved out of driftwood. Cake knives with 'Life is but a piece of cake' written on them in swirled script. It doesn't seem like anyone ever goes in and I always wonder how they sell enough to stay open. We drive past large Victorian terraced houses, tennis courts, green parkland – it's a place where GPs and lawyers live for comfort and quick access to the city centre. Down one of the roads is Mary's old house. Mary, the woman Grandpa was briefly engaged to before Granny. He met her at the rugby club when she came to watch his team play. He broke it off with her when he saw Granny at a friend's birthday party, laughing in the corner with a glass of wine. Black hair with a shock of white running through it. So beautiful she belonged in tobacco ads, or Hitchcock films, screaming, 'Don't kill me!'

I never knew about Mary when I was little. Grandpa and Granny fitted together so perfectly I never imagined there could have been someone else. But when Grandpa started to lose his mind to dementia he would often talk about old girlfriends he had. Pointing out of the car window at Mary's house so that I recognise it even now. I suppose he didn't so much miss Mary as the feeling of youth and vitality he had when he was with her. Granny stayed long enough to outlast that feeling. To the point in love where all mystery goes and you're watching them being helped down steps. Not being able to hear even with hearing aids in.

I'm sure Grandpa never loved Mary the way he loved Granny. I think whatever he felt stopped when he saw the love he was capable of with Granny. But his belief in what they had didn't wane just because he stopped seeing her. She just sat at the back of his mind until the movement of the everyday was rotted away by disease, and then Grandpa's mind made space for her at the front. So that he could remember what it felt like to blow someone away.

In Graham Greene's novel *The End of the Affair*, a woman loves a man and a man loves a woman. But she won't leave her husband for him. He's angry, so she reassures him, 'You needn't be so scared. Love doesn't end. Just because we don't see each other.'

She rings him the next day and adds, 'People go on loving God, don't they, all their lives without seeing Him?'

Perhaps Joe and I can carry on loving each other, even when miles of air and experience separate us. Not in the way of wanting to wake up in the same bed. Or needing to speak to each other when something goes wrong. But as a quiet love that endures out of respect for the impact he had on my life.

Perhaps one day this love will come out of me again, like it came out of Grandpa. My husband will be driving me to hospital for an MRI and I will point out of the window as we pass the Tottenham flat that Joe and I used to rent and my husband will humour my story because he will know I'm ill. I will tell my husband about how Joe slept with his face flat against the mattress, arms bolted straight next to him, in a position no one else would find comfortable. His big shark mouth. His toes that were long and thin like fingers.

I know that Joe never forgot his girlfriend before me even though she moved all the way to South America. It seemed like he had for a while, but then she came back. We were holding hands after leaving the cinema. She messaged him on Facebook saying that she found a box of photos from when they went travelling together. One showed a chimpanzee on his back. In another he's in a hammock reading a book. She's tanned and wears little blue dangling earrings. They climbed up volcanos together in the blue of morning. Ate noodles on the pavement while the endless limbs of passers-by threatened to push the paper plates out of their hands. He asked if she wanted to get a drink with him, but she ignored the message. His eyes misted up. 'We were both so *happy* back then.'

I let go of his hand. 'I'm jealous that you two got to do all that fun stuff together and we get gas bills and the Odeon.'

He looked tired before he'd even started talking but he knew he had to fix what he'd done. 'What we have is so much more important than a gap year,' he said. 'Jobs, hoovering, buying Tupperware – we are making it work. To me, that's the most romantic thing in the world.'

I believed him when he said it, but then a month or so later came 'I want to be on my own.'

Perhaps no one ever forgets anyone. We keep parts of them inside us forever and they come out in the moments we need them. Like ghosts who can't find their way to the afterlife.

30

My friend Hannah rings me crying a few days before Christmas. Her boyfriend just ended it with her and she's called to tell me what happened.

'It came out of nowhere,' she says, almost out of breath. 'We'd just had such a good time in Majorca – there was, like, one argument about him driving a motorbike when he was pissed, but aside from that we were great. Anyway, we get back and he's at mine and he's like, "I need to work on me. You can do better than I can give right now." Blah blah blah.'

When Joe ended it almost a year and a half ago now, I said it came out of nowhere too. And though I thought this was the truth, deep down I knew he was going to leave. I felt it in the soft, gelatinous marrow of my bones. Like how you can sense someone staring at you even when they're not in your eyeline, or the way animals run off when a storm is on the way. I had to, because otherwise how did I know to go to so much effort to see the opposite?

He told me he wasn't happy and I told his sister to get in contact with him because he was having problems with work or friends or family, not even thinking for a moment that the issue could be me. I felt a bit hurt that he didn't feel he could talk to me about his problems, but I assumed this was because I'm not the best at giving advice. He went to his mum's house for two weeks for a change of scenery and ended up staying much longer than planned. I suggested we move to a place where he didn't flinch every time he walked into a shared space, somewhere he actually liked – maybe a flat with just us two? But he wouldn't have a proper conversation with me about it. 'Shall we just stay on here for another year then?' I asked and he'd say, 'I'm tired, can we talk about this another time?' He gave similar responses when I tried to discuss going on holiday or asked if we were still off to spend Christmas with his dad. I didn't see his evasiveness as a sign of waning commitment but just him being lazy. I thought the same when I did all the food shopping and cooking for a month even though it was a clear sign that he'd stopped caring what I thought of his behaviour, hoping I'd step in and end it so he didn't have to.

I understand these events now for what they were: evidence of him slowly drawing away. There's one night in particular that I see from an entirely new perspective now that I've had so much time to think. I look at it and wonder how I misunderstood what I saw.

'Fucking hell,' I said, as I walked with you into our room holding my nose. 'It *stinks* in here.'

The bedroom opened out onto the front garden where our bins lived. The council hadn't taken them for two weeks so there were bags piled up outside with translucent white maggots crawling all over them, fat with the debris of our dinners. Mostly I blamed Danny; he was always throwing out whole packs of mince meat, having let them exceed their sell-by date. The bin bags he bought from ALDI were thin as tissue paper so were easily invaded. It was so hot that the weather had gently slow-roasted the contents so that the sweet, stale stink had leaked through the cracks in our window and clouded up the whole room like nuclear waste.

'Can you not smell it?' I asked you, your body now lolled face-down on the mattress, choosing to play Sleeping Lions like a school kid rather than talking to me. We'd been drinking all day, you more than me, and you'd stopped making sense during the last third of the bus journey home. 'I think we're going to have to re-bag all the rubbish and then drop it in the neighbours' bins. Moll did it last time so it's our turn. We don't have to do it now, but we need to do it before –'

You put your palm up like a stop signal.

'Are you listening, babe?' I nudged you on the bum with my foot. Bent down to look at you. There was dribble stringing out of one side of your lip. Your eyes slightly opened so that I could see your retinas vibrating back and forth. 'Babe?'

I slumped down onto the bed, almost giving up on you. All those beers and no water in direct sunlight meant the hangover was coming for me earlier than I would have liked. I could feel my jelly-like brain pushing against the front of my skull as if trying to escape the body that was hurting it so much. Other parts of me were numb. I got up and started to undress, knocking a leg hard into the chest of drawers, which was painful but not as much as the purple bruise the next day suggested it should have been.

'Babe?' I asked, louder, and you sat up furiously, quickly.

'I don't give a shit,' you mumbled. 'If you don't like it, why don't you just end it then? Just fucking call it a day if it's that big a deal.'

I laughed at the dramatic response.

'Did you just dump me over the smell of the bins?'

'Yeah, it's fucking over,' you replied, before flopping back down onto the mattress hard enough that you could hear the squeaks of the springs from inside it.

I didn't take what you were saying to me seriously. I looked at your furrowed brow, all wrinkled up like a map of the roads out of a city, the slightly clenched outline of your hand, and all I could think of was how adorable you looked. Your anger reminded me of a toddler's, when they're screaming and stamping and they're trying to scare you but it doesn't work because they've still got those chubby elastic-band wrists and those apple cheeks. You were too naturally kind to be angry. Too handsome for it. It didn't suit you.

'All right, Justin Bieber,' I said, which I often called you when you were in one of these moods because you reminded me of a spoilt pop diva. How they often become petty and ridiculous, asking for their coffee to be a few degrees warmer, complaining about the lack of foam.

'Leave me alone,' you said, turning away from me to face the other direction.

'You're dumping me over bin smell?' I asked one last time, and you didn't reply. I was already laughing in my head about how I'd bring up what you said over breakfast. 'How does it feel to be a single man?' I'd say, because it was so funny to me that you would end it with me over something so petty, or that you would end it with me at all.

Thinking back to that moment in the room, there must have been some truth to it. I guess he was planning on ending it for a while and in his drunken haze mistook bin smell as a good enough excuse.

'But you guys were getting on so well,' I say to Hannah, even though I don't believe this is true. They've probably stopped having sex, or maybe he's found someone else. But I don't say that because it's too early for her to be able to bear the truth. It's much easier to pretend there was no logic to any of it – that absolves us of the part we played. Makes the break-up seem part of this illogical scheme that we had no control over. But when as much time has passed for her as it has for me and she looks back at this moment she'll see that it was always coming from somewhere.

31

'It's actually getting quite serious,' Mum tells me over FaceTime that spring. 'They think if the virus keeps spreading they'll have to quarantine the whole country.'

'There's like two cases, relax,' I tell her, and then bring my hands up to my chest so they become little T-Rex arms because my brother and I always say Mum's like the hysterical T-Rex from *Toy Story*. The one that freaks out when they get Andy's birthday wrong or when he hears that the family might be buying a new dinosaur toy to replace him.

But then I see the news where there are heat maps of the country that show high infection rates of COVID-19 flared up in red and there are videos of people who've contracted it telling reporters that it feels like there are icicles in their lungs when they breathe. That's when I stop thinking it's one of Mum's 'things' and book a train back to Leeds so at least I'll have access to a garden during lockdown.

'We can't hear you, sorry, it's cut off, I can't – I can't –' It's Vicky's turn to ask questions on the Zoom quiz, but her connection is lagging. The time lapses between her movements so that she flashes through space. One second she's leaning towards the screen with one finger outstretched and the next she's bent over the side of the sofa to reach a plug. We can hear her asking us if it's getting any better but her mouth remains dropped open.

Something flickers again and she snatches back inside of herself. 'That better?' she asks and, after we nod, begins: '*I said*: who has adopted more kids? Madonna or Angelina Jolie?'

Mum and I spend every evening after dinner staying up late watching *Gomorrah*, an incredibly violent drama about the mafia in Naples. We become so used to the tropes of the show that we can pick out who is going to get killed by the end of each episode. The nervy account-ant perhaps? The girlfriend who's having an affair?

This time it's the boss's son's driver. He gets his dick chopped off and is left to bleed to death.

Dad's no longer having white wine spritzers like he usu-ally does every night, but rather a glass of wine followed by a glass of fizzy water. 'Is that a deconstructed white wine spritzer?' I ask him, raising my eyebrows.

'No,' he says. 'I'm just worried I'm becoming an alcoholic.'

At dinner we play this fun game we made up called Guess the Tupperware. It started one evening when Dad claimed, with genuine pride and admiration, 'Your mother has a great eye for the right-sized box for left-overs.' So now when she heads off to get the Tupperware from the drawer, Dad and I begin a drumroll. It starts off slow but as she approaches we get louder, until we're banging on the table like we are in the pub watching a football cup final.

She tries to pack all the food away but this time she's misjudged it; the carbonara needs an additional, slightly smaller box. And in response Dad and I hurl insults at her like lunatics.

They discharge Granny from hospital because they say she's better, which seems unlikely because she's been there nearly a year and nothing's changed about her condition. They must need the beds for COVID-19 patients. She goes into a home near Aunty Sally's house but no one's allowed to see her. They put up a painting of her and Grandpa's house but she misses home so much she asks them to take it down. Mum talks to her on the phone every day but she's going deaf. Even when Mum's at the other side of the house I can hear her shouting, 'ARE YOU EATING?' into the receiver.

After speaking to Granny Mum sits in bed scrolling on her iPad reading the *Guardian* news website even though she already read the paper copy this morning.

'What more could you possibly need to know?' I ask.

'Did you know a shipment of six million chickpeas has gone missing in Washington?'

Mum keeps cutting up her clothes and weaving the pieces of them into a rag rug. She comes into my room to show me when she's finished. Pink, blue, black and neon orange spliced up into jagged geometric patterns. 'I started this before 9/11!' she screams jubilantly. 'That's something!'

The writing shifts I'm covering at the moment start at 9 a.m. and initially I planned to use the time I would spend commuting writing or exercising before they began. But instead, I wake up each day at five minutes past nine, reach over with my left hand, which instinctively can find the mouse pad without me opening my eyes, and press it so that on Slack it will say I'm online.

Mum comes and sits on the end of my bed one morning and I can sense right away that something bad has happened. 'Granny's gone,' she says, her face crumpling into itself like tissue paper. I wrap my arms around her and her tears make her body wobble like a boat caught on a big wave.

We find a way to have a funeral service in the garden with six family members. But we're not allowed to hug, so from across the grass we face each other with these huge clown smiles. The coffin comes out of the hearse and it's so small it's weird to think she's in there all on her own. The next-door neighbour is a vicar and she comes over to officiate. She tells a story about how her kids were always playing football on the street and when they kept using Granny's hedge as a goal Granny didn't tell them to stop, she just smiled and waved from the kitchen window. We had wanted a proper funeral in a church, but it's actually nice saying bye to her here in the place where we knew her best. Where she would help me down from climbing trees when I only realised I was scared of heights on the way down, slipping me £10 notes, saying, 'Annie is fine just how she is,' when Mum went into a meltdown over my nose piercing.

It's May and you're allowed to meet one person outside now. Marisa gets her parents to drop her off at the beach and I steal a bottle of wine from the fridge and walk to meet her. So long has passed since we've seen anyone it feels like a night out, so she's in heeled boots and I've got fake eyelashes on. I ask her how she's doing since she broke things off with her ex and she says she's feeling better. The company she works for offers four sessions of therapy for free and they've made a big difference.

'At the end of our last session I was saying to him, "I feel like a completely different person," and he said, "Sometimes you've got to have a breakdown to have a breakthrough." I actually started crying.'

I used to hate the idea that I might learn from heartbreak. Comments like 'What doesn't kill you only makes you stronger,' and 'We're only given as much as the heart can endure,' would enrage me. I'd have the same reaction when people spoke about what they'd learned from the coronavirus: 'I'll never take hugs for granted again,' they'd say, or 'It just goes to show who is important in your life.' What they said was akin to telling me that all the pain I was feeling was justified. That I should somehow be grateful for it even as it tore me apart.

* * *

You stopped going into the barber's and bought an electric razor to shave your head with instead. We used to joke about how badly we fought when I helped you with the back. 'Do we dare?' one of us would ask. Hoping that if we acknowledged how much of a conflict point it was before starting it might make us more resistant to letting it get that bad in the first place. If you could see it coming, surely then we could move out of the way? But we always followed the same path and smacked into each other's bodies because of it.

'Is it straight?' you asked afterwards, your words a challenge, like a teacher talking to a pupil they know hasn't read the question properly.

I hated your tone. But rather than rise to it, I could have thought about why you might be speaking to me that way: because you care about your appearance and know if something goes wrong you will feel less confident about yourself. I could have calmly assured you. 'I promise, it looks great, would you like me to take a picture so you can see?'

But saying that would have been so hard for me. I didn't want to have to persuade you to see that I was competent. I thought you should see that by virtue of knowing me. So I just replied: 'Why don't you have a go yourself if you think I can't do it?'

I was walking back to the sofa when I heard you say: 'Can you just —'

Before you could finish talking, I spun around and shouted: 'You haven't even said thank you. In fact, you never say thank you. You haven't said thank you in weeks.'

I thought that would shut you up because you liked to see yourself as a polite person. Saying 'thank you' for each single action the corner shop did when serving you. Scanning the item, *thank you*. Telling you the price, *thank you*. Taking the money from you, *thank you*. Handing you back the item, *thank you*. I gambled that drawing attention to your lack of manners would be enough to eke out an apology. Not this time. 'It's not a big deal,' you said. 'Obviously I appreciate the help.'

Again, I could have recognised that your response wasn't meant to be dismissive, rather it was meant to encourage me to see that there was nothing to worry about. I could have acknowledged that the thank-you accusation was a complete exaggeration. I could have told you initially that I was too tired to help because I'd had a long day and was feeling particularly sensitive. I could have taken responsibility for the way me doing so much for you meant it was easier for you to do nothing at all. Tracked the ways in which my challenges had provoked the argument further. Walked away, saying, like they recommend in *Men Are from Mars, Women Are from Venus*: 'I don't like the way you are talking to me. Please stop,' or 'This is not the way I wanted to have this conversation. Let's start over.' I might even have done what you did outside King's Cross station, pulling you to the side and telling you, 'I want to be on my own.' But I didn't. I looked at you and thought, with full sincerity, *I want to fucking kill you.* I watched you sitting on your stupid chair. All the hairs scattered around you on the tiles.

'Are you going to sweep that up?' I asked, knowing that you hate being told to do things right before you actually do them.

'Obviously,' you said, spitting the word out at me like chewing gum onto a pavement.

I never feel that angry anymore. If someone does something I disagree with, like uses the last of my margarine when they know I like toast in the morning, or turns the oven off when I was warming it up ready to put something in it, I don't shout. I think about why they might have thought they could do that. Maybe they were worried about the house burning down. Maybe they thought I was finished. I follow the thought patterns until the red glow eases away and I can fall asleep on the pillow at night without gritting my teeth.

I'm still not sure if you learn anything from pain, though I do think you learn from what you do to get away from the pain. Finding ways to process your emotions better. Learning who you can rely on. No longer positioning your sense of self around another person. Months after lockdown first started, I'm like one of those people who comes off a TV survival show, turns to the camera and says, 'Now I know I can get through anything.'

32

'He's moved to Lowestoft. He's working as a youth worker now, I think.'

I finally find someone who knows where Joe is, what his life has become. They shrug their shoulders when they tell me, because when people leave the city to go somewhere quiet it's almost always read as a failure. But I know right away that Lowestoft means Joe's really happy. He always tried to sell the idea of living there to me. Said we could spend balmy evenings walking down the pier with polythene cups of cockles, turning to each other every time to say, 'They taste like the ocean.' There was an empty shop for sale on the high street and he said we should open a deli. One that sold expensive pasta shells and shut early. How there would be long evenings on the beach digging holes in the sand, watching as the tide smoothed them over. Heading to the arcade to shoot dinosaurs together on big plastic guns until our thumbs cramped up.

'He's talking about moving to Suffolk again,' I'd say to Moll, laughing. Because to me it was always a fantasy, like a character in a book who's always talking about running away but you know they never will. Like in *Revolutionary Road* where they're always talking about Paris and you know they're not going to make it. Or in *Death of a Salesman* when Willy wants to start that business. It didn't fit with my idea of who we were as a couple. He was always so good with people, I didn't know why he'd want to waste away his youth picking up wet tennis balls and throwing them for other people's dogs. I wanted him to start writing film scripts or something, apply for grants.

As we reached our fifth year together, work had started going better for me. Editors asked me to write things without me having to ask first. I went into offices and when they made me rewrite news stories I didn't think about how pointless it was, only at how much faster I was getting at sending in copy. I was invited to a book launch and complained about the bad wine and then thought to myself, *Wow, I'm the sort of person who goes to book launches and complains about the bad wine.* I called myself a journalist without saying 'sort of' first. People passed on their cousins' and younger siblings' contact details to me so that I could give them advice about how to get into the field. While people were talking, I thought of provocative questions to ask even if I already knew the answers. I'd become a 'success'.

It wasn't supposed to be like this. It was supposed to be him who made it. Or we were meant to do it together, like a plant whose stem broke into two halves that blossomed in different directions. The sort of famous couple who would come home from stressful days to collapse on velvet armchairs and bitch about their friend's one-man show being solipsistic. But he started to see these

338

dreams for what they were: fragile, meaningless. More about what other people saw than what we felt. He carried on with his job, which was easy enough to allow him to listen to podcasts through his headphones without anyone telling him off. On weekends he spent all his money forgetting about work.

I remember once we were walking in a park near our house. Cherry blossoms gathering like cotton candy on the trees. A tower block with clothes hanging out of it like Tibetan prayer flags blowing in the soft breeze. 'I was reading this thing about Tom Hardy the other day. He was saying that he likes being a dad more than anything, might just pack it in and be a house husband. I'd love to do that.'

'Do what?' I asked, knowing I didn't like what you were saying already.

'Have a simple life.'

'I think I'd want more things than that,' I said. 'I reckon you'd get bored. You're so talented, there's so much you could do.'

I never thought I'd be the sort of woman who wanted a career man. It was against my politics to require something so traditional. At university I wanted to get 'Never Work!' tattooed below my kneecap. The slogan was what situationist thinker Guy Debord scratched on the wall of the upmarket Rue de Seine in Paris. It later became popular during the 1968 anti-capitalist, anti-imperialist student strikes that swept across the city, things I was desperate to align myself with. I listened to a podcast and laughed when in a conversation about whether or not they'd go out with someone who worked at McDonald's, one of the guests said she'd only agree if they were the branch manager or looking to move up the company.

'I'd rather just go out with someone who works at Maccy's,' I said to you. 'Branch manager? They'd be such a neek.'

But what I thought I believed and what I did believe came to be at odds. I hated that he didn't have a career. Societal norms ventriloquised my body so that I was saying things I didn't know I cared about. I sent him applications for jobs he should apply for, asked him about funding for degrees he could do.

He hated how I pushed him, spending longer and longer at his dad's house in Suffolk, eating scampi and chips on the beach, sand gritting between his teeth. No phone reception to reply to me.

The problem wasn't him. The problem is that when you idolise men and they prove themselves to be normal, human, you're disappointed. I see now that I had built him up beyond something that he wanted to be. And now he was struggling, and I didn't like it because he was meant to be a god.

As Simone de Beauvoir says, '[Men] would not seem like dwarfs if they were not required to be giants.'

I picture him now in Suffolk, gazing into the blurring line at the end of the sea where the world looks like it stops. Throwing the last of his chips to the gulls gathering at his feet. Then I think of my life, staying up late to read books I can't put down. Going to galleries and taking pictures of the words by the paintings because it's an idea I want to think about more. I have all this energy now just from leaving him alone. And he's no longer tired because he can do as little as he wants without someone persuading him to do more.

Releasing each other might have been our greatest act of love.

33

I had a lot of fantasies about how I would look when I bumped into Joe again. None of them included him catching me hiding behind my neighbour's hedge. Nor did they dress me in dungarees with a big ink stain on the pocket or with a spot high up by my eye that's so swollen it's shifted the structure of my face out of balance. But that's how it is happening now on this warm evening in June a few weeks into my return to London.

'Did you just try to run away?' Joe asks as he walks up the street towards me, and I try to answer him but then I can't really explain why I acted like that. It's like this moment is such a big deal for me that it's wiped all my thoughts away until all that's left are blanks. It always surprises me how unshocking shock is. There's no action in it, no bite. For something that's meant to shake the core of your existence, it barely feels like anything.

'I think so,' I say, laughing.

His jaw tightens. 'Yeesh, that bad, is it?'

I try to think of something to say in response. But the words just cyclone around my brain. Coming apart until they're just letters. All of them moving so fast I'm struggling to put them back into an order that makes sense.

'How're your parents?' he asks, changing the subject to something we might both do better at.

'Same as always. They're thinking of installing a new shower even though the one they've got works fine. Your sister?' I ask, hoping his response will give me a bit of time to compose myself. But he answers almost instantly with something about the dog and it's already my turn to talk again because he's just asked me how work is going.

'Good, actually. I was on Radio 4 the other day.'

'That's cool.'

He brings his tobacco out of his pocket and goes to roll from it, but then stops and looks at his hands. 'God, why am I shaking so much?'

I can see that he's trying to find his way back to me. Looking for the right angle to settle on like someone patting grass, feeling out the best place to sit down for a picnic. I think about holding my hand out too so that he can see that mine are trembling just as much as his. But the end of the road is there before I can work up the courage to act, so instead I just ask him where he's headed.

'Just off to see some mates in the park. You?'

'Having dinner with my brother.'

'Well, send him my best,' he replies, hugging me and then walking to the middle of the road where he waits for a white van to pass. 'See you soon,' he says from the other side, and he shrugs when after a couple of seconds he realises his mistake. 'Or I guess I won't.'

While he was in front of me I couldn't process much. It all seemed to happen so quickly, as though we were on a TV running on fast-forward. But as I turn left, away from the road he carried straight on to, all my reactions settle down on me one by one until I feel as though I'm buried under them.

He looked really good.

So tanned that all the hairs on his arms and the tips of his eyelashes had bleached white. He was wearing clothes I didn't recognise again. Some really nice wool trousers that were worth how much he must be baking in them. A thin gold chain. Three-day-old stubble over his jaw. He looked more laid-back than usual, like someone who knows he doesn't need to impress people but can just wait for them to impress him in return.

Why did I say that about Radio 4?

It was so obvious I was trying to show off.

And why am I even showing off in front of him anymore? I don't need to prove myself. His reaction shouldn't be the arbiter of my success.

I can't believe I actually tried to run away. Do I think I'm in a Jennifer Aniston rom-com or something?

I remember once Aunty Sally telling me about bumping into an ex-boyfriend of hers. She said he was wearing these white cowboy boots. 'I was surprised because the guy I was in a relationship with would never have worn white cowboy boots. It just made it so clear how much we'd drifted.'

Who's he meeting in the park? He didn't say their names, which makes me think they're people I don't know. Women I might not know.

What upsets me the most, though, is how I don't care as much as I thought I would. And how he doesn't care even more than that. I guess because we don't know each other anymore. We asked questions you should ask and responded to the answers politely in the way I do when I'm talking to family members I don't like. When we hugged my chin bashed against his shoulder as though we've spent so long orienting around other bodies we've forgotten how these two are meant to slot together. I told myself there was too much of him in me and me in him for us to ever fully forget each other. But there we were, walking at different paces, heading in different directions. He's handed me back my arm and my leg and in return I've given him back the same. What's left in the end? Not even the charred ground after a volcano, the ruin of a battlefield, just empty sentences and good manners. What hurts more than missing him is realising I no longer do.

Later, at my brother's, when I've had a glass of wine and some food, and inside my stomach that same wine has been soaked up with more food, I start to feel a bit different. What would have happened if it had gone well? If we'd asked better questions that could help us see that we both still agree about everything. Like how it's funny that people keep complaining about the Tube-worker strikes when pissing people off is the whole point of protest because it shows how essential your services are. What if I had looked ridiculously gorgeous or was holding hands with some guy he kind of knows? Not 'knows' in the sense that I would've done something wrong in going there, but enough that it would sting, like they were in the same year at school or he's a friend of a friend. One who looks like Arsenal's Héctor Bellerín or Cillian Murphy circa *28 Days Later* and does something admirable like working for a charity or doing youth outreach work.

Jealousy and competition would have turned into texting, into 'What are you doing tomorrow?', into alcohol, into sex, into 'I've never got over you,' into commitment, but then those good things would have turned into arguments, because I wouldn't be able to resist the urge to punish him for having rejected me those times. Turning away from him in bed when he tried to kiss me, scream-crying on the way home from nightclubs. Asking, 'Do you promise you're not going to leave again?' until he's tired and misses the freedom he gave away so much that he's asking for it again. 'Sorry, I tried,' he'd say, while I'd loop all the way back around to who I was when I got off the train in Leeds after he first said it was over. When it comes to bumping into your ex there's just the way that hurts and then the way that ensures you're going to hurt later down the line.

'You never get the same girl back the second time,' I remember hearing Tolly say on *The Receipts Podcast*. 'You can get her back, but she won't be the same girl.'

The next morning he does actually text me.

'I went to a party last night. Your family friend Tom was there. South London is starting to feel a bit too small.'

'Yeah, I went to Haringey yesterday just to hide from you,' I say, able via text to curate a different version of myself, one who sounds unbothered, flirty. 'Annoyingly, I left the house looking really hot this time.'

He replies: 'I suppose you can save the outfit for the next party we're both at.' And then he asks me if I want to go with him to this Ethiopian restaurant with him on Friday.

It is really nice to think we could find our way back to that place, or somewhere near there. But it is even nicer knowing that I won't let myself. I like this new version of me too much for that. She doesn't need anyone else to be responsible for her happiness because she can find it on her own. I wish I could let the old me see this, though she'd probably be upset by my decision, always more willing to choose him than happiness. But she's not here anymore, so the Ethiopian restaurant and the two seats we would have sat in are filled with other people. Ones who are probably better off there than we would be.

In the first message you sent the night before we broke up you said, 'Hope you're having a good night, babe. Try to be quiet when you come in.'

Then: 'What time are you coming back?'

'Make sure you get a taxi.'

'Where are you?'

'I'm going to sleep now, night xx'

'Where are you?'

You rang me three times. I didn't pick up.

It was the night before you ended it and I was in a bar in East London, which has ball pools in it so repressed bankers can enjoy the feeling of being a kid for a few hours. My card had gone missing so I was passing my friend all the items out of my bag to try to see if it was still in there and getting annoyed at said friend for not panicking enough with me. One eye was open and one eye was closed as I leaned against a bus shelter, trying to roll a cigarette that would have made me vomit had I managed it. And then I was back in our bedroom trying to get the make-up wipes out of the drawer without you hearing me. Wincing as a water bottle I hit with my hands popped back into shape. You sat up, rubbed your eyes, asked: 'Why didn't you reply to my texts?'

When I got into bed I wanted to wrap myself right around you, but I could tell that if I did, you'd slip out from under me, a bit like Moll's cat when you try to pick her up. Your jaw clenched and unclenched so I could see the nerve quiver under your skin. I tried to kiss you.

'You *stink* of booze,' you said, slightly wincing.

'Smells like a bloody brewery in here,' I said in the mocking voice of a narky mother. You didn't laugh.

'I'm sorry,' I said. 'I'm so sorry,' and I cried, not because I felt that sorry but because I was at that level of drunk where it's so easy to tip whatever mood you're in into tears and I thought if I did it might stop the argument.

You turned back and faced me and kissed me, I guess because it was a better alternative to just lying there. Even so, I wanted to swallow those kisses right down into my stomach. I took my top off and you turned me over so that you were on me now, and when we started

348

having sex I shifted my hips so you could get deeper, but it still wasn't enough so I wrapped both my legs around you like vines twisting their way around a building, but it still wasn't close enough so I dug my nails into your back until I left pink raspberry-ripple streaks up and down your skin. You were pressing hard now, and as you did, your face seemed to tire as though some of your life force was fading out into me.

I wonder if you came to feel that you had nothing left to give. I'd taken so much of who you were: how to appreciate the colour palette of a film, to save the pasta water because it helps bind the sauce to the spaghetti, a lot of your friends, your identity as an 'I'. Eventually you fell off me and it felt like you were saying, 'There you go.' When it was happening, I liked taking it all, but now I felt like I had been given something I didn't deserve and I wanted to give it all back. You turned over and I fell asleep staring at the back of your head. It looked like a wall.

It confuses me that you were so worried about me going missing when not even twenty-four hours later you made the decision not to see me anymore anyway. Surely that in itself is some kind of a death? No longer able to warm your hands in the gap between my thighs, no longer smelling my fake tan on your T-shirts. In some ways it might be worse because you must imagine me doing all this stuff with other people, putting my tongue in places you wouldn't want it to be, laughing until I get a stitch.

Or maybe you were just worried for me in the way that you would worry for anyone you knew to be an all-right person. Like on TV when someone dies and their teacher tells the news reporter that they were a lovely, well-liked student with plenty of promise. Although it didn't seem that way. It felt like you worried about me because you really loved me.

Sometimes, when we were hanging out, if there was a lull in conversation I would ask stupid questions I thought would get a dramatic response. Often it was, 'Would you rather I die or you die?'

You would always answer the same way: 'I'd rather die.'

And you'd laugh at my more selfish response, which was always something along the lines of: 'It would be awful to lose you, but then there would still be the possibility of happiness further down the line. If I went then there would just be nothing.' Or, 'I'm one year younger so it's only fair that I be saved.'

You would imagine that his answer to my question 'Who would you rather die?' would be different once we had broken up. But based on his actions the night before he ended it, he might still choose to save me. Unless people don't end things because they stop feeling a certain way, but rather because the ending is a decision to try to stop those feelings being the case. It happens slowly: you stop saying 'Happy Birthday', you stop watching their Instagram stories, you stop expecting texts to let you know they got home safe, your computer forgets to autofill their details in on forms, you sign out of their Netflix. And once all the little things go, it's the big things: no longer wanting to call them when you have a bad day, when your wallet is stolen; no longer thinking of them at Christmas, and after a while you probably stop noticing the breaking of all the pacts you made together. He might still have died for me the day before he broke up with me, and maybe even now, but in a year or so if someone asks him 'Would you rather you die or Annie die?' well, then it really would be a joke.

'You can't go back to him after this.' That's what Moll said the night I came home after he broke up with me and I didn't know what that meant except that something irreversible had been set in motion. Not him no longer caring about me, but the decision to try.

34

A couple of weeks after bumping into Joe, Hayley and I are at the pub with Moya and a few more of their friends. We joke about how if Hayley was rich she'd turn into one of those wild health-food people who live off nothing but green juice and maca powder, which they snort through their nose so it hits their bloodstream faster. She says I'd shit it all away on handbags that would go out of fashion in a week. The sun stays in the sky long enough to convince us to get one more round before heading back to Moya's to listen to Taylor Swift's new album. A few of us squeeze onto the bed while Moya sits on her office chair. In between songs she turns in my direction, leans forward so that her elbows are on her knees and asks, 'So how are you feeling about everything?'

'I'm all good,' I say, but her face stays lingering on me as if there's more to the question. I wonder if I offended someone earlier on at the pub or if there's some political event I should have some opinions on.

'She means about the whole Joe's-new-girlfriend thing,' Hayley says, and as she moves through the sentence each word slows and breaks off as though she's reluctant to let them keep on forming.

'New girlfriend?'

Hayley looks back at me like I'm a dog about to be put down, then collapses forward so that her face is at my stomach and hugs me so tightly I marvel at how much strength is in those toned Gwyneth Paltrow arms of hers.

The dramatic response is required because this new woman she names isn't just a woman, but an imperfectly perfect woman who I can't dismiss the way I did with the others who came before. I can't say I'm just 'too much' for him and that she's just the easy option because she doesn't seem that easy at all. She's complicated and gorgeous with perfect hair that you can tell she soaks in Olaplex every night. You know she has one of those skin routines that's simple yet effective, that she says, 'Babe, you shouldn't be putting all those acids on your face, your skin is producing more sebum to compensate and *that's* what's breaking you out.' I bet she puts SPF on even when she's inside just in case a shard of light comes from behind the curtains. Her favourite song lyrics by Lana Del Rey about a man fucking someone so good they declare their love for him are also my favourite song lyrics. She looks like a French sugar-baby who sits outside cafés chain-smoking and telling leering men to fuck off. I'm actually annoyed to have to mute her Instagram because I respect her opinions on liquid blush and politics, but there's no other option because I don't want to see his comments underneath her pictures telling her how good she looks.

We stay until past 6 a.m. and when I get home it's awful walking back into my room because I kept my curtains open so sunlight fills the room, telling me to seize the day when it knows I can't. I want to torture myself so I go on Joe's Instagram where I can see pictures of her tucked up with his sister's Staffie on the sofa at his dad's house by the sea. There's another of them at the pub, his smile so big it nearly reaches right the way up to his aviator sunglasses while she looks at something beyond the camera, the sun glinting against her highlighter. *He never put up any pictures of me on his Instagram*, I think. And then I imagine things I can never verify to be the case, like him introducing her to all those friends of his he wouldn't let me near. Or saving up to go on holiday with her when he told me he couldn't afford to. The tears leak from my eyes now, relieving some of the pressure that's gathered in me like rocks.

'You make men better for the next woman,' my mum says when I tell her about what happened later after a pizza-induced short but unsatisfying sleep. She sighs. 'It's not fair but it's always the case.' I thought about the women Joe had been with before me. The one whose dad owns a big restaurant chain. The one who was always running nights raising money for important causes. The smart one who liked putting poetry on Instagram. I wonder how many ways these women worked to make him the sort of man who would take the day off work to help me sort my bad back. How they asked him to come with them to buy morning-after pills. And in turn, I wonder how many ways being with me marked him, made him better. Maybe for every stupid fight we had about him not washing cans before putting them into the recycling, he will just do it this time. Maybe he will make this new woman bowls of warm, salty noodles when her nose is filled with cold. Maybe he'll let her have more of her own life and give lots of his in its place. Maybe he'll take responsibility for his own happiness and not see it as the job of another to facilitate it. Maybe out of the mess we made they can make something perfect together, like building a house out of bones.

Things don't take as long as before to stop hurting. I come around to the idea of him and her together quickly. Perhaps because I watch a really cute video of two beavers, which makes me feel rather sentimental. Or perhaps, and more likely, because I realise I'm happy she's getting all the things I stopped getting, or never got. Because I can tell she deserves it and because one woman's happiness shouldn't have to take away from another's, even if it sometimes feels as though it does.

And when eventually I find another person to love, someone I want to be with for holidays and birthdays and long train journeys with no leg room, I'll think about the woman who made my boyfriend like that for me. Asking for things to happen that never would, crying over spilled milk. This new man will run me baths and underline all the lines from the book he's reading that remind him of me. And we will have a beautiful future together, the one he couldn't give her.

35

I spend the whole day with my friend Diyora walking around East Dulwich market. Buying spinach fatayers from a Lebanese food stall and licking pastry off our lip balm. Feeling the pavement warm under our bums. She takes a picture of me and I hate it because I'm smiling and it's making my lips look thin but she says I look pretty like my mum would. We don't talk much because there doesn't feel like there's anything to add to this moment. Instead, we just listen to the guy playing 'Home Again' by Michael Kiwanuka on the other side of the road. His voice is so beautiful it deserves to sell out Wembley, except at this moment I feel so good about myself I think us two deserve him all to ourselves. It's one of those days when you just run on from one thing to the next without anything feeling like it needs to be organised. She says she'll make me this lentil curry she saw on TikTok for dinner, so we walk back to hers and I lie back on her bed. And as I doze off to sleep I think about how easy it is to enjoy life; all you have to do is walk out into it and it comes running with open arms to greet you.

I'm awake reading my book when Diyora comes back into the room. She strokes my head with her tiny hands and says in that reassuring voice of hers, 'The curry's just reducing. It'll be twenty minutes or so.'

I nod. Then it's quiet, but not in the same way as it was before, in the way that it sounds as though something needs to be said. Her smile becomes the shape of a question and then she's asking one. 'How're you feeling about everything?' she asks, still stroking me but using her nails now.

'Fine, why? You mean about Joe having a girlfriend? Honestly, I'm really not arsed. I don't want to get back with him anymore anyway so it doesn't matter to me what he's doing. I guess the only part of it that hurts is that –'

I try to keep speaking but there's the familiar prickle in my eye sockets. 'I'm just annoyed because I can see her getting everything I wanted and it's not fair. Why was I not good enough for that? I deserve –'

And then talking is impossible because I'm crying so much that if I tried to speak I would sound like a wounded animal.

In her diary, Susan Sontag describes a time when she came home hungry and red-eyed.

> I prepared a bowl of pineapple to eat when P [her then husband, Philip Rieff] urged me to add some cottage cheese to it; he got the partly full container from the ice box + began to scoop the entire contents into my plate. I said (+ though I meant it), 'Don't, I only want part,' I took the spoon from him, + to my own amazement, scooped all the cheese out onto my plate myself.

Sometimes people see things in you that you can't even feel yourself. That's what Sontag's husband did when he saw that she needed food, and what Diyora did when she asked me that question. How did she know? Did she see something in the way that I walked? Was it hiding behind my sunglasses? I half wonder if she's hypnotising me; maybe the head-stroking has the same effect as scraping a spoon around the base of a teacup until I slip into my unconscious mind. Or maybe she's more like a wound dressing, pulling all the infection out when I didn't even know it was there.

After the crying stops, I take a deep breath and all this energy is expelled out of me so that I feel lighter, like I could float up into outer space. 'I can't believe I still get upset about this shit, you know?' I say, yawning.

Diyora sits up, nudges her watch out of the way to see how her tan lines are doing. 'Progress isn't linear, though. If you plotted it onto a graph, it wouldn't be this straight line up towards happiness. It would wiggle backwards, then forwards, up and down. You might feel worse in a month from now than you did a few weeks after it happened. But that doesn't mean you're not healing. It just means that we all experience emotions at different times. You were always going to feel this shit about him finding someone new, but you're also going to feel really good soon, I can feel it.'

I thought George was hot when I first met him at one of Adham's parties, but I gave up any hope of sex or even a relationship with him after I mistook the Leeds shirt he was wearing from the pub for an England one just because they're normally both white, and when he asked about writing I said, 'Sometimes it's so difficult I wish I did something easy and practical like working as a cleaner,' which is true but also makes me sound like a dickhead because I'm clearly only pining after this sort of work now that I'm so far away from needing to do it. But I kept turning up to things that he was at, and he kept slouching next to me on the sofa when he could have sat somewhere else where there's more room.

Last night we went to a pub in Tottenham together and I ended up staying over because I was too drunk to get the train and it would be too expensive to get an Uber back to mine. Now we're on the sofa together eating milk bottle sweets and fizzy cherries and I'm sitting in the other direction to him with my legs up on his lap. George holds my feet, pressing the pads of them until something starts to come loose; he pushes his knuckles into the knots at the backs of my calves, his fingers move up the bottom of my joggers, drawing shapes into my skin. I inch closer to him, but it never feels close enough. I want him to fold me up into myself like origami. Lie on me until I'm crushed through the bedframe. His flatmates start diverting their eyes so as not to draw attention to what's happening, and I like that it means we must be doing enough for them not to want to see it. I do basic things to try to get his attention, like saying, 'Look how big your hands are,' and then holding mine up to

his, feeling the way our skin seems to talk to each other.
I join in an order for an Indian and when it arrives I can
only manage a couple of onion bhajis and a handful of
butter chicken and I'm annoyed that I filled myself up
with all those sweets when I could have had one big satisfying meal. After we've finished George gets up to leave.
Outside we say bye and we hold each other for a while as
his jumper itches against my cheek. He pulls away and
laughs and then I laugh too, I guess because it feels as
though something else might follow the hug, but we're
too shy to invite it. I can't tell if I'm imagining things or
if I'm seeing exactly what I'm meant to see – what's lying
right there in front of my eyes.

A week later I'm at a gathering George is having at his
house in East London. At about 2 a.m. Adham and the
rest of his house say they're going to leave because it's late
and the only alcohol left is cooking wine, which tastes as
bad as you think it would. I tell them to wait for me,
then go upstairs to get my bag from where I hid it in one
of the bedrooms, but when I open the door on my way
out George is standing there in the frame of it. I move to
the right to let him through the door even though I can
tell from his face he didn't come here for anything but
me. He doesn't do anything right away and I would be
desperate for him to, except for how much I like seeing
how he's struggling to stop himself. His weight rocking
forwards and back on his feet, looking at my lips and
then down at the carpet. Eventually, something in him

snaps and he pushes me back through the door into the room. I feel the cold wood of the wardrobe on my back, one of my hands palmed against his bookcase to keep balance – a big volume falls off and lands crooked on the floor, another follows it. *It's raining books*, I think to myself, then, *Shut up, that's not funny, and why are you even thinking about funny things right now?* Until he silences all the words in my brain by picking up my jaw so that my face is looking up at him. We kiss like we're saying goodbye.

'They'll be wondering where I am,' I say after about five minutes. Except when we get there I realise they knew exactly where we had found ourselves. Adham's already outside, Rudy's scanning the table for his card, one of their other flatmates Jackson is putting in his headphones because he's planning on cycling. When they're out of the door we fall down on the sofa and my neck presses into the arm of it until it's crooked as my body tries to push it out to make space for what we're doing to each other. There's something slightly exposing about us kissing in this room, which only minutes earlier was congested with our friends sitting cross-legged on sofas talking about Adham's upcoming trip to Egypt and ignoring me while I tried to recentre myself with questions like, 'So who's the funniest here then?' – it's as though they are still here, haunting us. *I always thought there was something between them,* I hear one of them say. *I wouldn't have expected it,* says another. *They're too different.* Or, *I don't think she's ready for a relationship.*

You shouldn't shit where you eat. There's something scary in this, that they know both of us and if something goes wrong there will be two sides to this story rather than only the one I tell.

I ignore the voices and move over and sit on him and pull the string at my top so that it unravels and drops down, lean over to his neck and give long, ticklish kisses there. It all feels so intense for some reason – I think, because unlike anyone I've got with since Joe, he actually knows me. Part of me wants to say, *'Are you sure? Me?'* I feel like I've been turned inside out and someone's looking at the flesh underneath my skin. Like someone's rummaging through my bedroom. Or reading through my diary. But I carry on despite these worries because my body wants him so much there is no other option but to carry on, like I'm an insect swirling down the drain of a shower.

In the morning I wake up and look over at him. Normally I can't lie in when I've been drinking, but watching George's chest slowly move up and down with his breath, some of his calmness transfers over to me. I stop feeling like there's somewhere I need to be, or a message I need to reply to, and fall back into a hazy half-sleep, one where I'm aware enough to appreciate the support of his arm under my neck, the coolness on my legs from unexplored corners of the mattress. When my eyes open again, I'm not sure how long later, I look around his room: the wires from behind his projector tangled up in the ones coming from his speakers, a bike which always needs to be fixed in some way slumped against the wall, a desk with a dining chair he definitely shouldn't be working on if he wants to save his back, and then propped against the wall in a big wooden frame is a print of one of Monet's *Water Lilies*, which he told me he got from a charity shop for a fiver. It shows a pond that looks blue, but if you look more closely at the brushstrokes you can see that there's red and navy and neon green and peach and yellow and burgundy and turquoise and all the colours of the rainbow contained in that blue. Monet did 250 paintings of this scene taken from his garden over the last twenty years of his life, because he wanted to account for the way light changes a single image. George looks at me with this same focus, as though he's trying to see all the changing colours of me, when all the other men just see one thing.

'Could you see yourself being with him?' asks Ruchira when we're having coffee together a few days later.

'Hmmm,' I say and then tell her all about him. How he never sits down but always seems to find standing comfy, as though he were like a horse who can lock their joints and fall asleep on them. His quietness, which doesn't make him quiet, only louder, because when he does decide to speak everyone listens as it must be important if he's taking the time to voice it. The way he reminds me of that tweet I saw once that said, 'I just want a man who makes me feel really safe.' How I imagine being with him has the effect of what people believe comes from healing crystals, sending away bad energy, bringing good fortune.

'So you like him then?' she asks, seeing that I haven't yet answered her question.

'Yeah, I mean . . .' I pause for a moment. 'I don't feel like I've been hit over the head with a mallet, like I'll die if we're not together.'

'But maybe that's good,' Ruchira says, squirming slightly because she forgot to ask for vanilla syrup in her latte and she's got a sweet tooth. 'I'm not sure those feelings are real when you feel them. I think a lot of those desperate, *I-can't-live-without-you* feelings for Joe came in part because you projected so much onto him that wasn't really there. You were worshipping a man who didn't exist. This could be more real. You're meeting on equal terms.'

I nod.

'Sounds like you're holding yourself back a bit?' Ruchira asks. 'Like you're waiting for this feeling. But unless you give yourself over to this man, let him come to you, you'll never get it.'

Love isn't like Aristophanes said in that Plato story, like two people searching for their other halves. In fact, his speech in *The Symposium* was likely a work of satire aimed at mocking the sentimental and slightly ridiculous myths Greeks wrote about the origins of humanity. Plato goes on to define love as something different entirely, a reaching-up away from this world and into the good and beautiful of another dimension.

I don't agree with Plato's definition of love and I no longer relate to Aristophanes' version either. Love is nowhere near as inevitable as he makes out. It's not the electric reaction when you meet someone. It's not the 100 times you ring their phone when they're out late. Or the way you press your nose into their pillow because it smells like them. It's something you actively choose to do. Not an instinct, but something to nurture. It's a verb, not a noun. It's as difficult as a full-time job. It's extending your world view to encompass theirs. It's total generosity. It's doing things even if they won't notice them. It's making a fucking massive deal about their birthday. It's waiting before watching the next episode of something because you said you'd watch it together. It's trying to be a better person all the time. It's googling 'how can you tell if someone's depressed?' or 'what happens when you drink too much caffeine?' or anything else that might help them with what they're going through. It's making those 'uh-huh', 'mmm' noises when they're telling a story so they know you're still listening. It's challenging them. It's muting someone on Instagram because you know you're not looking at their thighs out of curiosity but because you want to be crushed in between them. It's every time-worn metaphor about the roots of two trees wrapping around one another. It's laughing at their Simon Cowell impression even though it's shit. It's subscribing to one of those flower-delivery services so that they will think you spontaneously decide to get them flowers every month. It's not checking their phone when they leave it unlocked.

It's telling them when something they said hurt and then interrogating yourself to understand why it hurt you. It's respecting them enough to understand that although you wouldn't have done it that way, they had their reasons. It's not pointing out that they just missed a really good parking space.

Joe and I weren't very good at love.

I choose to love – or choose to try to let myself love – George. When he stays over midweek I put half of last night's leftovers in a lunchbox he can take to work with him and smile at my phone when he says that all the boys were ribbing him for it. I call him when I'm walking home from a night out to ask him what he thinks bouncers spend their time thinking about when they stand in front of really quiet venues like galleries all day and then get upset with him when his only response is to order me an Uber home. I message him again the following morning and apologise for waking him up at 5 a.m. when he had such an important meeting later that day and he tells me I'm a dickhead but I sounded cute so it's OK. We go to the cinema and I go to pay and the guy at the till says, 'I wish my missus was like that,' and he smiles back, 'This is a one-off,' and I shove him and we both laugh and I realise I like playing this boyfriend/girlfriend game again. I go over to his in the afternoon and sit on the desk chair in his room and wait until he pulls it towards him by his foot so that I'm near enough to kiss him. Then we have sex and I realise only afterwards that it was the first time I've had sex sober since Joe. There's always been at least a couple of pints down me, a joint maybe. I spend enough time with him that he begins to notice things about me I've never thought of, like how I'm bad at saying no to people and avoid conflict so much I make problems worse. He doesn't say I look nice in person but over message he says I look absolutely fucking gorgeous today. I wonder if I make him shy. We get so comfortable around each other that he starts to feel like gravity to me, like something stable anchoring me to the ground. One time, when we're at a party, I look over at him and he looks back at me and we smile at each other and this feeling passes between us that no one else can see. As though we have just been cut loose into another dimension. I'm going home to Leeds for a while and I go over to his even though I've only got a couple of hours spare before my train. I was planning on having sex but then it feels like time would pass too quickly if we did and I want to draw it out, lying on the sofa with his arms around my shoulders as if they're an extension of my own spine.

These are all the things I let happen, but there are so many more that I stop in their tracks because commitment feels scary. Like when Jonny asked me to come to dinner with him and his girlfriend May and one other couple and he asked me if I wanted to bring George, but I said no because I was worried it might indicate something to him about the way things were moving forward between us that would be difficult to reverse if I changed my mind. Talking to everyone at the party except him because I'm scared if I don't keep up these other relationships then I might end up like how I was with Joe, with nothing but that other person. Like when he asks if he can come to mine after working late at the office and the prospect fills me with fear. But like that old saying goes, it's not him, it's me; it's the fact that I'm sleepy and quiet and just want to watch a period drama in silence. I'm in recharge mode, having been around too many people recently. My body is, too — I'm covered in so many different creams and oils I look like a baby seal. Not that he'd be bothered. In fact, I think he'd like seeing what I'm like behind all the anecdotes and shouting and straightened hair. But I'm scared to be that honest around someone, nothing standing in the way.

I let Joe see all this. I got so used to it that sometimes, when we were spending time together, it stopped feeling like another person was present. It still counted as alone time. So that when he actually wasn't there I felt anxious, as if I'd left something in the oven or had forgotten to lock the front door. When he left it was hard to enjoy my bed again. But, like everything that you scream and shout about and say will never be the same, it was. Now I sleep in here, starfished out or on my side with the duvet rolled up in between my legs. And as sleep comes for me and I drift off to a place where no one can follow, for the first time all day in a house of three loud women I feel truly on my own. No longer feeling like I have to put on a performance. Or voice questions I should ask or jokes

I feel pressured to make. I'm not sure there's anyone I could give that up for again.

'You never give quite so much of yourself the second time,' I remember my mum saying to me once, when I was still with Joe. 'You always keep a part of yourself back.'

I knew she was talking about love, but I didn't quite understand what she meant.

'What, though?' I asked, assuming she meant something specific, like secrets or something.

'You just keep something back,' she said, and I got bored of trying to make sense of her.

People ask me how things are going with George and their questions feel like accusations. When they ask how long we've been seeing each other now I think, *Why don't you go out with him then? Why does time need to correspond to the level of seriousness of a relationship?*

I guess I'm just angry because I can tell I'm pushing him away and I know it's something I'm going to regret.

When we were studying Thomas Hardy at school our teacher told us that Hardy spent the whole of his first marriage to Emma Gifford pining after this other woman called Florence Dugdale. His wife passed away of heart failure and he was able to marry his mistress. But then he spent the whole of his second marriage pining after Emma, writing fifty or so poems to her in the first year of his grief and another hundred throughout the remainder of his life. 'Beeny Cliff', from the collection *Poems of 1912–13*, recalls the first moment that he met Emma and came across her startling beauty.

> *O the opal and the sapphire of that wandering*
> *western sea,*
> *And the woman riding high above with bright hair*
> *flapping free –*
> *The woman whom I loved so,*
> *and who loyally loved me.*

I worry I'll become like Hardy. Always so held in the past I can't enjoy what's new and good.

I decide I'm going to tell George how I'm feeling. We meet at Victoria Park near his house and it's warm but the grass is wet from yesterday's rain so we sit on our coats while our bodies curl inwards as we try to conserve heat. He opens our beers with his teeth and the sound of them cracking against the enamel makes me wince. We start talking about fights because his friend has a black eye from the one he got into yesterday, how boxers' fists are legally classified as weapons so if they punch someone outside of the game it counts as manslaughter, then I tell him about how this girl punched me in the back of the head once and how everyone at school noticed me for the first time ever and someone even went into her class and said, 'Pick on someone your own size,' even though I started it by calling her a name. He said he used to be one of those lob-the-chairs-across-the-classroom-at-the-teacher sort of kids, which seems impossible to imagine given the sanguine way he seems to float through life now. I like hearing things like this because it makes the picture I have of him more three-dimensional; he becomes bigger before me as I connect the dots, more able to understand what it means when he says something is not his kind of thing. We laugh as he struggles to get the tobacco out of its plastic packet with his blunt nails. He puts his head on my leg and I stroke the back of his head in a maternal sort of way. Then he strokes my stomach and I pull up my crop top to show the big slash of pink over it. I tell him about how I got burnt taking a tuna pasta bake out of the oven and how it scared me. 'I was so excited to eat, I pulled the tray out too quickly and it hit me.'

He moves his finger over the raised, blistered part. 'I don't know why but that reminds me of Winnie-the-Pooh.'

And when he looks back up to my eyes again he looks drugged, even though he's only had one beer. 'I don't know why people aren't just staring at you all the time,' he says.

'What do you mean?' I ask, though I think I understand.

Then he sits up and kisses me and I realise then that I'm not going to say anything right now about our relationship because the moment's too perfect to ruin. Even if part of me knows that my fear of ruining this moment will guarantee that so many others end up worse.

The happiness I feel when I'm with him is good but also stressful. It clamps around my throat and says, *Are you sure about this?* I feel something heavy pressing into my chest, holding me to the bed like sleep paralysis. I want to run away and hide from it. I know where it's taking me. To shared toothbrushes, big shops where you include the hot sauce they like, sharing arms, legs. I'm scared of where this is going because the last time I believed in happiness it left and its departure did worse things to me than sadness ever could. I'm almost angry at how nice he is because I feel as though he's expecting something in return and I don't think I can give that right now. I want to scream, *'What do you want from me?'* so loud it rings in his ears like tinnitus. I shrink away from him on the bed so that we're no longer touching.

I remember once Ruchira and I were talking about giving birth. 'It's mad how your body goes through all that pain,' I began. 'Your vagina literally ripping apart, sometimes right down to your arsehole, and women actually decide to go through it all again, like a year later.'

Ruchira nodded. 'It's because your body releases all this oxytocin after the baby comes out,' she explained. 'The chemical makes your body forget all the trauma you've just been through. Otherwise no one would ever decide to have another child.' She paused for a moment and then said something that really made me laugh. 'It's kind of rude when you think about it. Your body basically gaslights you into thinking you'll be fine. Then you're on the hospital bed pushing a watermelon-sized object out of you thinking, *Not this again.*'

I thought it would be the same with love. That I would meet someone I like and the chemical reaction would be so strong that I'd forget how painful breaking up was and throw myself back in a second time without worrying about the consequences. But it hasn't been like that for me. There is something stopping me from getting there. I didn't think real people had walls; I thought that was just something people on *Love Island* said when they actually just didn't fancy the guy they were coupled up with.

But I understand it now because even though I like George, I can't let him get close to me. I start ignoring his messages and now I don't even reply when I've left it too late, so that we usually only end up talking when he's double messaged. I mention wanting to live abroad for a while so that he knows that some of my plans won't include him. Blaming everything annoying I do on drinking too much. Eventually the text arrives when I'm in between sets at the gym.

'Hey.'

That's all the first one says, but then he's typing for a long time. Then he's not typing at all, presumably because he's moved over to the Notes app. The next one follows seven minutes later.

I kinda wanna end things. We're just on different pages in life at the moment. I don't want to keep pursuing someone if they don't have any time for me. I probably should have communicated this earlier. I was just hoping things might change.

I want to beg for him back, tell him I will become what he deserves. But I know if I make that promise I won't keep it because I'm not capable of giving anyone but myself that time right now, that care. Part of me feels relieved to be all on my own. I'm free-falling, I'm light as a feather. Another, even more greedy part of me wants to ask him to wait for me, but you can't say that, can you? You have to let the universe take them away even if you're not ready.

> I just don't think I'm ready for a relationship right
> now. Something's holding me back and I think I've
> got some stuff to work through before I can be with
> someone again. I'm sorry you were on the other
> end of that. It must have been really frustrating
> and you're great and don't deserve that. I hope we
> can stay friends but totally understand if that's not
> something you're interested in.

He texts again, for the last time.

'Don't be sorry, I've had a great time with you. I just think for right now this is the best decision for both of us.'

And just like that I find myself all on my own again.

'Are you going to Ali's birthday thing?'

I know it's you even though I deleted your number a long time ago.

'Yeah,' I say. 'Don't worry, I'll be well behaved.'

Then I answer the phone when you start ringing me two minutes later.

'Hello.'

'Hello.'

'It's nice to hear your voice,' I say, even though I haven't heard you sounding like you properly yet.

'Thank you,' you say, the words stiff and tight as you hold the cigarette smoke back in your throat. Then the *shhhh* noise as it comes out on the tail of a 'how are you?'.

'I'm OK. Got pretty drunk last night and I gave my card to Ruchira to get money out at the machine but she put the pin in wrong three times and the machine ate it. To be fair I can't even be annoyed because I was the one who gave the wrong pin.'

You laugh, and it sounds like a seagull squawking.

The sound of it makes me laugh.

'You haven't changed much, have you?' you ask.

'Not really.'

'I can tell because your phone is still crackling.'

'That's just a bad signal.'

'And I can hear my own voice echoing in the receiver, which is extremely distracting.'

'Yeah, my tech game remains pretty weak.'

'Does the keyboard on your laptop work yet?'

'Yeah, I sorted that.'

'Good,' you say, and I get up from the sofa in the living room, move to my bedroom where I won't have the slightly invaded feeling of knowing someone might enter at some point. I want to be able to concentrate. I sit on the big box filled with all my shoes, a place I never usually sit.

'I've changed a lot,' you say.

'In what way?'

'I'm wedge now,' you say.

I don't believe it at first. Being skinny was part of your make-up. I'm not sure it is you if you're not skinny. Each of your ribs sticking out like piano keys. Like those stray dogs you see on holiday.

'The goal is to look like Jake Gyllenhaal in *Jarhead*.'

'That's mad.'

I try to think of your face, whether the sharp angles of your cheekbones have bloated out, your shoulders drawing from your neck. Decide I could think my way back to you through the difference.

'It's so nice talking to you,' I say again.

'Yeah, although it's annoying because I always think of all this stuff I want to tell you about, but now I've got the opportunity to say it I can't remember anything.'

'Do you remember when we were on that bus in Crete and that woman with the well-annoying voice kept talking about Cretan pies and Cretan wine?'

'Oh, memory lane, is it?'

'Buckle up, my friend, it's going to be a wild ride.'

But neither of us can think of much more to add except how funny it was when you used to try to peel oranges with those blunt nails of yours. The closer you look at the memories the more they blur out, as if you've zoomed into a picture so much that all you see are the pixels. It's as though there was no past leading up to this moment, nothing but us and our voices peeling away and locking around each other in the air. So much to say there's nothing at all to talk about.

'You been watching *Love Island*?'

'Naah, I've stopped all that shit since we broke up,' you say. 'I just don't think it's good for you – like, it's just boring and people try to make it seem valuable by intellectualising it, comparing it to Shakespeare and shit, or modern art.'

I laugh, not about what you said but what I'm about to say. 'I saw someone compare the neon writing around the villa that says "Eat, Sleep, Crack On, Repeat" to Tracey Emin's neon signs.'

'Christ.'

'No one needs to do that,' I say, moving to lie on the bed where I can get more comfy. 'It's just really nice watching people fall in love.'

'I get that.' You take a deep breath and I can hear the phone moving around in your hand. 'You still with that guy?'

'Naah, that ended, a few days ago actually. Turns out you all-the-way fucked me up and now I'm so scared of getting hurt that I hurt someone else instead.' I realise that was a bit intense so start what I'm saying again. 'Basically, I just think I need to be single for a while. I don't want to have to tell someone where I am or what I'm doing. I don't want to owe anyone anything because I know if I do, I won't be able to give it to them.'

'Who ended it with who?'

'Him, but it was me who made him do it. If that makes sense.'

'That's happened to me a few times. I was with this one girl, we got on really well, she made me laugh, she was really hot, but I was out all the time and dating other people and I carried on until she had enough.'

'Stop comparing us, I'm not like you,' I say, knowing he might be more right than I want to let on. I resent the idea that my behaviour is similar to his because that same behaviour hurt me in ways I don't like to remember. I don't want to believe I could be capable of inflicting that hurt on other people. There's never much justice in a world where there aren't good and bad guys, just victims passing their pain on to other people who become victims in return. Everything bad seems to come from trauma and there's no person you can point your finger at and blame. We're all guilty so much of the time, all innocent too.

'I'm a teacher now,' you say, and it pulls my mind out of the knot it was tying itself in.

'I heard. It makes so much sense. You've always been so good at explaining things, but you don't enjoy it *too* much. You know when sometimes you want to not understand someone because they're taking too much pleasure in correcting you?'

'That's nice. There's a girl in my class who really reminds me of you. She's always asking questions like, "Sir, why's the sky blue?" "Was Shakespeare hot?" "What you eating for lunch today?"'

'Do all the students fancy you?'

'Pretty much.'

I think of you in the classroom, pulling your top lip down with your finger like you sometimes did. Well-ironed seam on the front of your trousers. Leaning back against the desk and pointing at the kids who don't put their hands up to answer the question you just asked, encouraging them to the right answers. *'You're almost there, I want you to think about who the real monster is – Frankenstein's creature or the society that rejects him?'*

'I'm really proud,' I say, glad I can give this truth without it eating me up. 'You're doing so well and you absolutely deserve it.'

'Thank you. I'm gonna do some temp work for the NHS over the summer too.'

I laugh and you laugh and neither of us has to explain to the other why it's funny. You used to be so lazy with work, missing Mondays almost every other week due to extended hangovers. Walking out of jobs without warning because you didn't want to do them anymore.

'How are the rest of the family?' I ask.

'Honestly, life's great. I'm getting on with my parents, my sister's got a new business with a van and everything, the flat is all done up, her and Mike and the dog are happy.'

'Wonderful.'

'I don't even drink much anymore – like, I try keep it to every other weekend and I feel a lot better for it. You're doing well too, aren't you? *Vogue*,' you say, that last word held on your tongue much longer than any other. 'That fucking article you wrote about me, though – when you bumped into me I wasn't wearing a waistcoat – it was a padded vest. I've had so many friends be like, "Bro, are you a wizard?" since that came out.'

'You're funny,' I say.

'You're annoying.'

It's strange talking to you because we get on the same as we used to. It's as though I'm having a conversation with myself. I forgot that you used to be my best friend. I imagine that if people heard us talking they might say, 'You guys should get back together,' and I know that if we did these two versions of ourselves would do much better at the relationship than the former did. Able to express ourselves in arguments well enough that change would come out at the other end of them, you motivated to do things without my support, me no longer correcting and pushing but living my own life, one that doesn't require you in it, but loves it when you are. And yet too much has happened to allow us to go back to that place. I'm not sure what exactly it is – time maybe, or pain – either way, it feels impossible to move beyond it. It's like that line in Gabriel García Márquez's *Love in the Time of Cholera*: 'Wisdom comes to us when it can no longer do any good.'

As if you were reading my mind again, you say, 'It's difficult watching all of our friends fall in love. I'm jealous that they're doing it when they've grown up. I think if we met now we'd probably be together forever.'

'I dunno,' I say, and then I tell you about the wedding I was at the other week where the father of the groom said something in his speech that made me think about this. 'He said, "The best thing about getting married young is that you get to spend even more of your life with that person."' I know I'm not going to spend the rest of my life with you, but I am going to spend more of my life with the lessons we learned together, the person you made me into. So in that way, I'm so thankful we broke up when we did, because it means I get to spend more time with her.

'You know there's a deli now in Lowestoft,' you say, because that's the business we always talked about opening.

'Missed our chance, didn't we?'

There's silence for a moment and then I look at the time and I was meant to set off for Ali's ten minutes ago and I haven't even started my make-up. I tell you I need to go and you say you'll message me if you decide to come, even though we both know you won't turn up.

'All right,' I say. 'Love you, bye.'

You could just pretend not to have heard it but we both know that's not going to happen. You laugh again in a deep, throaty way. Say: 'Sorry, what was that?'

'Force of habit,' I reply, sighing.

I'm about to hang up when you say, 'I love you too.'

'Don't give me your sympathy.'

'No, like, not in that way, but I actually do.'

And it sounds weird, but I know exactly what you mean. It's a love that doesn't feel like it's going to burn through my chest, or bring me to tears, send me to your door in the middle of the night. It's a softer, mellow love that glows in my heart like a warm night light. It makes me proud of who you are now, proud of who I am. It doesn't ask for anything in return, and it doesn't ask for me to do anything to prove it. It's the sun on the back of your neck, it's the ocean lapping at my feet.

'I love you,' I say again, and I'm sure we will for the rest of our lives.

ACKNOWLEDGEMENTS

Thank you to my ex for showing me what love is. And for not suing me. Thank you Dad for the terrible jokes and the great food and for being proud of me even when what I'm writing about is sex. Thank you to my brother for seeing I was smart even before I believed it myself. Thank you to my granny for being the kindest woman I've ever met in my entire life. I used the five grand you left me to write the proposal for this book and I like to think you're proud of what I did with it. Thank you Grandpa for your brilliant laugh and tight hugs in that itchy jumper. I miss you.

Thank you to my lovely agent Florence for always making me feel like there was someone on my side. Thank you Rachel for seeing potential in my writing from so early on. Thank you to my editor Pippa for the feedback and for putting up with me when I kept fiddling with it when it was already done.

Thank you to Vicky, my best friend in the entire world, amen. Thank you Ruchira, you are my favourite person, I love you so much I could pop. Thank you Elliot, there's no one I get more excited about seeing enter a room. Thank you to my second mother Hayley and the rest of my rats and pigs Moya, Diyora, Bex, Hannah, Griff; your friendship is a lifeline and a blessing. Thank you to my day ones Aaron, Maris and Tom. Thank you Moll. Thank you Ali and Phoebe. Thank you Jonny. Thank you to Patrick and Eloise. Thank you to Adham, Jackson, Rudy and Georges. Thank you Grace. Thank you to my prunes Alice and Elle. And thank you to my schmoo, for literally everything. I can't really think of another way to put it.

ABOUT THE AUTHOR

Annie Lord is *Vogue*'s dating columnist. She also writes for *VICE*, the *Sunday Times*, the *Telegraph*, *New Statesman*, *i-D*, the *Guardian* and *Dazed*.

CREDITS

Trapeze would like to thank everyone at Orion who worked on the publication of *Notes on Heartbreak*.

Agent
Florence Rees

Editor
Pippa Wright

Copy-editor
Holly Kyte

Proofreader
Linden Lawson

Editorial Management
Rosie Pearce
Jane Hughes
Charlie Panayiotou
Tamara Morriss
Claire Boyle

Audio
Paul Stark

Jake Alderson
Georgina Cutler

Contracts
Anne Goddard
Ellie Bowker

Design
Nick Shah
Rachael Lancaster
Joanna Ridley
Helen Ewing

Finance
Nick Gibson
Jasdip Nandra
Sue Baker
Tom Costello

Inventory
Jo Jacobs
Dan Stevens

Marketing
Cait Davies

Production
Katie Horrocks

Publicity
Francesca Pearce

Sales
Jen Wilson
Victoria Laws
Esther Waters
Group Sales teams
across Digital, Field
Sales, International and
Non-Trade

Operations
Group Sales Operations
team

Rights
Susan Howe
Krystyna Kujawinska
Jessica Purdue
Ayesha Kinley
Louise Henderson